PRAISE FOR
GREENHOUSES OF HOPE

This collection of essays by young church folk is a primer on how to recover the vitality and fidelity of the church. These writers are deeply grounded in gospel hope, passionate about gospel inclusiveness, and convinced of a people-to-people gospel ministry. The "bottom up" perspective of this book is one to which attention must be paid.
—*Walter Brueggemann, Columbia Theological Seminary*

There are no quick fixes or magic programs in good youth ministry, just a cloud of witnesses of unique communities of faith all using their own special quirks, their context, and their gifts to cultivate a sense of God's call. This rich mix of stories from across the church will encourage you to find your own path in this crucial work. Refreshingly nonformulaic and unique, this collection feels like the messy work of the Holy Spirit.
—*The Rev. Dr. Lillian Daniel, First Congregational Church, United Church of Christ, Glen Ellyn, Illinois*

Where better for the church to find a fresh imagination for ministry than to stop, look, and listen to the words and lives of young people? And where better for young people in an age of isolation and disconnect to find a coherent life than in a worshiping, serving congregation? The authors invite us here into the language and practices of diverse congregations across the United States in which young people have a place to find themselves and their vocations, and having given us a sense of what it's like to be a young person in this congregation, provoke us to discover possibilities in our own.
—*Thomas E. Frank, Wake Forest University*

As you turn the pages, the stories in *Greenhouses of Hope* will nourish you and your ministry. From each context and setting, the voices call out to us and inspire us to cultivate meaningful, intergenerational connection with young adults. But it doesn't just stop with narratives of what's happening in other churches. This book also provides vital tools, probing questions, and significant resources to grow hope in your own community.

> —*Carol Howard Merritt, author of* Reframing
> Hope: Vital Ministry in a New Generation

This timely, vital, and well-written book shatters two destructive myths: that the current generation of young adults lacks moorings, purpose and passion; and that mainline churches are doomed because of their failure to connect with the young. Read a few chapters, and you will feel a new sense of hope for the church and the world. Read the whole book and you will have a set of well-tested "greenhouse" approaches to growing young adults who can help all of us flourish in this struggling world.

> —*Parker J. Palmer, author of* Let Your Life Speak,
> A Hidden Wholeness, *and* The Courage to Teach

Greenhouses of Hope

Greenhouses of Hope

CONGREGATIONS GROWING YOUNG
LEADERS WHO WILL CHANGE THE WORLD

Dori Grinenko Baker, Editor

ALBAN

Herndon, Virginia
www.alban.org

The Alban Institute
2121 Cooperative Way, Suite 100
Herndon, VA 20171

Unless otherwise noted, all Scripture quotations are from the New Revised Standard Version of the Bible, © 1989, Division of Christian Education of the National Council of Churches of Christ in the United States of America, and are used by permission.

Cover design by Tobias Becker, Bird Box Design.

Library of Congress Cataloging-in-Publication Data

Greenhouses of hope : congregations growing young leaders who will change the world / Dori Grinenko Baker, editor.
    p. cm.
 Includes bibliographical references (p.227).
 ISBN 978-1-56699-409-5
 1. Christian leadership. I. Baker, Dori Grinenko, 1963-
 BV652.1.G69 2010
 253.084'2--dc22
                                    2010038100

10   11   12   13   14   VP   5   4   3   2   1

This book is dedicated to
my father, Donald L. Grinenko, lovingly known as Ponce,
who taught me to plant seeds each spring,
water them,
and hope for what will grow,

and to

my father-in-law, Ronald H. Baker,
whose faithful tending of Scripture
makes a garden bloom
wherever he goes.

Contents

Preface

Daydreams pulled me regularly back to memories of my own vocational journey during my work on this book. Where was my path redirected? What communities of faith nurtured my gifts? What Christian practices awakened my passions and invigorated my search? At the end of a day filled with stories of young adults and their vocations, a dream in the night took me back to Angie, an old friend who is part of the reason I do this work.

Angie and I were both twenty-one when our paths crossed in the small Central Florida town of Crystal River, though we never actually met. I was a studious newspaper reporter freshly out of college, seriously pursuing a career I thought would last a lifetime. Angie was a fun-loving travel agent on her way to visit an old friend for a long weekend.

She never arrived at her destination. The call came over the police scanner on a humid May afternoon. I drove my Toyota to the other side of the county. There, the harsh yellow police tape marked off a portion of the Cross Florida Barge Canal where Angie's partially clad body had been found floating. Its driver-side window smashed, her car was found a few miles away, near a phone booth where she had stopped to make a late-night call in an era before cell phones.

For the next several hours, weeks, days, and months, I immersed myself in learning about Angie. I spoke almost daily with her brother, Chris, who lived in a small Illinois town where Angie had grown up. I talked to her friends, her mother, and other members of the loving community who cherished this vivacious blonde cheerleader and couldn't believe she was really gone. I felt myself becoming one of Angie's many grieving friends.

I dutifully filed stories reporting new details of her abduction, the search for the killer, and the outpouring of love Angie's death opened in her hometown. At the end of each day, I began my hour-long commute home. In the solitude of my car, the tough outer shell of the newspaper reporter melted. I shed tears. I prayed. I searched for (and usually found) the Holy One in the midst of a day filled with an almost physical sensation of evil and numerous levels of senseless loss.

Within my career in journalism, another way of life opened itself to me. The murder of Angie was part of a string of tragedies—including weekly accounts of sexual abuse of children by their mother's boyfriends, and a simple bicycle ride that ended with the death of eleven-year-old Natasha Seaman. These close-up looks at the endless stream of life's most painful truths caused me to envision myself differently. On those long rides home, I saw myself at the heart of a broken world, sent there not so much to report on it as to witness to and enter its pain on behalf of a divine creator who yearned for its healing.

It didn't happen overnight. I didn't have many companions with whom to discuss this quietly insistent voice inside me. But soon after Angie's killer had gone to trial, I had followed an inner nagging and was on my way to seminary, despite having never seen a woman in a pulpit.

My notions of who I was and could envision myself becoming were rather dramatically interrupted by the world's needs. People like Angie's friends and her brother helped me begin to name a gift that I urgently needed to express in the world. It was the community—yes, the church—that eventually acknowledged my rather fumbling search for an authentic response and allowed the brief whispers of a call to become fleshed out as an ongoing change in my life's trajectory.

Up until the time I entered seminary, I experienced church as concerned mostly with personal salvation, correct belief, and individual callings. After moving from Florida to Chicago, I naively stumbled into the nearest United Methodist church, which happened to be the avant-garde of its denomination in the late 1980s. This rather radical, politically active, and socially aware congregation redirected me. Sunday by Sunday, I came to critically examine what I ate, where I put my trash, whether I took the car or train, and how my husband and I spent our money. Over time, this kind of critical reflection became foundational in my understanding of how God calls individuals and communities to become agents of change in the world. Wheadon United Methodist Church was a reconciling community concerned with extending God's welcome to people of all sexual orientations, a sanctuary community offering safety to Central American refugees, and a nuclear-free zone. It claimed me and helped me find the substance of my call, fittingly reflected in a sign outside the church that read, "The Sign of God is that you will be led where you did not plan to go."

In this place, people moved the pews to form a circle so that we could see one another as we worshiped. People used words like *vocation* regularly. They set aside a special Sunday for all members to name their callings—out loud—as they received crêpe-paper stoles signifying God's presence in all places of work in the world. In this place I experienced what my colleague Elizabeth Mitchell Clement calls a "long conversation with friends—along the way, as life happens, between meals." Through small groups, in Bible studies in the pastor's office, on all-church retreats, and over fair-trade coffee in the fellowship hall, the people in this church—teenagers with whom I worked, an elderly woman who lived in a nearby retirement high-rise, and people of all ages in-between—noticed, named, and nurtured my evolving gifts for ministry. They cared for my evolving vocation not because I was special as one called to ministry; it was just part of who they were as a church.

They helped me find the place where God's dream for the world danced with my dream for the world to become something beautiful. That's what this book is about: congregations as people and places where young adults might discover a purpose that can make their lives sing.

Two decades later, after seminary, ordination, graduate school, and years of teaching and writing on topics related to adolescence, young adulthood, and faith communities, I came to work for The Fund for Theological Education (FTE). FTE's mission is to support the next generation of excellent and diverse leaders for the church. One way FTE does this is by providing fellowships for people who are exploring pastoral leadership and teaching in seminaries. Another way is through Calling Congregations, an initiative that sees congregations as seedbeds where young people's gifts might be noticed, named, and nurtured for the sake of the church and the world. At Calling Congregations, we have developed an approach called VocationCARE, a set of practices that invite congregational leaders to care about vocation in people of all ages, but particularly in the young. Among these young people might we find the very ones God is calling to be the pastors and leaders who will renew the church? That is our hope.

This book grows out of that work. May it awaken in you memories of your own vocational journey: When did someone notice your gift and nurture its tender emergence? What broken places in the world call forth God's desire in you? What makes your heart sing? By living in close proximity to those stories, all of us realize just how important it is to listen with deep and holy care to the still-emerging stories of the young people with whom we share a planet, a neighborhood, a church, or a home.

Dori Grinenko Baker
August 1, 2010

Acknowledgments

Collaboration makes my heart sing. The gift of working with so many fine friends and colleagues gives me deep joy. I thank the writers of this project for the energy they poured into the research and writing. Joyce, Fred, Katherine, Jeffery, Margaret Ann, and Sinai all put other projects on hold to enter into this work with one another and the churches we studied. Their range of experience as people, educators, pastors, and scholars reminds me once again that diversity is the most excellent way.

My colleagues at The Fund for Theological Education (FTE) surprise me regularly with the pure glee that occurs when people are living fully into their vocations. Stephen Lewis, Elizabeth Mitchell Clement, Jim Goodmann, Courtney Cowart, and Katie Oliff of Calling Congregations are an exceptionally creative team working under the visionary leadership of Melissa Wiginton. Their work is crafted daily out of passionate love for a renewed church, occasionally glimpsed dancing on the horizon. Their words and ideas appear liberally throughout this book. I am especially grateful to Melissa for her artful way of seeing patterns and gathering themes, woven together in the final chapter. I also thank Kim Hearn and Matthew Williams for ideas that helped shape the project, entrusted to me by the FTE, with funding from the Lilly Endowment. Serving with all of these folks is an immense privilege and pleasure.

As I traveled to conferences, retreats, and seminars over the past two years, many beautiful minds helped hone these ideas. I thank: Elizabeth Corrie of the Youth Theological Initiative at Candler School of Theology and participants who gave encouragement to our initial panel; students in my extended seminar at the April 2009 Princeton Youth Forum; students from my 2009 Wesley Theological Seminary course on youth ministry; the people of John Knox Presbyterian Church of Greenville, South Carolina, and all congregations who participated in the Calling Congregations "Notice, Name, Nurture" events; and Joy Crawford of Project Burning Bush at Union Presbyterian Seminary in Richmond, Virginia, as well as participants in its January 2010 conference, The Blaze.

For the third time I had the pleasure of working with Ulrike Guthrie as my editor. She is brilliant, and I am so glad our paths cross. I am grateful to Andrea Lee for her attentive copy editing and to Olivia Baker for helping with the commas.

In my small town of Altavista, Virginia, I walked this project as someone might walk a golden retriever. I know the exact spot on the sidewalk where I received a particular phrase, and I recall the moment of footfall when the title dropped down. I thank my friend Debbie Berger for the miles she walked with me, patiently listening to the intricacies of each chapter unfold.

On nights when there is no soccer, volleyball, violin lesson, or mom out of town, my family gathers for a meal around a table and a candle. We exhale, say a prayer, and enjoy the rhythm of these days we have together. Lincoln, Erin, and Olivia: thank you for that cozy feeling that is home. In it lies a deep knowing that God abides.

Green Shoots Emerging

Every single one of us has a good work to do in life.
This good work not only accomplishes something needed in the world,
   but completes something in us.
When it is finished a new work emerges that will help us make green a desert
   place.[1]

—ELIZABETH O'CONNOR

Make green a desert place. Take something barren and slowly tend it with the right amounts of water, sunlight, and nutrients. In time, green shoots emerge.

I have been looking for green shoots lately. I have been scanning the landscape of mainline congregations where youth and young adults *want* to be, where young people are heard to say, "If *this* is church, bring it on!" Despite somber news about the demise of denominations, I hear whispers of other realities.

I hear about a church where young people regularly shape the liturgy with words that speak their truth in ways that also inspire their elders. I know congregations that reach out in quirky new ways to their ailing urban neighborhoods, instead of locking doors and shipping out to a suburb. I find a church creating hospitable space that invites the live, wriggling questions and doubts of young people in unhurried, unworried ways. I see congregations where young

1

people's gifts are not stored in the basement or bracketed into "contemporary" worship services but are brought forth and celebrated. If these churches were gardens, they would have signs that say "Flourish" and "Grow" strategically placed where young people walk.

I name these churches "Greenhouses of Hope." A Greenhouse of Hope is a Christian congregation freeing itself to experiment with both newly imagined and time-honored ways of following the path of Jesus. Its members respond to God's love through practices that genuinely embrace the gifts of youth and young adults. Out of these greenhouses emerge young leaders who want to change the world.[2]

GREENHOUSE OF HOPE: A Christian congregation freeing itself to experiment with both newly imagined and time-honored ways of following the path of Jesus. Its members respond to God's love through practices that genuinely embrace the gifts of youth and young adults.

With that definition in mind, I launched a quest for such vibrant, life-giving, greening congregations and the diverse practices that grow there. I would have loved to journey across the country, visiting church after church, capturing their rich and diverse stories; but the telling would grow quite narrow, funneled through the lens of one white, female, seminary-educated, Protestant mother, minister, and professor. Instead, I invited six other scholars who care deeply about the future of the church and practice a method of research called *ethnography*.

In October 2008 a group of us gathered to dream about churches we knew and churches we didn't yet know that seem to be supporting young people in vocational discovery. Fred Edie, Katherine Turpin, Joyce Mercer, Margaret Ann Crain, and Jeffery Tribble, all of whom are professors at denominational seminaries, agreed to be part of the team. Sinai Chung, a recent doctoral graduate, and Melissa Wiginton, vice president of ministry programs and planning for The Fund for Theological Education (FTE), joined us. With assistance from the staff of FTE's Calling Congregations initiative, we came up with a list of diverse churches and began to spend time with them. Two years later, after conducting scores of one-on-one interviews, attending dozens of church potlucks, and spending hours immersed in worship, we have stories to tell about the Green-houses of Hope we explored.[3] In keeping with good ethnographic practice, each of us found a congregation with which our own journey resonated. Each church's story bears a connection to the researcher's own hopes, dreams, and biases.

Ethnography: Research done by people who immerse themselves in detailed observations of the ways of life of a particular people in order to learn about them, from them, and with them.[4]

I, *Dori Grinenko Baker,* grew up in Central Florida, where during high school I bounced between Southern Baptist churches with friends after Saturday-night sleepovers. I felt a tug toward some form of ministry throughout my adolescence, but back in those days, I couldn't imagine a woman in a pulpit. During college, I visited every imaginable church I could find, looking for a place that could help me grapple with doubts about the God I learned about at church. I finally landed as a United Methodist. Today I am an ordained minister who writes, leads retreats, and teaches about ministry with youth and young adults. The idea for this book emerged as I began working with FTE. In addition to convening the writers, I cowrote chapter 4, "Living Together: When Radical Welcome Reaches Out to an Interfaith World" with Katherine Turpin. We go to First Congregational Church of Berkeley, California, where a group of young adults found remarkable partners in discerning their call to extend Christian hospitality to people of other faiths.

Margaret Ann Crain sang in the adult choir as a teen and became president of her youth group at a United Methodist church in San Jose, California, yet she struggled with faith questions while growing up. As a young mother she was invited to join the staff of the congregation where her family was active. Finding herself with little but on-the-job training, she began to enroll in UMC training events: they led all the way to a doctorate in religious education and a commitment to ministry in the United Methodist Church. Margaret Ann is an ordained deacon on the faculty of Garrett-Evangelical Theological Seminary, a United Methodist institution, where she teaches Christian education. She wishes her children and grandchildren could have experienced the kind of ministry she writes about in chapter 2, "Staying Awake: When God Moments Echo in Community." She takes us to First United Methodist Church of Evanston, Illinois—a place where youth learn to talk about their "God moments" with fluidity and ease, and a place where a life of service seems to grow naturally out of ongoing immersion and explicit theological reflection on mission trips.

Sinai Chung grew up in Seoul, South Korea. She was an active youth leader of Chongshin Presbyterian Church, where her father served as a senior pastor. She loved to learn the Bible, to lead a worship praise team, and to hang out with her friends there. When it was time to choose a major in college, she didn't hesitate to enter Christian studies. During her freshman year of college, she became convinced of her vocation as a Christian educator and began serving as a youth leader of her home church. Her passion for ministry with young people kept growing, and she came to the United States for graduate study. Here, she continues to serve Korean American churches as a youth minister and is particularly interested in the Christian formation of Korean American young people who deal with cross-cultural issues. She writes about a first generation Korean immigrant church in chapter 3 "Mozying: When the Young Mentor the Younger." She currently serves as a youth pastor at Grace and Truth Presbyterian Church, Indian Creek, Illinois, as an adjunct professor at Trinity Christian College in Palos Heights, Illinois, and as a newspaper correspondent reporting on issues related to immigrant youth.

Katherine Turpin grew up in Charleston, West Virginia; Houston, Texas; and Birmingham, Alabama, where neighborhood United Methodist churches were the center of her family's social world. Because volunteer adult mentors in all of these communities invested in her, she moved into leadership first in youth group and later in summer-mission and campus-ministry settings. Today she teaches religious education at Iliff School of Theology (UMC) in Denver, Colorado, and serves as a volunteer adult leader mentoring the next generation of children and youth at her local church. She felt called in this book to witness to the strength of Christian formation and ministry emerging in our increasingly religiously plural urban neighborhoods.

Fred P. Edie grew up on a small island just east of Savannah, Georgia. As a teen he played baseball, swam and fished in the river, and hung out in the rumpus room of his church youth director's house. Serving as a summer youth worker during college, he was caught off-guard when he began to sense a call to ministry. Fred tells more of that story in chapter 5, "Converging Streams: An Island Congregation's Practices of Vocation Care." He takes us to Isle of Hope United Methodist Church near Savannah, the church where he grew up. These days, Fred teaches at Duke Divinity School and directs Duke's Youth Academy, an intensive program of deep Christian formation for high school juniors and seniors.

Jeffery Tribble grew up on the South Side of Chicago, where he was active in youth and music ministry in Baptist churches. He took his first steps toward ministry at Howard University, where he gave his life to the Lord, began to sing in the chapel choir, and became president of a campus ministry. While in graduate school, he felt another tug toward ministry, and so began to teach a Bible study for African American men while he was a student at the Massachusetts Institute of Technology. He tells more about his journey into ministry in chapter 6, "Embodying *Sankofa*: When Ancient Ways Inform the Church's Future." He takes us to First Afrikan Presbyterian Church of Lithonia, Georgia, a church that mindfully infuses African history, imagery, and ways of life into its practices of worship and education. Jeffery and his wife are both active ministers in the AME Zion Church in Atlanta, where Jeffery also serves as a professor of ministry at Columbia Theological Seminary.

Joyce Ann Mercer grew up near Richmond, Virginia. She found her way into a Presbyterian church when she was in the fifth grade. Although her congregation had no women pastors, and a few families even left over the election of the congregation's first women elders, Joyce eventually responded to a sense of call to ordained ministry shaped by youth leadership, mission participation, and the pastoral care of the congregation during a personal health crisis in her adolescence. A minister in the Presbyterian Church (USA), Joyce currently teaches at Virginia Theological Seminary, a seminary of the Episcopal Church located in Alexandria, Virginia. In chapter 7, "Calling amid Conflict: What Happens to the Vocations of Youth When Congregations Fight?" Joyce shares what she is learning about churches that are fighting with each other; some staying and some leaving their denominations over differing interpretations about the Bible and human sexuality. She takes us to two churches—one Episcopal and the other Lutheran—and helps us wonder, how do we care for the vocations of young people when we are busy disagreeing about things that really matter?

Melissa Wiginton grew up in Tennessee and Texas as the oldest of four children all well-formed by faithful parents and loving congregations. Her journey has taken her from a tradition in which women were to remain silent, but where she was given voice and leadership as an adolescent, to the United Methodist Church and the work of The Fund for Theological Education, where she gives leadership to the cause of young people hearing and responding to God's call to ministry. In the final chapter, "What on Earth Are We Doing? Young Lives Emerging to Change the World," she brings her decade-long observations of young adults entering ministry into conversation with the practices of the congregations described here and urges care for vocation even after age twenty-one.

Throughout this book, the authors balance two apparently paradoxical views. We are particularly interested in young people who answer a call to professional ministry in one shape or another, because we believe the church has something vital to offer a broken world. We want to see bright, creative, innovative young people answering a call to be pastors and preachers who will, in turn, help shape the imaginations and vocations of others. We believe that if the church is to thrive, it will need such young leaders. However, we also believe that Greenhouses of Hope open possibilities for living a life that matters *to all people*. We believe that all Christians have a call, by virtue of their baptism. We hope that congregations who practice care for vocation will give birth to a fascinating array of ways people can live and act fully out of their faith. Yes, some of them will become ordained pastors and preachers, but others will be accountants and engineers who find connection between their professional work and their Christian life. Others will be youth ministers, Christian educators, activists, teachers, or caregivers. People formed by congregations that care about vocation learn to find ways that all of their work in the world can be connected to their call as Christians.

The authors who collaborated on this book launched a quest for such vibrant, life-giving, greening congregations and observed the diverse practices that grow there. We are convinced that such congregations spring up from their particular context, history, people, resources, and crises. Each one looks different: there is no kit to buy, blueprint to copy, or curriculum to adopt.

We tell the stories of these diverse greenhouse churches in thick, rich detail to inspire leaders in other congregations to look within themselves and around at their context. What are you uniquely suited to do in this time and place? What is God calling forth from your congregation? In other words, what *must* you do in order to be faithful to God for the sake of the world, and how do you bring young people along on that adventure? By choosing to use ethnography, we enlarge the lens from one viewpoint to many. We avoid *pre*scriptions in favor of *de*scriptions. Let us show you what others have done, and let it awaken questions, dreams, and possibilities in you.

We tell these stories for an audience of congregational leaders, youth ministers, youth workers, Christian educators, and those who hold myriad other paid and volunteer positions in local congregations. We tell them for people who have found their church to be a "good enough home" to be worth staying put for a while.[5] And we tell these stories for people who *want* to care about church, but are tired of being disappointed and are tempted to walk away for all the good reasons all of us hear about in the news or witness on Sunday morning. These disappointments and temptations repeatedly hit many of us who love the church but hate its shortcomings: Last spring my heart ached over pain-filled letters to the editor in the *New York Times* about the Vatican's ongoing failure to investigate and punish priests accused of sexually abusing children. And just yesterday, I witnessed the worship hour tragically squandered: I sat with youth whom I had just accompanied on a mission trip exploring urban poverty and hunger in the city of Washington DC. Nowhere in the bland hymns or trite sermon was there a crumb of connection to the life-giving faith that had just been awakened in them. Indeed it was the most wasted hour of my week. In the midst of such disappointments and failures, I am not alone in needing stories of hope.

These are not bedtime stories to lull us into believing all is right with the world of church. These churches are not like sterile, tidy commercial greenhouses where everything is under careful temperature and humidity control. Rather, these stories take place in turbulent, tumultuous, and terrifying times. In the midst of such chaos, hope matters. Greenhouses of Hope are messy, organic, creative, inventive, and sometimes chaotic places. Nonetheless, they cultivate just the right nutrients to sustain and strengthen young people who want to change the world rather than flee from it.

We tell these stories so that readers will recognize familiar longings, catch glimpses of their own stories reflected, and be inspired to more fully imagine church as they *wish* it would be. Read the stories as you might visit a garden, noticing the native species and the kinds of care provided them. Wonder about what species grow in the soil of *your* congregation. What does *your* Greenhouse of Hope look like? What ideas might you nurture anew after having glimpsed green shoots sprouting up elsewhere? We urge you to think about the ways your congregation is creating space for the dreams of young people to be grafted into God's dreams for the world.

Churches with deep roots and ancient ways are catching glimpses of the future reflected in the eyes of their young. Teens and twenty-somethings are seeing visions. When adults who love them embrace this glimmer, when they nurture these young leaders, churches engage in God's good work of making green a desert place.

CHAPTER 1

Greenhouses of Hope

A GUIDED PILGRIMAGE

Dori Grinenko Baker

> We just said, "We're gonna stop complaining about the church we've experienced and try to become the church we dream of."
> We reclaim abandoned spaces.[1]
>
> —SHANE CLAIBORNE

Hope Emerging within Ancient Structures

The metaphorical roots of this project lie down the road from where I live in Virginia, at a six-and-a-half-acre renovated community garden called Lynchburg Grows.[2] As I set out to find churches across the country that are paying careful attention to new life emerging within their existing structures, I was struck by similarities between the lovingly restored greenhouses that make up Lynchburg Grows and thriving mainline churches. In this chapter I tell the story of the greenhouses that inspired me and the kind of hope that, in the words of Shane Claiborne, might help us "reclaim abandoned spaces" on our way to becoming "the church we dream of."

The nine greenhouses were, until recently, dilapidated and abandoned. When growing roses in the United States no longer was profitable, the owners simply walked away. Eight years later, a group of neighbors noticed potential in the abandoned greenhouses. A few committed, hardworking, and called people began a movement. They purchased the greenhouses and began removing years of accumulated debris. They wheelbarrowed out tainted soil and hauled in nutrient-rich compost. In what was once a wasteland, they began creating a multilayered oasis of hope. They recruited volunteers from churches and schools, began educational programs for local children, and partnered with at-risk teens who needed community-service hours.

Here is the oasis I saw when I visited in June of 2009: red Swiss chard, lemon trees, arugula, sweet aromatic basil, sage, and bananas all thriving in pots and raised beds; green peppers and tomatoes ripening in the warm air; a pond nurturing tiny bluegill, whose waste will feed the neighboring spinach. Marky, a special needs student from a nearby high school, showed me around, while Derek, a thirty-seven-year-old survivor of spina bifida, watered a green tangling cucumber vine heavy laden with fruit that would be picked, sold, and eaten on the same day.

As I emerged from one greenhouse, I found a dozen schoolchildren making fragrant bouquets of rose, sage, and basil to take home at the end of their field trip. As I stood outside another greenhouse, I met a recent college graduate who had just completed an internship at the garden. Enthused about how much fun he'd had teaching children where food comes from, that fresh food combats obesity, and that veggies straight from the garden actually taste good, he had changed his major to an emphasis on agricultural education. In yet another greenhouse, a sign celebrated the fact that 95 percent of the produce raised here by parishioners from St. John's Episcopal Church had gone to feed the hungry through local food banks.

In the final greenhouse, I was knocked off my feet by the fragrance of one particular rose—called a *lavande*—the ancestor of an ancient root distinctive among today's commercially grown roses because you can actually smell it. Found during renovation, the lavande rose was lovingly tended back to flourishing.

Next door to the lavande's home stands the one greenhouse that has not been renovated. In this greenhouse roses still grow. Given no fertilizer—only the water that seeps in the cracks and the sun that rises and sets each day—these roses nevertheless keep growing, bursting deep red right through the glass ceilings of the structures that would contain them. With only the most meager sustenance, these roses reach and bloom, but they do so in the midst of numerous obstacles.

I see in them an apt metaphor for God's calling in the lives of young people. God will call young lives, with or without the help of congregations. God will bring them bursting through glass ceilings as they grow toward who they are called to be. But how much better, and how much richer might the journey be if young people were not left to eke out their calling solo, but rather were given the best of their community's resources of attention, love, and nourishment toward their vocational flourishing?[3]

VOCATION: How a person responds to God with the whole of his or her life, including what he or she does to make a living, but also what he or she does to "make a life."[4]

Mainline congregations that are thriving and surviving into the next generations with strong young leaders will be like these renovated greenhouses in three particular ways: First, *they will see an "architecture of possibility" within their infrastructure.* Like renovated greenhouses, denominational churches have at their disposal centuries-old structures of grandeur and beauty. Because of the cost of maintaining old buildings, the word *infrastructure* usually has negative connotations in congregations. Plumbing, pipe organs, and stained glass windows need maintenance. That costs money, which drains the life out of aging congregations and away from missional opportunities that young people might heartily embrace.

Other more powerful, if less tangible, infrastructures are in place: denominations with a generation or more of global grassroots connections in places like Zimbabwe, Mozambique, Tasmania, and

South Korea; thriving partnerships that dig wells and provide mosquito nets to fight malaria; church folk who can respond meaningfully with speed and flexibility to an earthquake in Haiti, because they have spent decades making real friends there; a Korean American pastor who is called by a mostly white congregation in Houston because his denomination holds to hard-won decisions about the importance of fostering relationships across racial and ethnic borders. This kind of infrastructure can be of use to young people who want to change the world.

At the ground level, I see an architecture of possibility. Sometimes that refers to a spectacular piece of real estate located where young people are drawn to form community in collaboration with the economically vulnerable, such as Broad Street Ministry in Philadelphia or Mount Vernon Place United Methodist Church in Washington DC. Both of these were mainline churches on the brink of closing; now they are thriving centers for art, spirituality, worship, mission education, and outreach ministries that collaborate with neighborhood organizations.[5] But often, the architecture of possibility is quiet. It can be a church where a generation of aging activists share their stories of the Montgomery bus boycott with a youth group made up of Goths, hip-hop artists, and slam poets. In the Greenhouses of Hope you will read about, deep infrastructure is a valuable inheritance already being put to good use by young people who want to make a difference in their world.

Second, *thriving congregations will learn to look and listen closely to their context in order to ground themselves in what is organic and indigenous.* Greenhouses of Hope are learning from the Emergent Church movement that if you want to start a new church, you go hang out at the local coffee shop to hear what people care about.[6] You spend a month sleeping in the homeless shelter, befriending those who live there and learning about their struggles. You hang out in the bar around the corner and make connections with lonely people who are longing for a deeper sense of community. If you want to be an old church that has new life emerging within it, you will listen to your closest neighbors. Vibrant churches that are raising new young leaders from within listen and learn what ancient Christian practices are already close at hand, and then everywhere and always invite young people to climb into those practices with them. What is *emerging* within the existing denominational structures? How is the old church finding new life? In the stories told here, the answer to those questions seems tied to the particularities of the local congregation: its racial composition, its ethnic heritage, its neighborhood, its capacity for relationships across generations, or its deeply held historical commitments.

Sometimes, abandoned greenhouses are filled with debris. I remember the closet in the educational wing of a local United Methodist church where I organized the vacation Bible school one summer a few years ago. It was filled with filmstrip machines, egg cartons, and 1950s-era drawings of shepherds tending their flocks. This debris from a long-ago time needed to be removed to make way for the office of the church's first paid youth minister. Removal of debris can be painstaking because of the human stories associated with it. Removal becomes easier once one recognizes that the debris may be antiquated and even harmful theology or rigid institutional structures that no longer serve human flourishing. The Greenhouses of Hope you will read about in this book are places and people engaged in theological reflection that makes way for God's word to burst forth with new meaning for a *particular* time and place.

Third, *thriving congregations will be attentive to how they provide just the right nutrients for the young lives in their care.* An actual greenhouse is a seedbed. It provides the conditions for successful growth. In a greenhouse, young growth goes through a gradual process of hardening off. This is a time of slowly increasing exposure to harsh conditions outside the greenhouse, allowing the plant to become ever more able to sustain itself before it is transplanted to bring life to other places. If congregations grow their people to feed the world, then Greenhouses of Hope ask the question: How are we nurturing the young lives in our care so that they might go forth from us to change the world as agents of the transforming power of Jesus Christ? Hardening off takes many shapes and forms. It involves mission trips that expose young people to living conditions they never imagined, and then asks continually how this new knowing gets incorporated into their daily lives. It involves the messy work of navigating conflict in ways that nevertheless maintain, and maybe even deepen, relationship. Hardening off involves cultivating spiritual practices such as discernment, storytelling, contemplation, silence, Scripture study, conflict resolution, and community building that help young people embrace a distinctively Christian hope in the midst of suffering and despair.

Tony Jones, a leader in the Emergent Church movement, uses the term *old growth* to talk about the established church, from which he encourages young "cultural creatives" to flee for the exciting frontier of "New Christianity."[7] His ecological analogy depicts the old-growth forest as dispensable. Every day, actual old-growth forest in the Southern Hemisphere is destroyed to fuel consumption abroad and subsistence living for impoverished neighbors. The future of our planet, however, depends upon the preservation of this old-growth forest. It is the source not only of important biodiversity but also of the essential element, oxygen, needed to support life. While I, like Jones and others, am captivated by the beautiful adaptations springing up in Emergent Church and see there a promising new movement of God's reforming Spirit, I think it is also important to nurture what is *emerging within* churches that have existed for centuries.[8]

I redirect his metaphor to acknowledge the beauty of the old growth forest that is the denominational, mainline church. Perhaps this is the source of essential resources for the future of humanity. In its seminaries, people still learn to translate ancient Greek and Hebrew themselves so that they can unearth nuanced understandings of Scripture, which is critical if the Bible is to be a source of wisdom for our lives. Students learn to read the original writings of the Desert Fathers and Mothers so that they can bring them to life with authenticity and creativity, opening them to others as they lead a small group or a spiritual quest. Jones rightly empathizes with the young person, clearly called to be a pastor, who sees

seminary as a bothersome speed bump. I want to remind that
young person of a gift hidden there. Yes, seminary can slow one
down, but it can also clothe youthful aspiration in confidence that
comes from disciplined study alongside passionate action. Seminary allows time for mentoring relationships with wise peers and
elders. It steeps young people in a tradition, giving them ownership
of it so that they can then adapt and transform it to meet the complex urgencies of their day. Slowing down is one way of listening
to God's Spirit; it need not entail sluggishness. Seminary can birth
spiritual activists. Ordination processes can create leaders who are
impassioned and capable of restructuring institutions *from within.*
Keeping the resources that exist within the "old-growth" church
ready-at-hand will, however, require a new generation of gifted,
excellent young leaders.

So picture the ancient redwoods of Northern California towering
majestically toward a blue sky. Old-growth forests are where we, the
authors of this book, went looking for Greenhouses of Hope. We
found evidence that some congregations are reclaiming abandoned
spaces. They are clearing out the debris that no longer serves well.
In the midst of being "the church that is" they lean into "the church
that is becoming." Young leaders find here nutrient-rich soil, fertile compost out of which will sprout new, green shoots of promise.
They live out their calling to be entrepreneurial and creative in leading congregations into the future by letting their roots draw deep
sustenance from ancient structures.

I recently asked a group of young students in a seminary classroom to name the obstacles involved in answering a call to ministry
these days. I quickly filled the newsprint with their rapid-fire list of
reasons why a young person with any sense at all might ignore a call.
And yet, here was a room full of people pursuing degrees, taking on
debt, bypassing parental expectations, willing to work within im-
perfect structures—all in pursuit of an authentic response to God's
call. Answering the inner voice despite external pressures requires
courage. What inspires and sustains such courage? I suggest that a
peculiar brand of hope does so.

Hope Emerging with a
Distinctively Christian Aroma

At a 2008 commencement address, novelist Barbara Kingsolver urged Duke University undergraduates to "tiptoe past the dogs of the apocalypse that are sleeping in the shade of your future." She whimsically challenged the myth that success is made of money, status, and escalating isolation in cathedral-ceilinged dream houses, saying, "You could invent a new kind of success that includes children's poetry, butterfly migrations, butterfly kisses, the Grand Canyon, eternity. If somebody says 'Your money or your life,' you could say: Life. And mean it. You'll see things collapse in your time, the big houses, the empires of glass. The new green things that sprout up in the wreck—those will be yours."[9]

What kind of hope can sustain young people who must come down from the mountaintop of a glittering moment of achievement—such as college graduation—and begin the nitty-gritty work of carving out a future? This is a prickly predicament for young people living in a materialistic culture when all indicators predict less financial prosperity for future generations. Exactly how does one "tiptoe past the dogs of the apocalypse" with eyes ready to see the "new green things that sprout up in the wreck" when living on *this* planet in *these* decades? Young people called to reshape a world in which they envision a promising future could use a healthy dose of hope. Those being nurtured within congregations have access to a *distinctively Christian hope* sharpened through the ages. Christian congregations are uniquely positioned to provide: (1) emancipatory hope; (2) hope in action; and (3) hope resulting from an authentic response to human suffering. Together these might be called *emancipatory hope in action*.

EMANCIPATORY HOPE

Practical theologian Evelyn Parker writes about hope from her context as an African American scholar who grew up during the civil right era in a church that "bathed the youth in a social theology of involvement and confident expectation."[10] The black and white college students she saw coming to her hometown of Hattiesburg, Mississippi, as part of the Student Nonviolent Coordinating Committee incarnated hope. Out of this history and through her research with contemporary black teens, Parker writes of hope as "decidedly Christian and rooted in the experiences and beliefs of African American women, children, and men. That hope expects deliverance from economic, political, and racial oppression through the power of God, which requires one to live in the present *as an agent of change for God's justice.*"[11] Emancipatory hope acknowledges the role humans play in helping to bring about God's vision of human flourishing. Historical movements that seek freedom from domination—such as those led by Jesus and his followers like Joan of Arc and Sojourner Truth—illustrate emancipatory hope.[12]

Parker distinguishes emancipatory hope from two other approaches to the future. One is wishful thinking; the other is otherworldly, apocalyptic beliefs. Wishful thinking is desire and longing without the possibility of actual fulfillment. To Parker, wishful thinking is not negative; rather, it can be the "seed of hope" by nourishing action. The people who started Lynchburg Grows discovered the abandoned greenhouses after restoring an elderly man's backyard garden that had been accidentally destroyed. At first, they only dreamed of what they could do with the abandoned structures they stumbled upon. What started as a fantasy took on a hint of possibility as people began talking to neighbors, making contact with the owners, and getting legal advice. The wish took root and grew. Hope emerged as people began to experience expectation, confidence, and even assurance and faith that the project was possible. Because this hope was linked to the potential flourishing of the surrounding human community, this is an example of emancipatory hope growing out of wishful thinking.[13]

EMANCIPATORY: Related to human freedom and liberation.

Otherworldly or apocalyptic beliefs, on the other hand, are often obstacles to emancipatory hope. Parker found young people who expressed these beliefs to be "pessimistic and negative about the present." They tend to have low expectations for human agency because they see the world "ending before earthly dehumanizing conditions are transformed."[14]

Parker uses the work of theologian James Cone to nuance emancipatory hope as "a verb creating active expectation of the coming presence of Jesus." This kind of hope requires individuals "to live as if the vision is already realized in the present."[15] Emancipatory hope provides a framework that Parker uses to foster a spirituality of resistance in African American adolescents. In Parker's view, "it does not matter if they fully experience this new reality in their lifetime," but that they see their actions even now in light of faith in the Spirit of God who is at work transforming injustice. Like other liberation theologians, Parker locates hope-filled actions to confront evil on a "continuum of small acts of justice to monumental movements."[16]

HOPE IN ACTION

Hebrew Bible scholar Walter Brueggemann likewise focuses on human agency as an important factor in Christian hope. Like Parker, he acknowledges that hope need not accomplish its work in our lifetime in order to be reliable and worthy of our investment. He writes, "The hope that is God's gift to faith is therefore precisely *hope*—not sight, not inevitability, not finality. It must be grasped and implemented by the community of faith and by all who, from whatever sources of longing, imagination, and common grace, glimpse possibilities for what is *new*. It must become hope in action."[17] Hope, for Brueggemann, means human agency engaging with God's Spirit, which is at work transforming the world. Members of St. John's Episcopal Church, for instance, saw a group of citizens engaging a good work at Lynchburg Grows. Although the project did not originate within them, they embraced it as a meaningful way of enacting their faith. For Brueggemann, hope also means recognizing the "companionable presence of many others who, even if they do not move with us in obvious ways, are nevertheless in close proximity and seem to be journeying in the same direction." For this reason, he looks to "genuine faith in many different forms" as a source of courage in light of forces of economics and empire that seem to be shaping the future. "The hope that the divine Spirit breathes into our often skeptical and reluctant spirits translates itself ever anew into ethically concrete behavior whose object is to implement God's love for the world and all its creations. *Christians do not expect a perfect world, but they do expect and hope to change it.*"[18]

Finally, Brueggemann sees hope emerging not when we escape the world's suffering but when we engage it. He writes, "Suffering produces hope (Rom. 5:3–5) *but not just any suffering.*[19] Suffering that is recognized, admitted, voiced, and enacted produces hope. We do not know why, but it is so. Suffering denied and unarticulated produces numbness and rage irrational. Israel knew that." Hope, therefore, in Brueggemann's view, is deeply linked to the biblical tradition of lament, psalms of grief that express anger and loss. This seems especially important for mainline congregations today. Whereas one generation ago, these churches stood at the center of communities as undisputed shapers of belief, practices, and culture, today they are one voice among many at a noisy intersection where multiple meanings vie. Perhaps naming the loss of Christendom as a central force enables the mainline church to recapture a vision of Christianity as a living movement. What if grieving the failures of the institutional church is not the final amen at the end of a hymn but merely the necessary prelude to an ongoing song? For Brueggemann, loss that is voiced "emancipates from ancient anger, liberates from cherished rage, and permits new waves of God-given constructive energy."[20]

EMANCIPATORY HOPE IN ACTION

Emancipatory hope actively engages with God's Spirit in practices that liberate toward human flourishing. We borrow this term from its origins in African American experience so that it might be available to young people of all races and ethnicities who are inheriting a world in which numerous ongoing forms of oppression exist. Whether, for example, you were born into poverty or whether you come from a birthplace of privilege to align yourself with movements to eradicate poverty, emancipatory hope speaks to the uphill climb with a grounded optimism that is not naïve. Brueggemann's insistence that Christian hope must grow out of the recognition and naming of human suffering and be enacted in *this* world helps move us beyond disengaged pessimism. It fuels our desire to look closely at particular congregations that seem to embody the mantra "in the church tell the story, in the world live the story."[20] It is to these churches—greenhouses of a distinctive type of Christian hope—that we go looking for "sources of longing, imagination, and common grace" to inspire a movement of congregations that care deeply about raising up young people whom God will call forth to change the world.

EMANCIPATORY HOPE-IN-ACTION: Hope that does not abandon the world or seek to perfect it but does set out to change it. A worldly hope grounded in God's optimism.

In her speech to Duke graduates, Kingsolver advised a wizened optimism to an audience raised in the Age of Irony, an audience only too well aware that "we're a world at war, ravaged by disagreements, a bizarrely globalized people in which the extravagant excesses of one culture wash up as famine or flood on the shores of another." This reality and an accompanying widespread skepticism might lull us all—young people included—into an apathy that keeps us from large- and small-scale actions to reverse environmental destruction, species extinction, and the other harbingers of a seemingly dying planet.

But for this: In words that call to mind historical movements of human freedom fueled by *emancipatory hope in action*, Kingsolver says, "The arc of history is longer than human vision. It bends. We abolished slavery, we granted universal suffrage. We have done hard things before. And every time it took a terrible fight between people who could not imagine changing the rules, and those who said, 'We already did. We have made the world new.'"[21]

Both abolitionists and women suffragists were in part empowered by distinctively Christian hope to confront the evils they inherited, even as their adversaries misused Scripture to uphold structures of oppression.[22] Young people today are inheriting the evil of rampant consumption and a planet showing signs of demise; they also need to inherit a form of hope equal to the challenge of their age. It is *this* kind of hope—a worldly hope grounded in God's covenant—for which we go looking. It is *this* kind of hope you might recognize as you think about your own context in light of the churches we describe here. An emancipatory hope in action does not abandon the world or seek to perfect it, but it *does* set out to change it. Like the lavande rose in the greenhouse, this kind of hope has a storied past and an aroma that demands attention.

But how can we the church and its leaders best pay attention to hope? How do we listen to a congregation's stories? Ethnography, the art of immersing oneself in a place long enough to hear its unique rhythms, is one such way of paying close attention to hope where it emerges.

Hope Emerging within the Real Congregations We Know and Love

Ethnography is a specific way of listening deeply to congregations from a perspective of care and empathy, rather than pretending to be unbiased, detached observers. It is not only a research method but also a way of doing ministry. It opens the stories of people, congregations, families, and communities. Learning to listen to these stories can transform the way we minister.

LISTENING WITH NEW EARS

Ethnography is a rather humble art. It seeks to uncover small truths in discrete places, thereby helping to bridge the gaps left by big-picture research methods that sketch the contours of large cultural movements. In addition to using ethnography as a methodology here, we invite the reader to do research with us. Along the way, you will learn to listen with an ethnographer's ear to your own context. You will find yourself hearing stories of deep truth that were once just part of the background noise.

Big-picture research projects are immensely helpful to those who care about congregations and young people. Looking briefly at one such large-scale research project on young people's religious beliefs will help us understand what ethnography *is not* and why it is most useful to the task of exploring Greenhouses of Hope. The National Study of Youth and Religion (NSYR), led by sociologist Christian Smith, studied the religious lives of more than three thousand U.S. teens and reinterviewed them when they were between the ages of eighteen and twenty-three to see how their religious lives were faring as young adults. In a book reporting on the first study, Smith said that young people's religious beliefs mirror those of their parents, but not in a way we can be happy about. In a mouthful of words that nonetheless became common parlance in youth ministry circles, Smith defined "moralistic therapeutic deism" as a form of colonized Christianity that he finds prevalent among the young people he and his researchers interviewed by phone and in person. Moralistic therapeutic deism bears little resemblance to historic teachings of the Christian faith, instead reflecting a version of American civil religion in which God fixes things, roots for your team, and rewards good behavior with a happy afterlife. Despite reporting that much of religious formation imbues this sort of diluted, watered-down Christianity, Smith's findings did have an encouraging word for those involved in ministry with youth: the presence of faithful adults in the lives of young people makes an enormous difference. The follow-up study likewise showed that formative religious influences in the lives of teenagers had an impact on their embrace of faith in later years.[23]

All of this is useful information to people in churches that care about their young people. Smith's findings have stimulated conversation among congregational leaders who hope to reorient Christianity in the United States toward a more faithful living out of the gospel. In reviewing the book on Smith's most recent findings, youth ministry scholar Kenda Creasy Dean uses it to do just that: "While most American institutions drop out of young people's lives during, emerging adulthood, churches are uniquely equipped to practice the art of spiritual accompaniment, sharing a way of life with young people that participates in God's activity in the world before, during, and long after confirmation, until young adults are ready to spiritually accompany someone else. Smith's research offers us hope, but not a blueprint. Churches should take it from here."[24]

Many churches would like to follow Dean's advice and "take it from here." But how? If indeed moralistic therapeutic deism runs rampant in U.S. culture, how do we wiggle free of it long enough to provide alternatives that reflect the gospel more authentically? Dean reminds us that many mainline churches do not see themselves reflected in the limp theology Smith observes. Their young people may not have been the ones interviewed; they may have a very different story to tell. These are the stories that slip through the cracks of large-scale, mostly quantitative research on young people and the church.

Ethnography—with its detailed snapshots of real human communities—suggests a way forward. Rather than interviewing thousands of people over the telephone using standard surveys during the dinner hour, ethnographers move into the neighborhood. They take a close-up look at one particular pocket of church life, which involves attending worship services, educational hours, car washes, and bake sales. Ethnographers listen carefully to the music and the lyrics in the hymnbook and on the iPod. They look closely at the art hanging on the walls and ask question upon question of members at all levels of leadership. All of this takes place over months and sometimes years of interactions that involve face-to-face, participant observation and telephone, e-mail, and Web-based information gathering.[25]

After gathering field notes, recordings, and interview transcripts, ethnographers tell a story that reflects what they saw, heard, and learned. They don't craft the story alone but remain in conversation with their research partners, checking out their interpretations and altering them when necessary. As one ethnographer writes, "The findings are literally created as the investigation proceeds."[26] Along the way, they can't help but get involved. After listening closely and thoroughly, an ethnographer sometimes will make a comment here or a suggestion there that gets enacted, changing the very phenomena they seek to observe. Sometimes, the act of listening intentionally and empathetically breaks open an insight that can fuel impassioned action in the one who is speaking. In ethnography, all of this is okay. Not only is it okay, it is expected and affirmed. Ethnography is a way of learning about people that discards an earlier sentiment that research should be detached, unbiased, and scholarship-at-a-distance.

Each of the authors in this book was a minister, pastor, preacher, or Christian educator before he or she became a scholar. Each of us cares passionately about the future of the church, and we try to write transparently from this perspective. Often, though, loving the church means having to critique it. So as ethnographers, we try not to shy away from reporting the things that we may prefer to ignore. As much as we might wish otherwise, churches are fighting over scriptural interpretations of sexuality. The fight has an effect on young people. We talk about it. As much as we might pretend to ignore it, churches differ over whether the most important task is bringing souls to Christ or acting with Christlike hospitality in the multifaith world in which we live. Young people are listening with highly attuned ears to how we treat each other in the midst of this difference. We talk about that. Bringing these places of unease, deep suffering, or potential disagreement into the light can be part of the ethnographic task. In this way, ethnography becomes a form of activist research, with an agenda of helping congregations see themselves as they are, name their grief and loss, and move forward with renewed energy toward their vision of God's reign. It can empower congregations to respond to their communal call to more fully embody God's dreams for the world. We think that *all* research is tinged with the scholar's perspective. Practicing the habit of uncovering biases is part of the ethnographer's toolkit.

Cultivating an Ethnographic Disposition

Over the past decade, ethnography has become a popular way to engage in learning with people in congregations. The more researchers began using these tools unapologetically, the more they began seeing within them ways to improve the practice of ministry.[27]

Something beautiful happens when a skilled listener creates a safe space for stories to be told in an unhurried, unworried fashion. Ethnographers find themselves at times entering into a holy space, a space in which the speaker may be saying something brand new, even to themselves. In the pages that follow, you will read lengthy quotes from interviews. At times, you will catch a glimpse of that sacred moment in which the speaker seems to be coming to a new awareness. This is the beauty of deep listening. Although the authors of this book use ethnography as a research tool, we are well aware that we are also engaging in an art of ministry. We hold this tool carefully, even as we invite others into a deep listening that asks people to pause, take a deep breath, and reflect with another person about their lives, their values, their communities, and their commitments.

Thomas E. Frank, a seasoned observer of church life, writes about turning to ethnographic practices of listening as a way to escape what he perceived to be market-driven perspectives prevalent in church-improvement literature. He found most of that writing to be largely prescriptive, tending to depict a congregation "as a franchise in a service industry, completely missing the remarkable imaginative life of a community of persons who stay together over time, practicing a faithful way of life together." As an alternative approach, he favors a disposition toward ethnography that "honors this particular congregation, the one right in front of me, the one I am serving."[28]

Our aim as contributors to this book is to write lively ethnographic narratives of churches engaged in nurturing vocation in young people. It is a descriptive act that is not for the sake of sharing best practices of exemplary congregations alone, but, what is more significant, to help readers see *their own context* from a new angle. "The soul thrives on contemplating difference," Frank writes, "for if I see your place and symbols clearly, I can see my own more distinctively as well." In addition, he says, "Imagination is sparked by the juxtaposition of opposites, the collision of difference." Laying distinct worlds side by side can sometimes allow an unexpected view to emerge.[29]

In this book, we aim to engage you in imagining church anew out of an "ethnographic disposition." This means that even though you may be a leader in your congregation, you learn to occasionally practice being an observer, listening closely to the people in your congregation, at times withholding your immediate response in order to slowly and carefully tease out a full description of another person's way of seeing things. As Frank says, "Paying attention is . . . a spiritual discipline that not only centers one's life but opens the way to entirely unanticipated dimensions of experience."[30] Perhaps you will find yourself stepping back for a moment to really pay attention to a person who typically drives you crazy. Instead of retreating to a time-honored response, you may just pause, listen, and turn to wonder about the story that lies beneath a strongly held belief about the salary of the youth pastor or the designated parking space for ushers. You may even go poking around to see if you can unearth the story. If given a listening ear, the story may release its power into a form more accessible to being used by God's Spirit.

Practicing an ethnographic disposition doesn't mean you listen to everything with equal attentiveness. You become attuned to what matters most to you; and you listen carefully in multiple places for what may be connected to that. If you are a person who cares about the future of the church and you see the importance of engaging young people in falling in love with its future, an ethnographic disposition can help you apply this book and its humble offerings to your zone of influence. Questions at the end of each chapter will draw your attention back to the ethnographic disposition to think about how the narrative you just read speaks to the narrative you are in the midst of living.

Hope Emerging as Practice along the Path of a Shared Pilgrimage

The authors of this book use the framework of Christian practices to describe what we observe in congregations. Dorothy Bass reminds us that "Practices are borne by social groups over time and are constantly negotiated in the midst of changing circumstances. As clusters of activities within which meaning and doing are inextricably woven, practices shape behavior while also fostering a practice—specific knowledge, capacities, dispositions, and virtues. Those who participate in practices are formed in particular ways of thinking about and living in the world."[31] Understood in this way, a practice is a cluster of activities. For instance, the practice of worship includes such activities as singing, praying, offering thanks, preaching, and celebrating the Eucharist. Practices of hospitality might include working at a soup kitchen or hosting a drop-in center for neighborhood youth. The practice of congregations in calling people into Christian vocations involves a cluster of interwoven activities that are at times difficult to untangle from one another. As the authors of this book seek to get a close look at the patterns, we also observe some behaviors that just don't fit: these behaviors critique the patterns or seem paradoxical to other behaviors. Rather than ignoring these discrepancies, we note them and wonder what they might teach us about change, emerging practices, and the living, breathing character of congregations.

The authors in this book define specific practices they see at work in the congregations they studied. Like Bass, they found practices are not easy to separate into neat and tidy units; they overlap, race around, blend together, and become crystal clear for a moment before circling back. Speaking of congregations in terms of their

practices is a way of constructing knowledge that is admittedly partial and limited. This is not a complete picture: As ethnographers,
we don't go into a congregation wanting to gather all data. We have
particular goals in mind. Our goal was to identify practices that we
see as being fundamentally important for congregations that mindfully attend to the emerging vocations of young people.

We were aided in indentifying these practices by the work of
Calling Congregations, an initiative of The Fund for Theological
Education (FTE), which has over the past five years been hosting
"temporary congregations" made up of people from churches across
the country who are awakening to the need to care for vocation in
young people. Over the course of repeated multiday retreats, congregational teams learned to share stories about their own inchoate
yearning to be part of God's dream for the world and to elicit such
stories from others. They were ordinary people from all walks of life:
some were ordained pastors, some volunteered in church-sponsored
domestic violence shelters, some were youth ministers straight out
of college, and some were elderly, awakened passionately in their
grandparenting years to care about the young. They came from
Omaha, Nebraska; Lake City, Florida; Olathe, Kansas; Alexandria,
Virginia; Eugene, Oregon; and all points in-between. At the end of
each of these retreats, participants found themselves speaking a new
language steeped in the rich imagery of Scripture, overlaid with pictures of real lives they had glimpsed in one another's stories. Because
the gatherings were intentionally arranged to reflect diversity of age,
gender, race, ethnicity, and geography, people frequently reported
having tasted and seen, momentarily, the reign of God.

As my colleagues at Calling Congregations and I learned and
listened alongside these congregational teams, we carefully observed
a growing network of congregations that recognize what is at stake
in developing the next generation of gifted young leaders. We have
identified four core practices that congregations enact as part of caring for vocation. These VocationCARE practices are explained in
further detail below under "A Guide to Questions for Reflection."

The following chapters illuminate some of these practices explicitly and others more implicitly.[32] We hope your imagination will be sparked. Imagination is perhaps the most important nutrient available in a Greenhouse of Hope. As Frank says, "A deep river feeds the roots of congregations; the collective imagination expresses itself in a profusion of symbols, stories, rituals, and activities. Thus congregations themselves are springs of theological imagination."[33]

Pilgrimage, as distinct from tourism, is a way of visiting different lands in which the traveler remains open to the holy and, therefore, open to transformation. When on a pilgrimage, it is helpful to have a guide who knows the landmarks, can tell the stories behind places of significance, or knows where to be for the best view, just when the sun dips below the horizon. Often, these guides are people with deep connections to the place. This is the case here. Each of these guides has chosen a Greenhouse of Hope to live with, listen to, care about, come to know, and reflect critically upon. We embark on a guided pilgrimage with them now.

A Guide to Questions for Reflection

At the end of each chapter, I pose two sets of questions to promote discussion among readers. The first relates to engaging the Vocation-CARE practices. The second set of questions prompts you to take on the *ethnographic disposition* mentioned earlier. Such a disposition prompts you to wonder about your own context after having read a thick description of another congregation's culture. As you witness the ethnographer at work in each chapter, you may find yourself learning to ask new questions. These questions might encourage you to try listening in ways that invite people in to share new truths and voice meanings that are only beginning to come to expression. This is a way of practicing ethnography as a form of ministry.

The two sets of questions overlap and speak to each other. The first is more structured; the second more open-ended. You will find the one that best helps you think through the themes in the book and the ways you may use it to create a greenhouse culture in your context.

The four core practices conveyed in the acronym CARE in VocationCARE stand for:

C—Create hospitable space to explore Christian vocation;
A—Ask self-awakening questions;
R—Reflect theologically on self and community; and
E—Explore, enact, and establish ministry opportunities

Each of these practices takes on different shapes and forms in varying contexts, as we will see throughout the book. But some basic definitions here will help you identify the practices when you see them at work.[34]

Creating hospitable space for exploring vocational questions involves both inner space and outer space. It can mean covenanting to be fully present as a listener; to hold one another's stories in care and confidence; or to withhold trying to fix one another. It may mean a physical space in the church where young people find themselves welcomed and relaxed enough to share freely. It may mean a particular set of adults who regularly make young people feel at home. It is not an additional ministry program; rather, it is an ethos a congregation offers that allows people to listen generously across generations and walks of life.

Asking self-awakening questions wakes us up to our own lives, the life around us, and the life of God. These are questions that we are not always in the habit of asking, but that become more habitual with practice. Self-awakening questions help us hear God's call or listen more attentively for God's presence. They are questions that emerge when our heads and hearts are open to the holy. They might occur in a sermon, in a one-on-one conversation, or a small group setting. When we practice asking self-awakening questions, we often frame them to invite metaphors or images that help the storyteller explore who she is, what she loves, and what she cares passionately about. They help the speaker walk around in his story long enough to remember risks, challenges, choices, and outcomes.

Reflecting theologically on self and community is a disciplined practice of putting our lives and experiences in conversation with our religious heritage.[35] It happens when we look for the places where our stories intersect with God's story. We do this by paying attention to the feelings that arise in a story or life event and asking questions such as, Where did I experience the holy? What image of God from Scripture or tradition seems to hold meaning right now? When done in community, theological reflection can help provoke new insights about who God is and how God acts through us and in our world. Theological reflection can also lead us to wonder about how we are called to act *next*. What small step might we take as we seek to be co-creators enacting God's shalom in our world? In this way, theological reflection enables us to find meaning and purpose in our daily lives, in addition to imagining the trajectories of our lifetimes.

Exploring, enacting, and establishing ministry opportunities involves all that a congregation does to let young people try on a vast array of leadership roles. This ranges from including young people in the simple task of being an acolyte to creating year-round internships in which young people serve alongside the pastors to learn tasks such as hospital visitation, sermon-writing, and funeral planning. Do young people help collect the offering? Are they invited into real decision-making? Congregations teach in all that they do; when they invite young people *into the action* that is happening front and center, they teach that young people are a vital, necessary, life-giving part of the body of Christ.

CHAPTER 2

Staying Awake

WHEN GOD MOMENTS ECHO IN COMMUNITY

Margaret Ann Crain

> Authentic lives reflecting integral patterns grounded in religious wisdom and values result from seeking God's presence, not apart from the world, but in the midst of it. Seeking God's presence involves theological reflection, the artful discipline of putting our experience into conversation with the heritage of the Christian tradition.[1]
>
> —PATRICIA O'CONNELL KILLEN AND JOHN DE BEER

Emily, a college senior, is happy to tell me about herself, even though we have just met. Her brown eyes search the space between us as we settle in among the bicycles and secondhand furniture in her North Chicago student apartment. Her speech is full of stops and starts. She thinks carefully about each question, seeking to articulate her experience with authenticity. She tells me about playing guitar and writing songs. She talks about mission trips to build schools in Ghana and repair homes in the foothills of Appalachia. In the past few years, she has chosen classes, found summer jobs, changed colleges, and imagined her future career all out of a sense of God's call on her life.

As she grapples with the still unfolding details of her future, she does so with a feeling of connectedness. She knows she is part of something larger than herself. Her congregation is the source of that knowing. She says, "At First Church your Christian life and your daily life—it's all the same. I'm applying the same passion that I have from Appalachia to urban children. I'm taking environmental classes, learning about the horrible educational problems . . . I transferred [colleges] to do that. God is bringing something out of me."

She describes her congregation, First United Methodist Church of Evanston, Illinois (FUMC-Evanston), as a place that has shaped her so profoundly that a life of service is simply part of who she is. "I truly believe that I can make a difference. I don't feel that I *need* to keep doing service. It's just that it happens. Now service is a part of my life," she says. "It's like eating breakfast, lunch, and dinner."

Emily's life has challenges: she is the oldest of three children of color adopted by a white couple; she deals with identity issues as a person of black, white, and Puerto Rican heritage; a sibling suffers with mental illness and is not able to live at home anymore.

Emily works out these concerns by writing songs about them and by staying awake to what she calls "God moments."

THEOLOGICAL REFLECTION: The act of naming one's story as part of God's story, particularly as it is revealed through Scripture, Christian tradition, or an experience of Christian community.[2]

She describes a God moment as an instant of crystal clear knowing that God is present and active in the world. Emily and other young people at FUMC-Evanston have learned a practice of theological reflection that makes it normal to name and claim these God moments. When strung together, God moments create a story. Emily's story is part of her church's story. Her church's story is part of God's story.

Staying awake to the God moments is important in this congregation. Birthed through youth group mission trips, this alertness to God's presence is woven throughout this congregation's life as a community. It seems to be a central practice that helps young people nurture their sense of purpose in the world. As I eavesdropped on these God moments and the story they tell from many nooks and crannies of this congregation over the course of a year, I glimpsed the "soul of this congregation."[3] The soul of this congregation has nurtured a generation of young adults who are using the Christian story to help them map a future, rather than drifting away from church in their college years, as many of the millennial generation do.[4] The soul of this congregation cherishes deep relationships across ages, cultures, and geography. The soul of this congregation values the voices and leadership of its young people while it answers a deep yearning for an experience of community that, once lived into, keeps people coming back for more. The soul of this congregation has emerged over time, helped along by leaders who made deliberate choices.

As a member of this congregation since 1998, I chose to study it more closely when I became part of a research team investigating practices that nurture vocation in young people. As a grandmother with grown children, I had not raised my own kids in this congregation, but I had watched with great interest as teenagers seemed to be pouring enormous energy into mission trips—and finding *themselves* along the way. I wanted to tease out the practices that help Emily and others like her experience a depth of transformation *in church* that results in a life of discipleship *outside of church.* It is a formation process that has led several to seminary and others to vocations that serve the common good. Emily described her early experiences in the youth group: "What hit me really hard was going into church and being able to talk about some of the things that kind of made you uncomfortable. . . . I trusted my peers. I trusted Jane and the other youth leaders. It was a really cool place to express yourself, to talk about things that you might have done wrong. It was a place to really find answers. . . . I realized that Christianity was less about preaching and more about helping others and learning how to do that through this Christian community."

In this chapter, I will describe the practices that are forming young people like Emily who are seeking to live as disciples called forth to offer themselves and their gifts to the world. The thick description of this congregational culture I organize around five interwoven themes. They are as follows:

- Building heartfelt community that incorporates similarity *and* difference
- Experiencing and naming God as an ongoing act of shared theological reflection
- Integrating transformative mission experiences
- Using the language of call and vocation at key moments in the community's life
- Reversing hierarchies of age and status as youth lead the congregation in its commitment to mission

Together, these practices get acted out habitually over time. They inform and strengthen one another and result in a congregation that nurtures vocation in people of all ages, seemingly by second nature. As a result of years of immersion in this community of intentional formation, young people know how to recognize and name the presence of the Holy Spirit. In the experiencing and naming, they are transformed. They listen and hear the call of God on their lives. They become disciples who, like Emily, are finding their purpose in life in light of their Christian faith.

A Methodist "Hive" Revived: The Congregation and Its Context

The congregation that nurtured Emily occupies a towering, gray, Gothic structure near the commercial center of Evanston, Illinois. The imposing exterior of First United Methodist Church speaks to its central position in the community's history and belies the church's more recent struggle to survive. Evanston was founded by Methodists, a fact reflected in streets named after the denomination's founders, such as Wesley and Asbury. Methodists started Northwestern University, just two blocks from the church, as a school to prepare young men for what is now Garrett-Evangelical, one of United Methodism's thirteen denominational seminaries. Frances Willard, a Methodist woman who lived next door to the church, once described her town as a "beehive of Methodism." From that hive, she founded the Women's Christian Temperance Union (WCTU). At first focused solely on the link between poverty and intemperance, the WCTU later widened its reform agenda to mobilize leaders for the women's suffrage movement.[5]

The founders of Evanston also started this congregation. Its sanctuary is graced with beautiful stained glass and a wood carving that stands more than thirty feet above the altar table. The famous Chicago Prairie School architect, Thomas E. Tallmadge, designed the building in 1911. More than nine hundred people can be seated in its worship space. In 1952 it was the largest Methodist Church in the United States.

By 1990, however, the congregation had shrunk to only a few hundred people who could not afford to maintain the huge building. Walls crumbled from water damage. Dark hallways led to large classrooms that people rarely visited. Inadequate bathrooms threatened to cease working at all. When Rev. Dean Francis came in 1995, he found a congregation with a great past but an uncertain future. The education program consisted of classes for children that took place at the same time as the single worship service on Sundays. Adults found little opportunity for structured learning, although their desire for intellectual stimulation was strong. Rev. Francis described the church as "an intellectual, in-your-head kind of place," not a "hands-on, confront-poverty-and-oppression-directly kind of place." Vestiges of the church's grand history lived on in two important ways: annual rummage sales that produced forty thousand dollars to be sent away for missions, and strong lay leaders involved at the denominational level.

The city of Evanston is located on the north border of Chicago; Lake Michigan is its eastern border. Today, Evanston is the beginning of the area known as the prosperous "North Shore," but it is not nearly as affluent as towns a few miles further north. Kenilworth, about three miles north, is one of the highest per capita income towns in the United States. Dominated by Northwestern University, Evanston is diverse both economically and culturally. In 1995 the university was healthy but the town was struggling. All the major retailers had left the central commercial district. People passed along the sidewalks without a pause as they hurried to catch commuter trains into the Chicago Loop for work.

The commercial district came back to life, however, in the late 1990s when an eighteen-screen movie theater moved in and an upscale grocery store opened a half block from the church. New restaurants and businesses flocked in. Several high-rise condos brought young professionals and empty nesters. Today sidewalks are bustling at all times of the day and evening. A website describing the area asks, "Are you craving Japanese, Chinese, Irish, or Greek food? The North Shore's got it. Do you have a taste for French, Italian, Middle Eastern, Spanish, or Thai cuisine? You'll find that, too!"

The congregation could have been left behind, as have many high steeple churches in reviving neighborhoods across the country. Instead, it kept pace with the neighborhood's renewal. I witnessed firsthand the resurgence of this grand old congregation. Its worship today is powerful and meaningful. Its congregation is diverse and enthusiastic. In the summertime, one service moves to the grassy park across the street, where worshipers look out over the dazzling blue waters of Lake Michigan. Joggers and dog walkers join in for a hymn or prayer.

What had been a white, upper-middle-class congregation became more diverse both economically and culturally. Currently the congregation is about 75–80 percent Anglo, 15 percent African American, and has a few Asian Americans. A high educational level provides one unifying factor in the diversity. Francis says, "The interesting thing about the congregation is that we have more diversity among our children and youth than we do among our adults. On Sunday morning you might not see the depth of that diversity in the sanctuary, but if you go upstairs into the Sunday school classrooms, you see it much more." The congregation's mission statement posted prominently on a street sign highlights this value: "We celebrate our diversity of personhood, including age, gender, race, education, economic status, sexual orientation, and special needs. We are glad you are here to experience our theology of faith and love put into practice."

During my research within this congregation, I frequently went "upstairs into the Sunday school classrooms" and beyond and discovered the pervasive presence of youth, children, and young adults who seem to lead the congregation in more than just diversity. Integrated into the life of the church, ministry to children and youth instills a sense of vocation as it builds community and engages in service through mission trips. As Rev. Francis describes it, the "presence [of youth] here is not some afterthought. In that sense as we've moved along, the youth are leading us, not the other way around."

Participants in a recent adult mission trip echoed this story: Hearing about God moments from young people made adults hungry for similar experiences. When a group of adults decided to take a mission trip of their own, the experienced youth became their teachers.

Building Heartfelt Community
That Incorporates Similarity *and* Difference

A heartfelt sense of community is often a hallmark of a strong youth group. But when such a youth group flies solo, disconnecting one age group from the rest of the congregation, it can create an unrepeatable longing as youth grow older. FUMC-Evanston has found a way to live out a deep sense of community that begins among peers, but spreads intentionally across generations, expands to include far-flung neighbors encountered on mission trips, and encompasses communion with God.

The intergenerational connection is often highly visible during worship services. An event last winter is a good example. The January children's sermon drew about twenty young children to the steps leading to the chancel. The usual scrambling for seats next to Rev. Jane Cheema, pastor of youth and family ministry, worked out peaceably as she began her children's sermon. The text was the story of the call of Samuel (1 Sam. 3:1–10). Cheema began by holding up her cell phone and asking, "Can you hear me now?" Alluding to a well-known television commercial, she asked the children if they knew of times when their moms or dads had trouble getting good reception. She likened the calling of Samuel to this: his reception of God's call was poor. He couldn't really understand the message. Cheema laughs as she tells what happened next: "I was talking with the kids. I told them, 'This guy Samuel kept hearing all these funny things from God. He was about the same age you are.' I was using my phone to illustrate that sometimes the message doesn't get through. Just then, I looked down and I saw that my phone was actually ringing." The small red cell phone she was holding to make her point buzzed unexpectedly, startling her. She looked quizzically at her phone, and then glanced up to the balcony in the back of the sanctuary where the teenagers all sit together. She knew from the caller ID that it was one of them calling her. As if on cue, the teens had whipped out their phones, speed-dialing Cheema the moment she held up her phone. One of them got through.

Laughter filled the sanctuary as Cheema revealed where the call had come from. Cheema remembers this as a powerful moment of connection drawing people together throughout the huge sanctuary and across the gulf of generations. Cheema ended the children's sermon with a prayer that all of us might hear God's call when it comes.

This unscripted moment captures a deeply held belief in this congregation that children and youth are a part of an alive and spontaneous worshiping community. Although many of the teens sit together in the back of the balcony, the worship leaders almost always refer to them. The teens also act as readers, ushers, liturgical dancers, and worship leaders. As Francis says, "The youth program is not something that we do separate from the life of the church. Youth are a deeply engrained part of the life of the church." Cheema echoes this, saying, "We're gathered together and we're sent out together. We don't have a little satellite youth program that runs around adolescent issues that aren't connecting to the worshiping life of this community." Along with this practice is the belief that God calls all of us, even the very young. A sense of fun, a bit of unpredictability, and a connection across generations exists alongside worship that is quite formal and deeply liturgical.

Regular practices such as a children's sermon on the chancel steps, an honored space in the balcony where teens congregate, and a pastor who has teens' phone numbers on her caller ID may seem commonplace. On closer examination, though, they reveal a congregation that values relationships across generational lines. These worship practices help create space that offers hospitality and honors each person.

Both of the clergy leaders recall a decision early on to intentionally create space for deep community in this congregation. Cheema recalls, "We had a year where we played name games until you just wanted to fall over. Everyone had a chance to say who they were. Everyone had a chance to say where they were from. Everyone had a chance to start telling their story and connecting their story to our community. Telling story and connecting story is what we do in so many ways." Creating community across boundaries of age required commitment. Cheema told parents, "We can assure you that if you can get your children here, we can help them find a way into this community of faith. We can help them find a meaningful way of belonging here as adolescents. But if you don't get your children here—if you don't make it a family priority—we really can't do any of that because what we do happens *here* in this gathered community on Sunday morning."

CREATING SPACE: A practice that offers hospitality and honors each person where they are on their journey.

Because the only opportunity to gather as one church family was the primary worship service on Sunday morning, leaders faced a *choice point*: move the time of the Sunday school hour, a significant change in the church's culture, or risk losing the sense of community among generations. This fundamental change in the congregation's life finally happened only four years ago, after one earlier attempt failed.

Don Baker, a member of the congregation for more than forty years, observed that deep community, once tasted, reorients lives:

"It's fascinating the way we've proven some of the myths wrong. For instance, that kids and families are way too busy in the summer so we can't possibly schedule something: We have kids who plan their summers around Appalachia Service Project," he remarks with amazement. Youths' commitment to service through mission defines their summer schedules, and the high level of commitment is actually required year-round. Youth prepare for summer missions through regular gatherings for training, prayer, fundraising, service, and community building.

CHOICE POINTS: Moments when a decision is made by an individual or a group. The choice affects the future. Sometimes choice points are deliberate, even prophetic. Sometimes they seem to happen as if by accident.

Undergirding this commitment is Francis's understanding of his primary responsibility as a leader: "My job is to create among the staff a vision of Christian community. Community is a place where joys and sorrows are shared, where we support one another, where we stand up for one another and don't let other people trash-talk us, where we stand firm with each other." His respect for Cheema is evident in their shared leadership. "I couldn't ask for a better colleague. We've trusted each other with our lives." Their mutual affection and respect is evident each Sunday as Cheema and Francis share the announcements before worship begins. Their good-natured ribbing and laughter invites worshipers to join in the fun.

In the summer and fall of 2009 the banter between Francis and Cheema included reports on who walked to work the most. Later they invited the rest of the congregation to join in this challenge, which began with a committee's decision to urge folks to lower their consumption. These two have served together for nearly fourteen years, a longevity of staffing that begets trust and can seed deeper levels of community among congregation members. "I don't think that you elicit from youth or adults a willingness to step out and feel called by God when church leadership changes over. You need that sense of trust," Francis says.

I began this research thinking that mission was the key practice that is helping the young people of First Church to hear a call to ministry. Now I see mission as deeply related to the more primary practice of community. The intentional seeking of community, one relationship at a time, organizes the life of this congregation. The effects of community formation spread through the congregation and have an important formative effect on children and youth.

It then extends to the places youth and adults offer themselves in mission. When the first youth group travelled to the Appalachia Service Project (ASP) in 1998, church leaders saw mission more narrowly, as simply a good way to begin building a youth program. Over the years, however, they began to see that entering with solidarity into the lives of people who live in poverty had birthed a significant relationship. In 2006, the year after Hurricane Katrina devastated New Orleans, the youth considered changing their plans to go to Appalachia, responding instead to the urgent need in Louisiana. One of the boys reported that ASP was struggling because so many churches had directed resources toward Katrina relief. Almost immediately, the group decided that their relationship with ASP was primary: they wanted to honor that relationship.

The youth now embody this understanding of mission as relationship. As Emily says, "These connections that you make on ASP, they're family. They truly love you. It was bigger than just your blood family or your home church family. I really do think we are all together: we are all one, we are all friends, and we are all really brothers and sisters."

Cheema sees a link between a sense of belonging to a larger community and the desire to find one's purpose in the world. "One reason these mission trips are important is that it gives the kids a chance to belong to something that is bigger than their own adolescent stuff. Your own drama of who's dating whom, your own little cadre of friends who are all picking at each other, your own issues with your parents . . ." Instead, she says, the congregation sends youth out expecting that something important will happen: both the mountain residents and the traveling suburbanites will be transformed as they experience the human connection that is part of the reign of God.

Heartfelt community begins with clergy who truly care about each other and enjoy one another's company. It extends across generations as people come to know one another by name. It then creates a sense of unity in worship and in mission that reaches out to include the people in Appalachia. These mission partners, who are very different culturally and economically from the congregation, come to be included in this sense of community through an ongoing process of reflection on the experience of mission as it intersects Christian Scripture and as it is interpreted through the naming of God moments.

Engaging in Theological Reflection That Integrates Mission Experience into Everyday Life

In sharing their mission experience, youth frequently talk about God moments—discrete memories of connection with the divine or times when one glimpses the reign of God. These occur regularly on the ASP trips when hearts and spirits are especially attuned to the presence of the Holy Spirit. Cheema began helping youth name their experiences in this way, and the youth caught on. Now they teach others that these God moments cannot be ordered up; they come unbidden. They are easily missed, however, in the busy-ness of daily life. Emily explains:

> When you *ask* for a God moment, it's not going to happen. You're looking for this huge thing, and you overlook moments and brush off other feelings when you set your sights on something. I tell people just to be. Just live in the moment when you're on ASP. Work hard. Make an effort to talk to your homeowner. Everything falls into place. Everyone has experiences. You can't measure who had the cooler or greater God moment than someone else. That doesn't exist. That's applying the human form of measurement.

Young people learn to recognize and name such moments as God moments through the disciplines of Bible study, prayer, service, and careful nurturing of community. Experiencing and naming God moments then provides an alternative measurement to those of status and consumption that can create angst and anxiety during the high school years. Emily describes the feeling that "someone had just given me this gift of being happy and not clouding my ear with noise." For Emily, the God moments are the natural outgrowth of relationships that honor others, even across differences of age, status, and culture.

Emily talked at length about these moments and how important they are to her. She described one that occurred after returning from a trip with forty-five people who ranged in age from high school freshmen to college students to middle-aged adult chaperones: "It was a moment of true community, where everyone is equal. We all learn, and we're also all teachers. We influence everyone around us; that's one of the mysterious ways that God works." Emily calls this "a very spiritual high."

Emily taught me that during ASP, members of her congregation learn to name God moments at the end of a workday when everyone gathers for group time. Accompanied by guitar, they sing songs that have become favorites over the years. They pray as well, and each person present has an opportunity to share something important that happened during the day. Emily said: "Year after year, the community creates this space that is so open and honest that you feel like you can totally let yourself go. At youth group you can trust in everyone. That's why there are these God moments.

Cheema sees the naming of God moments as directly related to a young person sensing the seeds of a call to ministry, mission, and leadership:

I think call comes in the lived experience of being present in the life of someone whose situation is so dramatically different from yours. . . . When we talk about this in the evenings, these high school boys who are such adolescent big guys will start using words like "I experienced God today in the way that George talked with us about how bad his situation has been. I realized that even though my life is really different, I can't fix George's situation, but I can listen to him. I am sharing his life for a week. I can remember that when I go back to where I live, and I can keep trying to do that." So I think it's that sense of the lived experience, opening hearts and minds to that being a faith experience, and then taking that back to our home and continuing to live that out.

In addition to gathering time in the evenings, when God moments are named and shared in relation to song and Scripture, sermons become a place where the gathered community continues integrating the experience into back-home life. Francis shared in a sermon, just four weeks after ASP: "[Living as a Christian] does not mean isolating yourself, far removed and decontaminated from the squalor and mess of the world. It is rather that caring for the vulnerable and marginalized has a purifying effect upon us. It clarifies our vision, shifts our perspective on the world. It refocuses our vision. It readjusts and realigns our priorities. It reconfigures our perception and has a transforming effect upon us." God moments transform young lives—here as they care for vulnerable and marginalized people while on a mission trip. Youth return from the trip with commitments to live differently in light of the transformative learning. The senior pastor is aware of the transformation and supports it by weaving it into the experience of the entire congregation, mentioning it in worship, in the church's publications, and in other congregational forums.

LAMENT: A key biblical motif that allows people to express regrets, grief, and longing. Lament acknowledges suffering and can clear the way for God's Spirit to move in new ways.

This recurring practice of sharing intense moments of connection to God's world and one's role in it is *not* how youth ministry has always worked here. About ten years ago leaders heard many of their most active members lamenting that their adult children were not choosing to be part of a faith community. Kids who had grown up as active and happy members of a seemingly effective youth ministry program had little or no interest in continuing to be part of the church. As one of the volunteers with that youth program observed:

> I worked with the youth group from 1971 to 1977. We were overfocused on social and political issues without the theological base. I look at that with a fair amount of regret. We talked about community. We never gave them the theological vocabulary. We didn't have them in the worship service. We did almost nothing with them around biblical literacy. They're in touch with each other now, but almost none of them are part of a Christian community.

Christian Smith's 2009 research echoes this awareness. He found that mission experiences in one's youth are not particularly strong indicators of strong young adult faith.[6] A slightly different picture emerges from my close look at the young people in this congregation today. Mission trips *alone* might not have a formative effect, but when a congregation carefully creates space for meaningful, ongoing reflection on the experience, we hear youth testifying that the practice becomes embedded in the stories they tell about their lives. In Emily's case, she is writing that story into her future, allowing the practice of naming God moments to help her sort out who she is becoming and to what she will remain committed.

Many youth who are part of an intense summer mission never experience a call to a life of service or professional Christian ministry. Yet, FUMC-Evanston's ministry has enabled a number of young people to recognize such a call. How does it happen?

Hattie is a first-year seminary student. She became active in the youth ministry and mission trips just as they were beginning to emerge within in the congregation. She describes this journey:

> ASP was the pivotal way for me to become involved in the church community because it created a place for me very directly. I would come to anything the youth group did that was related to ASP, and then . . . I started to want to do other things with those people. Because of my first

ASP trip, and the subsequent two trips I went on, I developed a geographic place I loved traveling to, as well as a spiritual space with these other
kids in my youth group. I've learned this year to translate that same type
of service, the same emotions as experienced on ASP, into other work and
other geographic places. Now it's become the church community where
I'm working.

What Hattie terms *translation* is key. She makes a connection between the experience of service, community, and the communion
of the Holy Spirit and her choice to find ongoing ways to engage in
ministry. She is shaping her life's story in response to the God moments she was invited to first experience and later reflect upon.

Using the Language of Call
and Vocation at Key Moments

The sense that God is calling is constantly present in this congregation: it is lifted up in the language of sermons and children's moments, and it is especially visible at key moments in the community's
life. On Pentecost Sunday eighth graders join the church after a season of preparation. A short biography of each new member appears
in the bulletin. Cheema coaches the young people to create a bio
that mentions a way they have experienced God or grown in their
faith. She is confident that they are ready for such a testimony. She
tells them, "I know you know these words. I know you can say this."
Her confidence reminds them of their immersion in the language
of faith through Sunday school, worship, and the fellowship of the
congregation. "They're learning about our liturgy and the language
as connected to our worship, our ritual, how we live out our baptism, and how that relates to call."

Part of the confirmation ritual every year is the choir's singing
of an anthem that lifts up the theme of call. "Because you are God's
chosen ones, Christ's peace must reign in you," the choir sings.[7] At
the end of the service, the congregation sings a hymn commissioned

for its 150th anniversary that reiterates the call that the confirmands have just claimed:

While zealots worship flag and gun and beat the domination drum,
We'll teach the ways of peace 'til justice walks in mercy's shoes,
the poorest eat, and hear good news, and war and terror cease . . .
Carry the flame, sister and brother, living the faith, passing the praise
From one generation on to another! Carry the flame, carry the flame! [8]

This peak moment of the liturgical year often finds many of us tearful, moved by the words of the hymn embodied before our eyes.

Taken together, I witnessed a rich year-round cycle of community formation, mission immersion, theological reflection on life experience, and liturgical affirmation of the community's role in helping one another on our individual journeys as we journey together as a church. This movement reminds me of the base communities of Latin America and the action-reflection methodology of liberation theology, which they practiced. As Brazilian educator Paulo Freire showed, we engage in action and then reflect upon it, creating a circle of action and reflection that leads to more action in the world. The result is transformation of ourselves and of the situation in which we find ourselves. God moments do not exist for a momentary high: they are the impetus to go back and reflect on how the experience shapes the next action. This happens in the year-round reflection on mission that gets restated in liturgy and ritual using the language of call and vocation.

Reversing Hierarchies of Age and Status

One final theme suggests itself as I look back over my learnings: this congregation abandons the usual hierarchies of age and status. Two examples illustrate this. First, after about ten years of sending youth to ASP, some adults in the church decided they wanted to organize a trip to the same area in the spring of 2009. During the months when

I observed the training sessions for those preparing for this trip, I repeatedly saw youth teaching these adults. Cheema positioned the experienced folks, both youth and adults, to teach the rest of the group about the root causes of poverty and how to respect people whose culture differs from the culture of Evanston. At one such session Cheema asked, "Why is there poverty?" At first, the group cited illiteracy and lack of transportation. "No, those are the *results* of poverty," Cheema observed. Experienced youth then led all-ages small-group discussions focused on case studies. The discussion revealed absentee landowners hold 80 percent of the land and mineral rights in the region; little revenue is generated for schools, roads, or social services because the land is undervalued. I marveled at the excitement and energy in the room and the acceptance across generations of wisdom and ignorance alike as they learned about the socioeconomics of Appalachia. Normal age hierarchies were replaced with a respect and willingness to learn from those who knew firsthand how to sensitively cross the boundary into the Appalachian culture. Throughout this event, youth were accorded authority by Cheema and by everyone else. I detected no patronizing of the younger folks; youth were experts and teachers.

The second example of youth leading the congregation in mission is Emily, who was preparing to lead a group of young adults on a mission trip to Ghana in the summer of 2010. Emily shared many stories of how the youth ministry of First Church has shaped her. Now, as a senior in college, she is equipped to organize and lead an international mission. She says, "The church provided me with role models. Once you knock down the barrier of the age boundary, then for a young person the sky's the limit. You unlock this vault of life tools." Emily's goals for the mission in Ghana are genuine and not patronizing. They reflect the loving relationship model she learned in summer trips to Appalachia: "It's not about changing the way people live there. I don't want to change them, because I love their lifestyle. This first project is geared toward bettering education in the villages. I'm not going to set their goals for them. I just want to motivate them. People in Ghana have high hopes. They have dreams. We work alongside them." Emily has integrated the values of relationship and community and has applied it to another context. She will model this approach for the adult group as they travel to Ghana. She is leading the way.

All Along Life's Journey

In conclusion, I invite you to imagine with me what it might be like to raise a child in this church.

When you bring your newborn son (or daughter) home from the hospital, the congregation provides your first meal. You will celebrate his baptism at the front of the sanctuary, just steps away from where your three-year-old will sing in his first choir. The minister of music will teach him, while still in preschool, that he is leading worship, not performing for an audience: "I'm always emphasizing to them, 'You are leading worship. You are a worship leader. You are helping people pray and praise,'" says Jerry Jelsema, minister of music.

On Sunday mornings, your five-year-old will rush to the front of the sanctuary with his friends to get a seat beside Cheema or Francis for the children's moment. After taking part in the all-ages worship, he will follow a leader out of the sanctuary to a carefully designed children's church that age-appropriately engages him in practicing the elements of worship. Once a month, however, he will remain by your side during worship, walking forward with you for Holy Communion. When your son enters fifth grade, he will no longer go to children's church, for he will know his part in the congregation's worship practices.

Along the way, your son will take turns with the other children *being* the players in an ancient story they now know by heart, the biggest event of this church's year: The Christmas Pageant.

When he reaches the age of confirmation, he will take a summer mission trip to nearby Rockford, where he will stay over several nights to take part in an inner city mission led by high school interns from the neighborhood. By the end of the week, your rising seventh grader will count one of these high school interns as a new friend.

At his confirmation, adults will sing together a familiar hymn as they welcome a new group of baptized children into membership. As these teens rise into the ninth grade, they will be eager to *finally* be old enough for the church's annual trip to ASP, something they have been hearing about since they were children. The year-round training events begin. Your son will learn to do construction and home repair. He will role-play about cultural sensitivity, group building, and safety procedures. Each time they gather to raise funds, he and his peers will also practice the art of community building, strengthening the ties of connection they will need for the intense week of sharing. The peak fundraising event is a dinner and silent auction. For this night, your teenager will write a brief story expressing a way he has experienced God. A few of his older friends will give a testimony, sharing out loud why they care about ASP.

The trip takes place, and a brief hiatus from all youth group activity will follow during the rest of the summer. But in August, your son will stand up in church, telling a story about a God moment. Then he and his cohort will begin planning anew for the next summer. Along the way, adults of all ages will get to know your son as they have served side by side at the spaghetti dinner or shared a long journey along windy, curvy Appalachian roads in an eleven-passenger van. When another group of adults decides to make a pilgrimage to Appalachia, your seventeen-year-old might show up on a Sunday afternoon to teach a forty-eight-year-old how to identify assumptions about class stereotypes that get in the way of befriending. The adults will have learned from your son that sharing one's time and energy in this way is nothing short of life-giving.

The elements of ministry named here are hardly unique. Ministry in many congregations would include such descriptions of building community, connecting youth to the life of the congregation, or celebrating rites of passage and service beyond the church. But I detect a rhythm, an intentionality, and an ongoing pattern that creates a space where, over time, in Emily's words, "You learn to love yourself and those around you."

Yearning for the Reign of God

My theory is that being a part of such genuine Christian community is something for which we all long. When Emily speaks of her God moment as a feeling of peace, of some burden being lifted, of a lightness of being—I recognize what the old hymn calls "a foretaste of glory divine."[9] We long for those moments. When we experience one, we want more. This small transformation leads people to make different choices in their lives. The choices are motivated by this yearning: they want to find places to be in community with people where they make a difference and have moments of connection to one another and the divine.

Hattie, who is now in seminary and working as a youth minister, testifies that it all began for her on a mission trip: "We went to Rockford the summer after eighth grade, and I very clearly remember a devotion about hearts of stone and feeling this heaviness in your heart . . . how to turn that into energy and a positive outcome, not to lose that but to use it as a foundation to build upon."

Bonny, who has gone on the trips as an adult leader and who has two daughters who have participated, told me this:

> These kids most certainly *do* experience the reign of God. That is key to the idea that it is hard to come back home, to leave this space and time filled with God moments, this space in which to claim—unapologetically, without hesitation, without embarrassment—that one has experienced a God moment. There are frequent tears during our church's "private" devotional time at night. Kids have some of that "summer camp religious experience," except that they are having that experience with their own church in front of their peers, so all have witnessed and supported one another in the process.

And when they come home, they continue to journey with others who have heard their testimonies and who share their commitment to community across the normal barriers of age, race, class, status, and culture. They have been awakened in this community to a vision of the reign of God.

Questions for Reflection

ENGAGING VOCATIONCARE PRACTICES

1. Congregations are *creating hospitable space* when they learn to listen generously to the stories of people across generations and walks of life. FUMC-Evanston creates hospitable space through an emphasis on "heartfelt community that incorporates similarity and difference." In such a space, the gifts of young people are likely to be noticed, named, and nurtured.

   - What are some of the intentional ways FUMC-Evanston has created such space? How does the creation of hospitable space help sustain the transformation that teens experience during mission trips?

   - How does your church or faith community create hospitable space? Where have you experienced it? How do you name it? How might you imagine it becoming a more intentional practice?

   - FUMC-Evanston experienced a few stumbling blocks on the way to "heartfelt community," such as changing the Sunday school hour and challenging the myth that teens are too busy in the summertime to do mission trips. What are some of the obstacles to creating hospitable space in your congregation?

2. *Asking self-awakening questions* helps people hear God's call or listen more attentively to God's presence within them. They are questions that emerge when your head and your heart are open to the holy. They might occur in a sermon, in a one-on-one conversation, or a small group setting. One way FUMC-Evanston engages young people in this way is by asking confirmands to write about a time when their faith grew.

- When in the life of your faith community do you ask people to think back over the sacred experiences of their lives?
- Imagine a few self-awakening questions that might help you think more deeply about the way you are currently expressing a sense of your life's purpose. Then imagine how you might ask similar questions of someone whose gifts you notice and care about.

3. Naming God moments is a context-specific way FUMC-Evanston engages young people *reflecting theologically on self and community*. As they do so, young people in this congregation begin to see the story of their lives overlapping with what God is doing in the world.
    - When might you invite young people to reflect on how their dream for the world intersects God's dream for the world?
    - How does your culture or context specifically practice theological reflection? In Bible study? Through testimony? In what other ways does it do so?

4. FUMC-Evanston invites young people to *explore ministry opportunities* by having them serve as ushers, readers, liturgical dancers, and worship leaders. Young people also try on more significant leadership roles as they mature. Emily is leading a trip to Ghana. Other young people regularly teach adults how to cross cultural boundaries in Appalachia. In this way, being in ministry begins to feel like a normal part of growing up in this church culture. For some, that has led to lifelong leadership roles.
    - What ministry opportunities do young people in your congregation regularly take part in? How does your congregation begin conveying at an early age that young people can contribute to leading worship rather than simply performing in it?

- If a young person in your congregation seems particularly gifted for leadership, who, in addition to pastoral staff, may be likely to notice and nurture them?
- Think of a time when a young person discovered a gift through participation in the life of your faith community. What support or encouragement was given him or her? By whom?

PRACTICING ETHNOGRAPHIC LISTENING

"Congregations need to be far more deliberate about understanding the depth and power of their own culture as well as its capacity to help transform larger communities. . . . They can help create spaces in human society where larger, more visionary questions about the purpose of human life can be asked."[10]

- How might you see differently "the depth and power" of your own culture because of the thick description Margaret Ann Crain shares with us from *this* congregation? Who in your congregation might have stories like those told by Emily and Hattie? Or who might have stories that need telling? How would you imagine yourself welcoming those stories?
- What practices of nurturing young people in your congregation (perhaps rather invisible because they occur so naturally) did this congregation's practices call to mind? How might your congregation be creating space where "visionary questions about the purpose of human life" arise?
- Margaret Ann Crain is writing about a multicultural congregation in an urban neighborhood. Given the racial, ethnic, geographic, and economic background of your context, how did any "juxtaposition of opposites of collisions of difference" (Thomas E. Frank's phrase) spark your imagination?

CHAPTER 3

Mozying

WHEN THE YOUNG MENTOR THE YOUNGER

Sinai Chung

> We have forgotten that the self is a moving intersection of many other selves.
> We are formed by the lives which intersect ours.[1]
> — PARKER PALMER

It is Friday night at Choongsuh Korean Presbyterian Church (USA).[2] Every room is abuzz with one small group or another. I am immersed in a Bible study with four teenagers and their pastor, when he calls for a break shortly before 9:00 p.m. A stampede ensues. Down the stairs and around corners the teenagers run. I follow, curious about where they are headed and why they are in such a hurry. As a veteran in youth ministry, I have my hunch that food must lie at the end of this quest.

The teens arrive in the children's room. At the center of the table is a basket of steaming Korean yams and a large pitcher of orange juice. I think smugly that I am right—food, indeed, was the destination of this exuberant race. But the actions of these teenagers then surprise me: one at a time they take a cup and fill it with juice, not for themselves, but to hand to one of the twelve young children seated around the table. They carefully peel the skins of the yams, again, passing them along to the children. "They are feeding the kids—not themselves?" I ask myself "What on earth is going on here?"

Jeremy, a five-year-old, begins to eat a yam. Grace, a high school freshman, stops him with a warm smile and a gentle voice. "Honey, Jeremy, pray first." She mimics the iconic posture of prayer—putting her hands together and closing her eyes. Right away, Jeremy imitates her motions, praying, and then begins to enjoy the starchy staple of Korean American church potlucks.

As my learning at Choongsuh progressed, I witnessed older youth engaging regularly—and with delightful abandon—in such acts of role modeling that both cared for and shaped the behavior of younger children. The scene that so impressed me on this particular Friday night was merely a hint of a particular kind of mentoring practice that has a long and powerful history here. The *mozies*—a Korean word for older siblings—take care of the young.

MOZYING: A traditional Korean practice in which elder siblings help care for younger siblings and that functions as a culturally specific form of mentoring.

I name this practice *mozying*, after the Korean word for "the oldest sibling," because it resembles what Korean eldest siblings traditionally do for their younger siblings. In this chapter I will describe the congregation and the youth group where I observed this *mozying*. Then, I will bring this practice into conversation with its congregational and cultural causes. Finally, I will delve into how young people's vocational calling is nurtured by this traditional practice recycled for a new day. Through this thick description, readers might be awakened to see practices operating within their own congregations that, at first glance, may seem like nothing more than hungry teens racing toward the food line.

Korean American Congregations and the Next Generation

Korean American congregations face the stark challenge of reidentifying themselves: they can no longer exist simply as first-generation-centered congregations that served well for so long. The number of first-generation members is gradually decreasing due to the decline of new Korean immigrants in the United States.[3] At the same time, second-generation people have grown to be an emerging body within congregational life.[4] To sustain themselves, these congregations must transition into places where "the first and the next generations grow together."[5] In the midst of this transition, most Korean immigrant churches struggle with the issue of ministering to their second generation.

The struggle centers on making space for a generation of offspring who speak English as a first language and are culturally more American than their elders. In addition to the task of providing faith formation and spiritual growth of their offspring, Korean American churches in America have a unique mission: they hope to transmit Korean spiritual traditions and cultural values to their offspring, even as those offspring assimilate to their North American context.[6]

In the ideal, Korean American congregations move through three stages of ministry to accomplish this task. The first step is to provide pastor-led educational ministries in English for their young people, from preschool through high school. Later an English-speaking ministry for college students and young adults develops. Both of these first two stages are under the supervision of the "mother church"— the first-generation congregation—and both stages offer separate, age-level ministries. The final stage is a separate English-speaking Korean American congregation with its own senior pastor and its own identity operating as an independent church. Such a congregation evolves from being an English ministry of a Korean American congregation to being strong enough to function as an independent congregation in terms of membership, ministry, administration, and finances.[7]

Except for a few huge congregations, Korean American churches rarely reach the final stage of this ambitious plan. In fact, many of them have a difficult time performing even the first stage. Although the reasons are many, the main issue is often the lack of qualified ministers. Korean American congregations are well aware that the best people to minister to its young are second-generation Korean

Americans themselves—young adults who grew up speaking English and who share similar identities with the people they seek to serve. A key ministerial gift is the ability to bridge first-generation adults with their offspring through bilingual and bicultural fluency.[8] Korean American churches always hope to hire such second-generation ministers. The unfortunate reality is that the number of second-generation pastors has not been enough to satisfy the needs of all Korean American churches. This is due in part to a cultural reality: like many other Asian immigrants, Korean American parents urge their children to pursue professions that will guarantee economic and social stability. Rarely do Korean American parents encourage their children to pursue professional ministry, hence the shortage of qualified second-generation pastors to minister to their second-generation people.[9]

In struggling with these issues, Korean American churches recognize the need to nurture from within a new generation of ministers. Adding to this complexity, second-generation Korean Americans who do answer a call to pastoral ministry are often called to serve beyond Korean American churches to all the people of God in every situation, including multiethnic congregations.

A Congregation of Brothers and Sisters

Choongsuh is a congregation that takes seriously the desire to meet the needs of younger generations. Founded in 1972, it is a medium-sized Korean American church in a northern suburb of Chicago, having grown to 333 registered members and an average of 160 regularly attending members. Inspired by the conservative evangelical theological tradition of its homeland, it began when several young pastors emigrated from the same region of South Korea (called Kyoungsang) to the United States.[10] Most of the active members are now in their fifties and sixties. Some are in their thirties and forties. Missing almost entirely from membership are people in their twenties; many of them are away at college or graduate school, but some maintain a loving presence, visiting regularly and helping with youth activities for the thirty-five youth and children who attend.

For this chapter, I interviewed more than a dozen former members of the youth group who now range in age from twenty-five to thirty-three. These people were raised in Choongsuh and now find themselves serving in many different church and campus settings as professional and volunteer ministers. As I studied the context and practices that shaped this generation of young leaders, I also interviewed and observed current members of the youth group. Although much has changed in the past seven to ten years, I saw many of the formational practices the former youth told me about still at work at Choongsuh.

The members of Choongsuh describe their church friends as being "like family." Most of its adult members come from the same village of Korea and have been close friends since before their immigration. In many cases, they truly are brothers, sisters, and cousins. They have grown with one another through the life of this congregation. In and out of church, they and their families have shared lives together. In this way, all members of this congregation have experienced what they describe as blessed closeness, a genuine love, and a strong bond with one another. Indeed, this congregation has truly functioned as an extended family, where all members enjoy genuine familial relationship with one another. Peter, a member for more than twenty-five years, says:

> For us, our church is like a big family. Old members are like grandparents, parents, uncles, and aunts for its young members. Young kids are like grandchildren, children, nieces, and nephews for its older people. Members in the same age group are like brothers and sisters and cousins to one another. There are actually many real relatives as well. The old love the young; the young respect the old; the older take care of the younger; the younger learn from the older. When someone needs help, we take care of that one together. On holidays, we celebrate together. We are just like a family.[11]

Perhaps because of this feeling of solidarity, members of Choongsuh take to heart the vision of ministering fully to both the first and the second generation. This hope is reflected in its motto: "A community where the first and the next generation grow together." This motto is lived out in a concern of the first generation to provide high quality Christian education for their younger members. The second generation has returned the favor by filling this congregation with youthful inspiration. Older members experience the active and energetic presence of younger generations as a gift. Peter reflects:

> We adult members wanted our church to be a giving church to our second generation. We did not want to gain something from them but just to give, support, and feed them like all mothers do to their babies. But we have gained a lot from our second generation. They have kept this congregation younger and more active. I have a wonderful memory of a joint prayer meeting that we had with youth group members and with some college kids too. We were impressed by their pure faith. We learned a lot from their passion, courage, and energy in their praising and prayer. We looked back on our own faith and recommitted ourselves to God through them. I was personally very touched when they as a group prayed for their parents and all adults with their whole hearts.

When it was unable to offer English-language services to its younger people, Choongsuh ministered in an unusual way: by explicitly sending their offspring elsewhere, to congregations that could better meet their needs. Some of these young adults went with the blessing of their parents' generation to larger Korean congregations with English services, to Korean American second-generation congregations, or to other churches with multiethnic or mostly white membership. Many of them went to churches in other states where they study or work. A good number of young leaders who were nurtured in this congregation have been sent as pastors, missionaries, and church workers to various other places of the world. Consciously or unconsciously, the first-generation congregation sent forth its second generation as a form of ministry to others. In this way, Choongsuh's adult offspring learned from and contributed to the larger community of faith beyond the boundaries of this one specific congregation.

At the same time, however, Choongsuh welcomed its grown-up offspring back and carved out places for them to serve in pastoral roles. Even without an English-speaking ministry in the congregation, a large number of the second generation has served this congregation during and after their college years. In recent years, three young leaders have accepted a call to professional ministry. Two of those ministries got their start at Choongsuh: one person served as an associate youth pastor here before going on to campus ministry; the other was called in 2007 by this congregation to be a children's pastor and still serves as the congregation's youth pastor.

A LONG HISTORY OF CALLING

From the late 1980s to the present, vital youth ministry flourished at Choongsuh. One of the twelve young people to accept a call to full-time professional ministry from this context is Dave.[12] In conversation with me, Dave said, "We were so blessed with so many passionate leaders coming out of Choongsuh. But we don't know why God did it to us. It was God's providence, and we cannot explain. All we know is that we are only 1 percent of this picture and God took the 99 percent. And he made this thing happen."

Not completely satisfied with this answer, I responded, "You're right. We do not know *why* God did that to you. But we can try to understand *how* God did it and *how* God used the human part to make that happen in this specific congregation, in this particular youth group. Then others might learn from that *how*."

In order to understand this *how*, I began to ask about the practices in which these potential young leaders most passionately engaged. What was going on in this youth group that formed and re-formed their faith, fostered their spiritual growth, cultivated their Christian virtue, and developed their leadership potential? What nurtured their sense of call? I will focus on four interrelated practices I heard again and again in the stories of previous and current Choongsuh youth: (1) sibling love, (2) inclusion, (3) passionate prayer, (4) student leadership. I will end with a fifth practice, one that grows out of the earlier four and yet sets itself apart as something altogether different: *mozying*.[13]

THE PRACTICE OF SIBLING LOVE

Members of this youth group experience one another as real brothers and sisters, in keeping with all church members' close, intimate, familial bonds with one another. Chris, who was born, baptized, and raised in this congregation and currently serves as its youth pastor, explained:

> I have always felt like our church was a second home. A lot of older men and women at the church are like aunts and uncles and grandparents. We have learned from the adults that church feels like family. Our church is not just a church, but we share life together. That is something that I always remember. A lot of us grew up together. . . . I am an only child but I felt like a lot of folks at youth group were the closest things that I never had— siblings, the *Hyoungs* and *Nunas* and *Dongsaengs*.[14]

In my interviews, over and over I heard the phrases "like brothers and sisters" and "we spent a lot of time together" when people described their years as youth here. They shared positive memories of hanging around one another in and out of church, on weekends and weekdays. Dave joyfully shared:

> We spent a lot of time together. We met Friday nights for youth group and Sunday mornings for youth group but we oftentimes also spent a lot of time together on Saturdays— all day Saturday, all day Sunday, and all day Friday. We would just always spend time just because it was fun and we enjoyed hanging out with each other. We lived so close to each other. . . . Instead of spending time with friends from school, we were spending time with each other from youth group. We loved each other like brothers and sisters. To this day we treat each other like brothers and sisters. We created that? I don't think so. It created itself.

Dave's story allows us to grasp the peculiar intimacy nurtured in this immigrant community. Such a siblinglike relationship entails understanding and trusting one another, enabling individuals to frankly open up to one another as they are. Judy, a current youth group member, told me:

> They just know you and love you as brothers and sisters. And so they understand who you are, and trust you when you do something. For example, while praising, if you are opening your arms and raising your hands, they won't say, "Oh my gosh, she is so weird! What is she doing?" They would just understand and trust your heart when you do it. They won't care about it because they know who you are and your background. They just accept you and love you as you are.

Of course, sibling love is not always easy. Bickering and moments of disagreement also occur. And within the congregation, conflict has also arisen over the years, but the predominant memory shared by the young people who grew up here is that of familial love and bonding.

THE PRACTICE OF INCLUSION

A practice of inclusion seems to grow out of the practice of sibling love among Choongsuh youth members. Both the former and the current members of the youth group describe it as a clique-less and hospitable space in which there exists an explicit intention to include one another. Timothy, who grew up in this youth group and became a youth pastor of a Korean American church, told me, "I took a lot of pride in this: the shy people, quiet people, uncool people, they got a lot of attention because a lot of people were trying to reach out to them. So many people who would be alienated in other groups were able to be the core part of our group. When we had fellowship activities, people who were in leadership made sure that there would be no one who was being left out."

The practice of inclusion is particularly meaningful considering the fact that the members of this youth group might often feel exclusion within U.S. society. Timothy's story implies that as part of an immigrant community, some of these teenagers "would be alienated" and "left out" in other groups. They often felt marginalized in their schools and among their American peers. At the same time, they often also felt alienated when visiting Korea. For the members, this youth group has been one of the only places where they feel included, welcomed, accepted, and recognized because the members intentionally tried to include one another as precious "core parts." Furthermore, their youth group seemed to function as a comfort zone where people with a similar background, experience, and identity felt they belonged. Eric, a former youth group member, who is now a worship leader of a multiethnic congregation and training to be a missionary, said:

> I always felt I was not accepted in this land. I remember when I was in high school. I visited Korea during the summer. That was hard. Kids there didn't like me just because I grew up in America. When I came here though, people didn't accept me because I don't look "American." All the second-generation kids from our youth group actually had experiences like that. But we had such a specially blessed experience here. We were family like brothers and sisters, and we shared many things. And so, you know, all of us were accepted there and all of us were welcomed there—only there. Definitely, my youth group is meaningful to me for this reason.

THE PRACTICE OF PASSIONATE PRAYER

Passionate prayer is a characteristic practice not just of Choongsuh youth but also of many other Korean American churches. Passionate prayer is characteristic of Korean spiritual traditions and is highly likely to be transmitted by Korean Americans to their offspring. The youth members of Choongsuh recognize that their passionate prayer practice was inherited from their Korean Christian ancestors. Joshua, a college pastor who was nurtured here, said:

> You know our prayer was very passionate. It is a more typical Korean style of praying. We pray for hours and hours, we pray aloud, we pray with

crying and all that stuff and sometimes speaking in tongues. It is always very dynamic and spiritual. Americans do not do so, and they might even think this is weird. But our prayer was always like that. That is our style. You know the Korean churches are very different from American churches in so many ways, and a lot of what the Korean churches do is hours and hours of prayer meetings. Sometimes I felt it went on too long, but overall once we got into prayer, I would typically think it was good.

As Joshua testifies, the youth of Choongsuh prayed passionately and earnestly as a group; they did so frequently and for many hours at a time, to the degree that such prayer became the norm within their faith life. Bible reading and praise accompanied the practice of praying. Dave describes a love-hate relationship with this norm:

We prayed forever. I got so mad sometimes because always there were prayers, which was good, though. In American churches, they pray for fifteen minutes. But we would pray for hours sometimes. We prayed and worshiped and prayed and read the Bible together and prayed together. I think we did a little bit of everything—all kinds of prayer practices, like in groups, individually, and in small groups. When we met in groups on Friday nights before the youth group, we had prayer meetings thirty minutes before the meetings. On Saturday mornings, there were prayer meetings. As we prepared for retreats, we had prayer meetings. When we went to retreats, we had prayer meetings and all that kind of stuff. We prayed individually and collectively.

Laura, a current youth group member, describes a prayer tradition currently practiced:

The most impressive thing for me is when we come in the morning on Sundays. We have a special time before the Sunday worship starts. Youth group members gather before we have morning services, and we have time to pray. That prayer time is influential because it is always very passionate. We can open up our hearts before the worship. But to me, the more impressive thing is how many people actually come to the morning prayer meeting before the Sunday worship service because it is early in the morning. In our youth group, people actually come early in the morning to gather together and to pray together and to read the Bible together and to prepare for the worship together.

THE PRACTICE OF STUDENT LEADERSHIP

The leadership of Choongsuh youth grew in the face of what could have been adversity: a consistent lack of pastoral leadership. Despite the hard work of adult members to retain staff, youth pastors came and went frequently. This high turnover was a result of young pastors being called to senior pastorates or on to another state for further study. In fact, this instability of pastoral leadership is a common and chronic issue among many Korean American churches; they strive to find stable pastoral leadership for their youth groups.

This often causes huge problems. The void of leadership can leave a youth group flailing as its members struggle with the confusion resulting from the lack of ministerial or organizational direction. But in the case of Choongsuh, the inconsistency and instability of pastoral leadership actually fostered leadership among teens and college students. It served as an opportunity for the congregation to train leaders from within who would then be given real responsibilities. People had to step up to fill the void. These young leaders cultivated ownership among members, and their leadership skills continued to grow. For the most part, teens took charge of tasks such as organizing functions and facilitating groups. College students stepped in to provide spiritual leadership and teach Bible studies.[15] Timothy gave an example of this practice:

> Back in 1993, the youth pastor left. We didn't have a youth pastor for a
> long time. And then we had one person. He was there for a few years and
> then was gone. We would have another, and then he too would be gone,
> and so on. So from 1993 on, if we were going to have fellowship activities,
> students organized it. Otherwise it wouldn't happen. I think sometimes
> being underresourced as a church gives opportunity for people to step up.
> There were about ten leaders out of thirty kids. And I think that allowed

for leadership roles. I remember when I got to college, some people that I met, they had a really hard time in organizing hangouts for ten to twenty people. And yet anybody from Choongsuh could have done it, because we did it every week. People just had to learn administration and organization and had to have some discernment for people who were not being asked or were being left out.

Mozying: A Revised Mentoring Practice of Choongsuh Youth Group

The practice of mozying is a culturally specific way of mentoring that has been uniquely practiced in Choongsuh youth group where older people take care of, invest in, and serve as role models for younger members as part of a genuine sibling-love relationship. As explained earlier, the term *mozy* originates from the Korean word meaning "the oldest sibling in a family." In its linguistic sense, *mozying* simply means what the oldest sibling practices. I call this practice mozying because it resembles what the oldest siblings in Korean families do for their younger siblings. I use the term *moziers* for the older group of people who are mentoring, and *moziees* for the younger group of people who are mentored.

MOZIERS: A group of older role models who care for and mentor their younger peers.

MOZIEES: The younger peers who are cared for and mentored by older youth.

Mozying was the most recurrent theme I heard during my study of the youth at Choongsuh. I see it as a key practice fostering spiritual growth and nurturing the vocational exploration of young leaders. In addition, it is a kind of legacy—something practiced throughout the history of this particular youth group and still being practiced in the current youth group. In closely examining the practice of mozying, I posed the following four questions:

- In what ways is mozying practiced?
- What are the characteristics of mozying?

- What caused mozying to become prevalent within this particular youth group?
- How did mozying influence the vocational exploration of the young leaders?

WAYS OF MOZYING

In the stories of those I interviewed, I saw three prevailing ways of mozying.[16] First of all, *moziers take care of moziees*. One can see that moziers truly and intensively care about their younger friends, just as older siblings in a family take care of their younger siblings. Eric explained, "It is like having older brothers who are always taking care of you. . . . I felt I was a young child and I that I was loved and safe." Through mozying, younger people experience older, more mature people who really care for them. Timothy said:

> Older people took others under their wing and cared very individually for the whole person. They were like real older brothers. People did that very well in Choongsuh. When I first came into the youth group . . . we didn't have an [English-speaking ministry] and so anyone who was passionate about God, the way they expressed it was just by taking care of younger people. You could tell, "Oh that younger person is taken care of by that older person." You look at anybody and you could kind of tell. It wasn't formal. It was just like having older brothers who love a lot of younger brothers and sisters.

Second, *moziers invest in moziees*. They do so by pouring their life into moziees, even outside the church setting, in what can be described as life-on-life ministry. Older people would get into younger people's lives, selflessly investing time and effort in order to be with their younger friends. Here is an example from Timothy's experience:

> I would say the biggest impact on me was through the one-on-one investment from older people to younger people. Many memories are clear in mind. I remember someone named Matthew. He wanted to do a Bible

study with junior high boys who were serious about their faith. He lived in Chicago. He picked up someone in Chicago. He picked me up in Skokie. He picked up another in Northbrook. He picked up another in Glenview. And then he did Bible study with us. On Saturday, every single week, he probably spent two and a half hours of driving just to do that. These older people were some of the most self- less people that I'd ever met in my life.

Eric described a similar experience: "They invest- ed a lot of their time and their efforts . . . their life. Just the time spent together in the car. There were two or three years like that, going back and forth. That was probably the most memorable moment for my soul, because of the time he invested: the time we spent together."

"That was probably the most memora- ble moment for my soul, because of the time he invested: the time we spent together."

Finally, *moziers act as role models for moziees*. Moziers become examples for their young friends, showing them how to live out the Christian faith. Younger people learn through seeing what older people do. The process of transmission of prayer practice might be one of the best examples of the way this role modeling works. Joshua explained:

> The older people were really influential. When I was a young youth group member, when we went to retreats or something, there were just kind of old-school Koreans there, praying for hours and hours. They came out three and four hours later. That's how it was. . . . I just saw the way it was. When I was a kid, while they continued to pray, I would just lie down and go to sleep, because I was just a kid. But I found that I was doing it too, later.

Joshua testifies to the fact that it was meaningful for him, as a younger person, to watch the life and the spirituality of older people around him. That experience was what he used to craft his own way of being with young people when his turn came. Especially when moziees see that moziers really believe their faith, they become transformed by the examples of their elders. Joshua continued:

> When I was much younger, there was a guy called Paul. He was always faithful and passionate and very genuine and sincere about what he believed. He was always a strong role model. He was a college student, and now he is an ordained pastor. He role-modeled a lot. He was one of the college kids who came back every summer and helped out and spent a lot of time with students. I looked up to him as a spiritual role model because he was very devout. He was always there, always very focused and straight on.

CHARACTERISTICS OF MOZYING PRACTICE

In its specific characteristics, mozying differs from other forms of mentoring in three distinctive ways. First, it is based on intensive and genuine sibling love. Although other mentoring practices are done on the basis of a "meaningful relationship" between a mentor and a mentee, the relationship on which mozying rests is very different.[17] By definition, it requires a much more intimate level of relationship. As a matter of fact, mozying does not occur unless there are interactions at a very personal level between older and younger people, just like those between older and younger siblings in a family. Joshua emphasized this aspect, saying:

> Older people were getting involved and just spending time with us. The relationship was very personal, and we knew the older people as our brothers and trusted them in that way. I think it is the most important key for me and in all of my ministries. We could see that older people were genuine as we spent time with them, and we could realize that they really cared about us as we enjoyed fellowshiping with them. They really met our needs at the personal level, because they got to know who we are through that kind of intensive relationship.

Second, mozying differs from other types of mentoring because it is a practice that benefits both parties, in several ways. While other mentoring practices tend to emphasize "assisting mentees in learning the way of life,"[18] mozying clearly benefits the mentors as well as the mentees. One can easily assume that the practice would be beneficial for moziees, as it provides chances for them to have older siblings in Christ who shepherd them in their young Christian walk at the most intimate level. But one should not overlook that this same practice also had great meaning to moziers. The first benefit is that this youth group functions as moziers' own community: it is an extension of the youth group in which they felt at home, and it is a place to which they belong, have a role to play, and feel needed. Community has a big influence in how people grow spiritually and how they find their vocation. For moziers, youth group might have been the only place in which they experienced such a welcoming community. Timothy pointed out, "The youth group—that's their church. We were their church and their community when they didn't have their own [English-speaking ministry]."

Another benefit is that moziers enjoy being part of the growth of moziees whom they have known very well for a long time as brothers and sisters. For moziers to actually follow the growth of their younger friends and to accompany them in the course of their growing is a blessing. Chris said, "It is exciting to see how the students that I had seen when they were very little have grown. It is exciting to have the chance to be a part of their lives and to minister to them, watching them grow physically and spiritually, because I want them to make their faith their own. That's really cool to me, being part of that."

A third benefit is that mozying develops moziers' faith, Christian living, and leadership. Being examples and role models calls forth the best in them. They learn to make small sacrifices for the sake of their moziees. For example, when investing their time, moziers told me they did so with pleasure and without expecting rewards. Moziers might feel stretched by the role, because they are human beings and investment always calls for high commitment and sacrifice. Eric frankly pointed to this issue, saying, "When I was in college, a lot of us came back and we did the same thing—like the older brother role. Sometimes, that really stressed us because, you know, it is not always easy, especially when we are tired or busy with school." But through it, moziers described becoming more disciplined and refined as leaders. Eric continued, "But it really caused us to grow up because we had to take care of our little brothers and sisters for whom we were responsible. So that's a good thing. And so I feel like in the future, whatever I decide to do and envision, I would continue to do like our older brothers did by taking care of us and investing their lives in us. I feel like it is the most valuable thing I have learned as a leader—to be willing to invest in people."

Finally, the mozying practiced by a group of older people differs from other types of mentoring because it has a highly contagious chain reaction throughout all age groups. While other forms of mentoring are done "between two individuals" or at best "between a teacher and a small group of students,"[19] mozying is done between a small group of mentees and a small group of mentors. Furthermore, while other forms of mentoring might focus on only one generation of mentoring, mozying is about a chain of mentoring that continues from the older generation to the next in a repeating pattern. Throughout the history of this youth group, in every generation, a group of older siblings has always taken care of, invested in, and been role models for their "younger siblings." When the first-generation group of moziers left, the second-generation group of moziers took their place. This pattern keeps on going from generation to generation. Moziees from every generation come back to this youth group to be moziers for the next generation. As Chris commented:

> It's fascinating because every time a class of leaders graduates, there is always new leadership ready to fill the gap. It's always strange to me that every generation that has left Choongsuh has come back. They come back during summers and winters and even during the school year . . . oh, including myself. While I was in college, and even nowadays as a youth pastor, I myself did the same thing that my older youth group members did for me and my generation.

Specifically, how is this pattern replicated? Timothy recalls:

> They would talk to us all the time about more serious issues and talk to us about our faith, and invariably their passion and love and selflessness became contagious, and we did the same. There are a lot of key people like that, and they are all in ministry now too. That image and that memory for me stayed with me, and I just did the same for younger kids in Choongsuh youth group during my college years and even when I did my youth ministry. It is very easy for me to do it because the experience was such a part of my life. I copied what these older people did for us.

CONGREGATIONAL AND CULTURAL EXPLANATIONS OF MOZYING

What congregational and cultural norms caused mozying to be practiced at Choongsuh? First, the birth of mozy practice within this particular youth group might be a result of its unique and special situation. Three situational aspects need to be considered in order to understand the development of mozying. The first and most unique aspect is the intensive and genuine sibling-love relationship between members of this youth group. In essence and by definition, the genuine siblinglike love relationship is a prerequisite for mozying, a practice in which older people play the role of older siblings for their younger people by taking care of them, investing in them, and being role models for them. Mozy practice is possible in a youth group because of such a sibling relationship.

The second situational aspect is the absence of an English-language ministry in Choongsuh congregation. In general, a relatively small Korean American congregation is not likely to be able to have a separate English-language ministry to serve college students and young adults, as is the case with this congregation. Since Choongsuh has never had an English-language ministry for the older age group, these older people had to be involved in the youth group if they wanted to serve their home church. These people, who have loved their young youth members as real younger siblings, naturally became part of the youth group and the youth group became their community. This gave them specific opportunities to carry out mozying within this youth group. In this sense, the development of mozy practice could be fostered specifically within this particular youth group.

The last situational aspect to take into account is the lack of consistent pastoral leadership in the Choongsuh youth group. Despite the endeavors of the adult congregation to provide it, this youth group, similar to youth groups from other medium-sized Korean American churches, was not able to enjoy consistent pastoral leadership, either because of frequent changes of youth pastor or the complete absence of youth ministry. What distinguishes this particular youth group from others is that, although it did not have consistent pastoral leadership, it did nonetheless enjoy consistent spiritual leadership. When the group was without pastoral leadership, it had to, wanted to, and actually did fill the void to help their beloved younger siblings to grow spiritually. These older youth or young adults became moziers. In this way, the lack of a consistent pastoral leadership actually enabled mozying to take root in this youth group.

Second, the development of mozying can be explained in the Choongsuh youth group by Korean cultural values about siblings, which have been actualized in this youth group. There are two Korean cultural values pertaining to sibling relationship. One is a Korean familial ethic that siblings are to be on very friendly terms with one another and that such sibling love is the foundation of humanity. Such relationships have been strongly influenced by Confucianism, according to which sibling love and filial piety are praised as two great values at the root of all benevolent actions.[20] This teaching is prevalent throughout Asian countries, including Korea, and has influenced the people's ethical life.

Another Korean cultural value is that the oldest sibling is to take care of his or her younger siblings. In Korean society, the oldest sibling in particular, and older siblings in general, have a special responsibility to take care of and be role models for their younger siblings, something they actually do. Although the oldest sibling has a right to be respected by younger siblings, and although the firstborn son in particular enjoys many benefits that his younger siblings and even his older sisters cannot enjoy, the most prevalent theme of Korean sibling relationship is that the older ones take care of the younger ones.

As a Korean American congregation that has retained a great number of Korean cultural values and norms, Choongsuh congregation has continued to promote these two Korean cultural values about siblings. Through its adult congregation, the two values of sibling love and sibling responsibility have been embedded in the thought and life of Choongsuh youth group members, and this in turn has resulted in the development of mozying as a practice within this youth group.

One might justifiably ask why mozy practice has developed only in Choongsuh congregation and youth group even though other Korean American congregations and youth groups possess the same Korean cultural values about siblings that are the foundation of mozy practice. Here, we need to recall that the entire congregation of Choongsuh has been like a family and its youth group members have been like real siblings. This has enabled youth group members to actually love and treat one another as real brothers and sisters within this Choongsuh family. Mozying, which is based on Korean cultural values of sibling love and responsibility, most likely only develops where these two values are practiced.

VOCATIONAL EXPLORATION THROUGH MOZYING

All my respondents who have been nurtured as young pastoral leaders in the Choongsuh youth group agreed that this mozying was the most influential aspect of their vocational exploration. Specifically, how did mozy practice nurture their vocational exploration? First, mozying built the foundation for their understanding of ministry—as owning one's faith. In the course of being mentored as moziees, these young pastoral leaders experienced that they were growing in faith as they became more and more enthusiastic in fellowshiping with God through fellowshiping with moziers. Eric mentioned, "Having older brothers, that's why I felt I kept growing and growing spiritually." Even a current youth member, named Karen, claimed that mozy practice made her grow in faith: "I believe [moziers] are a major part of our Christian life in many ways. I know they really take care of us and really love us. I think they brought a lot of fun into our lives, but not only fun: they also brought Christ into our lives. I think that is really special to me personally. I became more serious in my faith. Our faith grows by learning from older people. . . . We see how they think and what they say and do."

Second, mozy practice nurtured the spirit of ministry. At the heart of pastoral vocation is having a passion for people, without which no one can pursue ministry. The young pastoral leaders learned such a passion for people in the course of being involved in mozying. Eric mentioned, "In terms of being shaped, I think having older brothers is why I discovered such a passion for people." For people like Eric, to have pastoral vocation basically meant to expand the scope of mozy practice beyond the boundaries of their own group. When they saw that their moziers so loved and cared for them, these young people learned from their moziers' example and in turn loved and cared for their moziees. In doing so, when their hearts went beyond the bounds of love for their own younger brothers and sisters in their youth group to all their brothers and sisters in Christ in the world, the young pastoral leaders learned about passion for all the people of God. Eventually, ministering to people became an "inescapable burden" in their heart, and they went into ministry. As Timothy put it, "God has given me such an intense burden to love church and people that if I did not do it I would go crazy."

Third, mozy practice exposed the value of ministry. Through it, the young pastoral leaders came to understand how rewarding ministry can be. Says Joshua, "Doing ministry is a meaningful job. I think I learned this from the dedicated older people and from their consistent involvement in church and in serving people. So I guess it just became part of my life. It's just what I did or what I liked to do and who I was. I learned that it is valuable to spend time with people and help them grow." These young people found that many youth members changed and grew through the work of their moziers and through their own work as moziers. They realized that seeing people change and grow is extremely joyful and meaningful. Such experiences compelled them to dedicate themselves to exploring pastoral vocations.

Fourth, mozying provided a model for ministry. The young pastoral leaders took mozying as their ministerial example while they refined their vocational callings in their practical ministerial settings. They used what their moziers had modeled for them as the basis of their ministries. From their own experience they knew such practice to be effective. Timothy remarked, "That image and that memory, for me, stayed with me even when I did my youth ministry. And it is very easy for me to do it because I had experienced it in my own life. I copied what these older people did for us. . . . Investing in people stuck with me so deeply that I took in three foster kids from youth group who lived with me when they went through changes and bad times."

Finally, mozy practice developed traits of ministry, such as love, spiritual maturity, responsibility, administration, organization, discernment, hospitality, and leadership. Let us take leadership as an example. The Choongsuh youth group lacked consistent pastoral leadership, but precisely because of this, young people could develop their leadership skills. As moziees, they could learn to be student or organization leaders. As moziers, they could learn to be spiritual leaders. Then, the next step might be to prepare for being pastoral leaders. Eric said, "I feel like I have certain strengths and gifts that God has given me and that I feel I am using. And some of that—especially leadership—was certainly cultivated from my early years through being a mentor in my youth group."

Implications of Mozy Practice

Each congregation has its own culture and practice. No matter how good it may have been for the Choongsuh congregation and its youth group, mozying cannot be replicated elsewhere. But others can learn from it, adapt it, and see if it has benefit in their settings.

In hopes that it might stimulate the imaginations of others, I suggest that congregational leaders might (1) become agents of mozying themselves, (2) create atmospheres in which mozying might flourish, and (3) teach others to take on the role of moziers.

A Greenhouse of Hope is a congregation that nurtures young leaders using the gifts and resources at hand. It makes use of its particular context. Choongsuh is just such a place. A group of immigrants brought to their new community the beliefs and practices integral to their identity. In addition to passing on their faith, these first-generation Korean Americans passed on the unique cultural practice of investing eldest siblings with a privileged role. This mentoring role carries with it a burden to care for younger siblings. As young adults practiced mozying in the family-like setting that is Choongsuh, they became leaders. They tried on roles played by professional ministers and teachers; some were even hired to serve as youth ministers when they finished college. Today, many of these young adults are serving the church as chaplains, pastors, educators, and missionaries. A new generation of teens is mozying, continuing to adapt an ancient practice, recycling it for a new day.

Questions for Reflection

ENGAGING VOCATIONCARE PRACTICES

1. At Choongsuh Korean Presbyterian Church *creating hospitable space* happens largely through a network of relationships that function as family. Indeed, numerous members describe their church friends as feeling like brothers, sisters, cousins, aunts, and uncles.
   - What are some of the intentional ways young people at Choongsuh Korean Presbyterian Church benefit from this familial space?
   - How does the presence of hospitable space serve a particular function for youth who must navigate across cultures as

the children or grandchildren of immigrants? How might this be similar or different in churches that do not share a common story of recent immigration to the United States?
- Does family imagery surface when people describe your congregation? What other imagery surfaces when people talk about the faith community of which you are a part?

2. *Asking self-awakening questions* helps people hear God's call or listen more attentively to God's presence within them. They are questions that lead deep into the heart and soul of what matters. They might occur in a sermon, in a one-on-one conversation, or a small group setting.
- Where do you see evidence of this happening at Choongsuh?
- How does the intimacy that grows between a moziee and a mozier seem to lend itself to conversations in which such questions might be welcomed? Do such mentoring relationships exist in your congregation?
- Where do you see opportunities in the life of Choongsuh or your own congregation for self-awakening questions to be asked on a more regular basis? What are some of the obstacles to this?

3. Members of Choonsguh are *reflecting theologically on self and community* during what they describe as characteristically long and passionate prayer services. In this practice, the details of everyday life are placed alongside God's unfolding story.
- Where else do you see theological reflection happening in the story of Choongsuh?
- How do church members in your culture or context specifically practice theological reflection? In Bible study? Through testimony? In what other ways is it done?

4. A signature gift of Choongsuh is its adeptness in inviting young people to *explore ministry opportunities*. In fact, a lack

of paid pastoral staff has often provided the entree for a young
person to step into a leadership role.

- How does the repeating cycle of mozying uniquely prepare
  young people to accept ever-more-demanding leadership
  roles?
- Does mentoring for leadership occur in your congregation? If so, what does it look like?
- Are the young people in your faith community looked
  upon as having gifts to share with their younger siblings,
  or are they more likely to be segregated by age? What are
  the challenges of each model?

PRACTICING ETHNOGRAPHIC LISTENING

"The soul thrives on contemplating difference, for if I see your place
and symbols clearly, I can see my own more distinctly as well."[21]

- What do you see more distinctly about your ministry context
  because of the thick description that Sinai Chung shares with
  us from this congregation?
- What practices of nurturing young people that you "know by
  heart" did this congregation's practices call to mind?
- Sinai is writing about a Korean American church made up
  of second- and third-generation immigrants in a suburb of
  Chicago. Given the racial, ethnic, geographic, and economic background of your context, how did the "juxtaposition
  of opposites of collisions of difference" (Thomas E. Frank's
  phrase) spark your imagination?

CHAPTER 4

Living Together

WHEN RADICAL WELCOME REACHES OUT TO AN INTERFAITH WORLD

Dori Grinenko Baker and Katherine Turpin

> I am far more open to Jews and Muslims and Sikhs and humanists and all kinds of other human beings, including self-declared atheists, *because* of Jesus than I should ever have been apart from him.[1]
>
> —Douglas John Hall

The day after 9/11 a young seminarian named Shelly Dieterle noticed a mosque in her community offering open worship. "I remember being really nervous about going to the mosque and not knowing at all what I was going to experience. But for whatever reason, I felt a deep urgency to be there," she says. She brought a few friends along. They were given scarves to cover their heads and were gently assisted in understanding the Farsi-language service. "We were greeted with a wonderful welcome and excitement about our presence. I came back to church and talked about how powerful my experience was. We then invited someone from the mosque to come worship with us, especially to be present during our prayer time." The following year, folks from Dieterle's church, First Congregational Church of Berkeley, California (FCCB), fasted and celebrated Ramadan at the mosque.

Some Christians responded to the 9/11 tragedy with "God Bless America" bumper stickers and increasing suspicion toward Muslim people. Others congregations quietly went to work, getting to know their Islamic neighbors or deepening the ties they already had. Almost a decade later, one such congregation sees its interfaith relationships as a key marker of its Christian identity: at this church, to be Christian includes embracing people of other faiths. Young adults who find their way to FCCB, a United Church of Christ congregation, say they are drawn to practices of Christianity that welcome engagement with religious difference as part of the path toward living fully into one's own religion. Young people in this congregation echo the sentiments of religion scholar Judith Berling: "Just as coming to know other persons helps me understand myself, so learning other religions brings my Christianity into sharper relief and helps me notice and own what I earlier took for granted"[2]

New friendships formed between FCCB and its neighbors in the pain of the 9/11 tragedy. Members who were students at UC Berkeley and wanted to learn to "know and love neighbors of other faiths"[3] found supportive infrastructure in their church: a generation of post–World War II adults who had created such friendships in response to an earlier tragedy, the Holocaust. This web of friendship allowed FCCB to imagine immediate responses to the escalating violence against people of Middle Eastern descent that happened as the United States was preparing to go to war against Iraq and Afghanistan. A first step was the formation of a group of women from different faiths called "From Fear to Friendship." Later came a week of educational emphasis called "Peace Not Prejudice." A course called "Food, Religion, and Hospitality in the International Community" invited participants to different expressions of ritual, feasting, and hospitality. All three of these initiatives were campuswide events that drew leadership and sponsorship from FCCB. When the daughter of a prominent family at the mosque Dieterle had attended after 9/11 proposed an Interfaith Action Initiative, Dieterle and her church immediately stepped in to help, and now provide ongoing support.

Threads of interfaith friendship are so deeply embedded in this congregation that it has become integral to who members are, while not diminishing their decidedly Christian way of being. This distinctive way of following Christ seems to be particularly important for people under the age of thirty who find a home here. Dieterle, who is now ordained and the youngest clergy on staff here, says she is often asked what churches must do to attract people in their twenties and thirties. "Right now, much of the Christian theology that is out there is oppressive toward people who are not Christian. Many young people have a hard time with that. They've grown up in this mix," she says.

A New *Convivencia*

This mix. Young people living in the United States, the most religiously diverse nation on earth, bump into competing worldviews daily. They embody a new *convivencia*—a living mix of a multitude of religious beliefs and practices. During adolescence and young adulthood, Christians often begin to see a troubling paradox: while religious traditions are a primary source of human values such as peace and hospitality, religious differences are also a primary source of the world's warfare, violence, and bigotry. In the midst of "this mix," Dieterle finds young people hungry for a lived Christianity that embodies the advice of Old Testament scholar Walter Brueggemann: "In church *tell the* story, in the world *live* the story."[5]

CONVIVENCIA: The historical period between the ninth and twelfth centuries in Spain, when persons of Jewish, Christian, and Muslim faith lived and worked in relative peace together, sharing their cultures in rich cross-fertilization of art, technology, and ideas.[4]

When we, the authors of this chapter, went looking for a church that was leaning into this new convivencia, we hit stumbling blocks. College campuses with interfaith collaborations were easy to find, due in large part to a movement launched by Eboo Patel's Interfaith Youth Core.[6] We found individual Christians and community-based youth programs called to interfaith work, but congregations?[7] We almost gave up.

Both of us are Christian ministers, theological educators, and students of youth culture. Both of us as young adults were lucky to find United Methodist congregations that welcomed our doubts and questions when we were discerning our vocations. As we ponder the issues and opportunities posed by the new convivencia existing in the United States today, we sense a hunger among young people who have doubts and questions about how to live as Christians while explicitly respecting the faiths of others. We had a hunch that a church living into the wriggling question of religious pluralism would be a place to which young people might be drawn and a place where young people would find help integrating their faith with their everyday lives. Since such integration is key to vocational discernment, we kept looking.

We noticed FCCB. When we looked more deeply, we found exactly what we had been looking for: a Greenhouse of Hope completely at home within the new convivencia.

Embracing Diversity in the Land of Hippies and Flip-flops

Just a few blocks from the University of California-Berkeley, FCCB inhabits a stately brick building that looks like a prim New England matron awkwardly transplanted into this eclectic neighborhood on the east side of San Francisco Bay. Across one street, the volunteers of Berkeley Free Clinic give away clean needles by night and provide dental exams by day. On nearby Telegraph Avenue, you can hear a Rastafarian drummer, eat authentic Indian cuisine, or buy a handcrafted Peruvian hat from one of hundreds of street artists who set up shop daily. The city of Berkeley is home to a diverse population of people on the move—immigrants from Asia, Africa, and the Pacific Islands, as well as aging hippies and young Americans of all ethnicities who come to join the 35,000-member student body of the university.

FCCB embraces this cultural mix. The stories parishioners tell of the interfaith relationships they have fostered over the past twenty years reveal desire for relationships of reciprocity and mutual hospitality. Their interfaith practices are not random samplings of the world's religions at their doorstep: rather, they grow out of "accumulated trust" that comes out of repeated invitations "into their home," in the words of one of our interviewees.

The practices of interfaith hospitality appear to flow in and out of the hospitable space created in services of worship. Worship at FCCB explicitly welcomes the life experiences, questions, and emerging identities of all people, but especially of children, youth, and young adults. In the following reflections, we will describe these two sets of hospitable practices—interfaith engagement on the one hand and intentional welcome of the young on the other—through the lens of Dori's visits, interviews, and focus groups with members and leaders of the congregation. After a thick description of the congregation, Katherine and Dori reflect together on how FCCB embodies *interfaith Christian practice*—a term we craft to describe how this church lives out an ethic of hospitality that forms young people's vocational imagination. We hope it might help other congregations to imagine hospitality in their contexts.

Worship as Extended Family

It is a Sunday morning in early November 2009. During the past week, congregation members watched news reports of the shooting death of U.S. soldiers at Fort Hood, Texas, by a Muslim of Palestinian descent. The first version of a health care reform bill had just narrowly passed in the U.S. House of Representatives. About 250 members of the community gather to worship in a lofty sanctuary flooded with light from windows high above. A team of pastors sits on a rounded stage behind a jazz ensemble.

The first spoken words to the congregation come from two lay members who have been asked to speak as part of the stewardship campaign. Sam, a bartender in his midtwenties, tells about being raised a Southern Baptist but dropping into a completely secular life during college.[8] He describes moving to California to hike the mountains, deserts, and coasts. There, to his surprise, he found his creator. As his testimony becomes more heartfelt, his voice grows shaky. The young woman by his side gestures support and the congregation leans in, sensing his vulnerable moment and quickening their attention, as if to encourage his speech. He continues to talk about the community he has found at FCCB and its significance in his life: Coffee hour—specifically *the hugs* at coffee hour—is what gets him out of bed to worship on Sunday, following the brief sleep he gets after working until the wee hours of the morning.

Hugs, laughter, and connecting glances punctuate the service. A string of unspoken connection between the people seated around me is momentarily articulated by a woman's whisper at the end of the greeting time. "Don't worry, I'm not going to cry *this* Sunday," she says to a friend. Her friend tells me that last week's service, an honoring of All Saints' Day, was particularly emotional for everyone. But moments earlier, as we listened to Sam's heartfelt testimony, many worshipers had already experienced tears. The next speaker, Sena Perrier-Morris, shares a ritual called Milestones: "Good morning, Church. This week we celebrate these exciting changes in our children's lives: Tiffany attended her first middle school dance and reported that her feet hurt from dancing in new shoes. Tara mastered a new rung on the monkey bars . . ." The brief ritual ends with Sena reminding members to e-mail her with milestones to celebrate next week, as the children come forward to sit on the floor between the front pews, facing the pastors and musicians.

Phil Porter, minister of arts and communication, then engages the children in a lively telling of the story of the widow's mite (Mark 12:38–44). At one point, fake dollar bills are flying from Phil's hands as he illustrates a point. A few brave children step forward to check them out. Others follow. Phil engages them in conversation about the story, collects the fake money, and invites the group of twenty children to follow a team of five adults for the young children's Sunday school hour.

A sermon on right giving, in keeping with the stewardship season, follows. The preacher of the day, minister of community life Adam Blons, speaks without notes or a manuscript, including in his sermon a story from his life as a sixth grader: in a year when his parents had divorced and money was tight, Adam gave his mother a bathroom scale—a gift he came to regret. He challenges the congregation to consider the ways in which their giving reflects their deepest values.

Following the sermon and pastoral prayer, a time of impromptu testimony occurs. Senior pastor Patricia de Jong and intern Geoffrey Gaskins walk to the front pews, look out at the congregation, and ask from the floor for a few volunteers to answer the question, how you have experienced God's light shining in your life? A mom in her midforties shares the importance of the church community during her decision to have a child with her same-sex partner. She tells about the meals, care, love, and support that poured in during a long serious illness later suffered by that child. She wonders aloud who she would be if she had not found her way to this church decades earlier. Two other people share their brief stories. One of them is Charles Townes, a scientist, now in his nineties, who won the Nobel Prize for his work developing the laser. He speaks eloquently for a few moments about God's presence as evidenced in the expanding universe.

At the close of service, a minister invites those who wish to join in a brief celebration of Holy Communion. As most people leave the sanctuary, a dozen or so people gather at the front. A woman prepares bread and cup. Joys and concerns flow when invited among this intimate little band of folks whose ages range from their twenties to their nineties. A young woman weeps as she prays for the families of the perpetrator of the violence at Fort Hood and for all Muslims in the U.S. armed forces who may be victims of discrimination in the aftermath of this tragedy. A middle-aged man prays his sorrow over the chasm dividing the nation over health care reform. After the words of blessing have been said, an elderly gentleman with an unsteady hand eats the bread, drinks from the cup, and passes the Eucharist to a woman beside him. During a fellowship hour after worship, I learn that communion is offered weekly in this cozy space, in addition to regular communion among the whole congregation on first Sundays. This weekly sacrament is a reminder for those who have migrated here from Roman Catholicism that they have found a home here.

Through my researcher's eyes, the practices just described reveal deep commitment to radical welcome.[9] Voices of laypeople join those of professional clergy. Life experiences of children receive attention, and leaders depict Scripture in a way that evokes meaning for elementary school children. One young adult commands rapt attention as he tells the story of his journey to meaning and community. The sermon, while addressed to people of all ages, does not neglect an opportunity to connect with a middle schooler's experience. The preacher makes the risky choice of preaching without a manuscript and telling a story that reveals his vulnerability. The service begins and ends with laypeople telling stories from their lives out loud to one another. While this church does not claim the label "emergent," its Sunday morning gathering engages the heart and mind, creating an experience of the holy that is often touted as a necessary mark of Christianity that will succeed in reaching younger generations.[10] At the same time, the congregation honors the rituals of its elders and appreciates their vibrant presence. The once-a-month leadership of the Spirit Band sets a lively rhythm for worship. All of this contributes to a strong pulse of lives being quickened in this place.

The worship practices at FCCB reflect a community that cares about its young, values the vocations of laypeople and clergy alike, and creates adequate space for sharing the stories of real pain and joy that lie at the heart of the human quest for meaning. These observations are echoed by Michael Huston, a seventeen-year-old who wrote his college application essay about the influence FCCB has had on his life:

The banner suspended above the sanctuary doors boldly affirms to all who enter, "Whoever you are and wherever you are on life's journey, you are welcome here!" The community is comprised of people of all ages, races, sexual orientations, and political beliefs. We listen respectfully to and honor each person's life experience. Each member of the church brings their unique gifts and open spirit to celebrate life and a power larger than themselves.

Every Sunday morning, I look forward to the privilege of passing through these open and affirming doors. A warm smile spreads across my face as I am greeted by members of my "extended family" with a kind affirmation, handshake, or hug. This unconditional support is also evident after church at fellowship hour where people with a genuine interest in my wellbeing continue to inquire about my life.

Michael goes on to write: "As I have grown into a mature young adult, I have transitioned into a role of leadership in these programs. Aspects of this leadership include my passion for inviting others into enriching conversations and motivating persons into action." Michael found at FCCB a community that *noticed, named, and nurtured* his gifts. The movement he traces—from welcome and inclusion to leadership and action—is a movement that can result when a congregation affirms the gifts of young people and lovingly watches as those gifts continue to emerge.

NOTICE, NAME, NURTURE: Three verbs used to describe churches that care for vocation in young people. They are key components of a leadership development model that helps churches better accompany young people on the quest for vocation.[11]

Two UC Berkeley college students—Lisa Coronado Morris and Tinley Ireland—echo portions of Michael's story. They, too, were noticed by the FCCB community and called into acts of service where their gifts could emerge. The ground for them was tilled by a preceding generation and its practices of interfaith hospitality.

Interfaith Practice as "Sharing Our Homes"

"My experience in Berkeley is that belonging to a church is odd." "It is extremely radical in the Bay Area to be a Christian." "It's totally countercultural to be Christian here!"

These comments flow in rapid-fire succession during a conversation with a group of veteran lay leaders of the congregation. I asked them to talk about the church, its ministries of interfaith practice, its ministries with youth and young adults, and its attention to vocation in people of all ages. But first, these members needed to tell me just how countercultural it is to espouse faith in their corner of the world.

Boisterously, they all agreed that in the secularly steeped culture of the San Francisco Bay Area, it is natural to share a connection with someone tied to *any* faith tradition—since the vast majority of people they encounter through work, service, and play do not affiliate with religion at all. "If I meet anybody in any faith community, I feel an affinity and a connection to them. There are people who have a faith tradition, and then there is the secular world," says Bonnie Hester, a lifelong resident of Berkeley who grew up in this church. She describes her entry into interfaith friendships as a natural progression that occurred while working alongside two Muslim women in a child-care cooperative years ago:

> It was a slow kind of getting to know each other. It was very comfortable. There was a lot of relaxed being together and joking. Then I was invited to their home for a celebration after Ramadan. I didn't know what that would be like. But the overarching lesson for me was how ordinary and relaxed all cultures are in their homes. To be invited into that was an expression of accumulated trust—that we would be accepting of whatever was provided there. It was a broadening in an ordinary sort of way.

Alice Clark, the grandchild of progressive Christian missionaries to India, shares a similar story.

I've been influenced by Hinduism all my life, but a change came when I visited a dear old friend in her home a few years ago. I asked her if I could attend her morning worship with her in her kitchen shrine. She was perfectly happy for me to do that. It was a practice that had a lot of ritual elements, but she was doing it in a very relaxed manner. I began to feel very comfortable with that and bring it back and share it with people here, just to try to help people become more comfortable with the incredibly different rituals of Hinduism.

Over the past years the church has engaged in this sort of interfaith home sharing by visiting temples, mosques, and synagogues and sponsoring classes in Hinduism, Buddhism, Sufi dance, and Buddhist meditation. While individual members were forming friendships with coworkers, learning about one another's rituals, and experiencing stories of various pathways to God, conversations at church sparked and ministry teams formed. Over the years, groups have traveled to Turkey, Israel and Palestine, India, and Spain and Morocco. A peacemaking trip to Iran, taken by senior minister Patricia de Jong, helped lead the UCC denomination to adopt an "Axis of Friendship with Iran" day, celebrated with numerous partnering institutions for the first time on September 12, 2009.[12] "We try to encourage people who travel to share their experiences with each other from a spiritual place. I see travel as a real opportunity to open and share the world," Alice says.

This distinction is sometimes described as the difference between traveling as a tourist and traveling as a pilgrim.[13] Experiencing that distinction has been deeply gratifying to Bonnie:

Some of the things I've done in this world I've done only because I've been a part of this church, and it's been wonderful: for instance, traveling to Morocco and Spain and looking at those places where Jews, Christians, and Muslims lived peacefully together. We've had a chance to talk to Jews and Christians living there. We have an attitude that the world is a small place, and we want to have connection. We're now talking about a trip to South Africa.

This framework of hospitality toward the world as a small place was long at work at FCCB, but it heightened in the aftermath of 9/11, particularly as a response to subsequent anti-Islamic rhetoric and actions. Leaders in the congregation who were already steeped in the value of Christian interfaith practices were then poised to support a new generation asking *its* questions.

Interfaith Practice as "Becoming Better Christians"

What kind of young Christian leader emerges in this milieu? How is Christian identity formed in a place of robust conversation with Jews, Muslims, Hindus, Buddhists, and people of no faith at all? The influence of FCCB's embrace of convivencia on young adult vocation became particularly visible to me through the church's committee on call and discernment. Rebecca Wright, a lay pastoral counselor, leads that group. She notes that the church is located near the Graduate Theological Union, a consortium of nine seminaries in a neighborhood sometimes called "holy hill." It is not unusual for a church in such a location to become home to people moving through seminary. During the past few years, FCCB has nurtured fourteen people as they've moved from discerning a call to ministry, through seminary, and into ordination in the United Church of Christ. Many of those candidates for ministry have been young people, drawn into the FCCB congregation through its on-campus presence—an intentional witness to what the pastors describe as a form of "bilingual" Christianity that can converse "at the wall" of public life.[14]

Shelly Dieterle, who began attending here before she started seminary and who currently serves as the congregation's minister of campus life, claims her vocation as a pastor was nurtured by the church's willingness to engage with her in interfaith practices: "Interfaith action is central to my life as a Christian. I don't always *out* myself as a Christian in public settings. I prefer that people experience and observe my way of relating and later learn what inspires it. I try to create opportunities and environments for people to live and experience progressive Christian values."

One year the congregation established an internship for Tinley Ireland, a recent college graduate considering seminary, so that she could try out her gifts in a loving, supportive environment. Ireland, twenty-three, told me, "One of the things that attracted me to this church was its interfaith slant. Our church is very Christian, but also very interested in working with other faiths, especially for the betterment of the community."

Ireland was raised as a Unitarian Universalist but converted to Christianity in her freshman year of college, after enjoying the highly experiential worship she found visiting an Assemblies of God congregation. On one of her early visits at FCCB, a rabbi spoke during part of the service. On another occasion, Ireland remembers hearing a portion of the Koran being read alongside the Bible. Judaism and Islam were "not given equal authority with Christianity, but the fact they were present resounded with my interest in maintaining relationship to other faiths, while being distinctly and decidedly a follower of Christ. I think it is very important to be so comfortable and so sure of your faith that it is possible to comfortably interact with people of other faiths." She remembers an interfaith text-study in which a rabbi explained that, although for him Judaism is the best and truest expression of faith, encounters with differing interpretations deepen his own reflection. It is only in coming from a place of openness about other religions and certainty about one's own that difficult conversations about living together peaceably can take place, she remembers him saying. That approach became foundational in her own way of living out Christianity. "There are people who will take different parts of different faiths and combine them within their own faith practices. I push away from that. It works for some people, but I see my goal in interfaith action that my Christianity not be diluted. I am Christian, but open—open to other faiths and moving toward a fuller understanding of who God is."

Through the internship, Ireland discerned her vocation, but it was not to professional ministry as she once imagined. "My vocation is to be a layperson rather than a representative of the institution. I'm a follower of Christ. I love Jesus. I do that in the interfaith world." She is currently pursuing a Ph.D. in medieval Italian literature, while remaining active in her church's Spirit Band and interfaith outreach.

Lisa Coronado-Morse, twenty, is another UC Berkeley student who found particular sustenance through FCCB's practices of hospitality, nurture, and interfaith action. Nominally Roman Catholic as a child, she began to explore Christianity more intentionally during late high school and then in her early college years, when she found her way to FCCB.

> I really found out what Christianity was when Shelly [Dieterle] would have dinners for students and we would talk together: Community. Community with other Christians. It was in those moments when I felt their lovingness and their compassion extended to me in every way. I found acceptance and a complete interest in who I was. I came to feel that I don't have to know exactly what Christianity is and I don't have to be solid in my faith. I just have to be with them and those things will come.

Coronado-Morse describes this immersion in community as linked almost imperceptibly with an interest in her unfolding vocation. "So Shelly, when she meets you, she scopes out your interests and forwards opportunities to you," she says. In the spring semester of Coronado-Morse's freshman year, students created the interfaith action initiative. She became involved in leading a dialogue group that evolved into creating an art project intended to stimulate conversation about faith on campus: "I felt I was led into interfaith work. I fell into it, and then I embraced it. Shelly led me. My curiosity led me. My desire for friendship led me. In interfaith work, I got a much deeper desire to find out what Christianity is. Interfaith work developed a hunger for me to know my own story."

Through leadership in the campus interfaith movement and supported by Dieterle as her advisor, Coronado-Morse also came to discover gifts she didn't know she had. "I kind of wowed myself," she says. "I found I was really good at finding faith-based questions and in making things happen. I am a doer."

In a prominent corner of the FCCB sanctuary sits a large Tibetan singing bowl that when struck signals all to enter into a brief time of centering on a passage from the Bible. This bowl has a story: it belonged to the now-deceased husband of a congregation member who brought it back during a time of earnest spiritual quest. Blons, minister of community life, explains that the bowl is a symbol of this congregation's lived theology. "The key for us is relationship. This bowl and its place in our worship grows out of a connection. That's why it feels authentic. We live in this multicultural, multireligious environment. It's who we are. Its presence here honors who we are."

The presence of a singing bowl in worship also teaches. Like inviting someone's Jewish dad to a Sunday school class to describe *Shabbat* or inviting a couple in the congregation who meditate to share their practice with the youth group, interfaith moments invite questions, questions invite reflection, and reflection leads to fresh insight about one's own path. At FCCB, that is a path marked, in Blons's words, "by God's radically inclusive love, best understood as Jesus's mission to break open the idea that God's love is meant only for a chosen few."

Choosing Embrace

Members of FCCB make a direct link between their relationships with people of other faiths and their Christian practices of hospitality, sometimes called "radical welcome." In the words of senior pastor Patricia de Jong:

> Our call is to magnify the longings of Jesus. The longing of Jesus was for everyone to come to who they are and to move out of the presence of the holy into the world. I come to these relationships so open to other traditions because I know how important mine is to me. I know who you are. I know how profound the experience of the sacred and the holy has been

in your life. So let's meet. I can't think of anything more blessed than to sit
with them at table and participate in eating a meal together.

Theologian Miroslav Volf describes the practice of "embrace" as a
response to exclusion prompted by religious difference.[15] The members of FCCB we interviewed echo Volf in rejecting a "false sense
of purity" in creating Christian identity. In other words, Christian identity does not require one to separate fully from those who
are religiously "other." Instead, Christian identity includes both
separation from and binding to the other. As Volf notes, "We are
who we are not because we are separate from the others who are
next to us, but because we are *both* separate *and* connected, *both*
distinct *and* related; the boundaries that mark our identities are both
barriers and bridges."[16] Indeed, Volf argues that the boundaries af-
forded by religious traditions undergird the moral arguments for
engaging in embrace. Our research collaborators described the importance of their religious identity as decidedly Christian, and yet
they articulated a sense of Christianity that does not exclude people
with commitments to other religious traditions. In addition, the
Christian practice of hospitality—particularly the habit of listening
to one another's stories in this congregation's worship and fellowship
life—provides a recurring pattern that shapes people over time. This
pattern provides a template for engaging in hospitality and embrace
with people outside the community.

Stephanie Spellers, in the book *Radical Welcome,* uses Volf's metaphor of embrace to talk about churches in the United States that
are embodying an emerging theology of welcome across lines of race
and ethnicity, generations, sexual orientation, and class privilege. We
see a parallel movement at work where Christian congregations are
stepping into the emerging practice of convivencia. Although Spellers does not name non-Christians as a focus of radical welcome, we
extend her concept to apply to the practices of interfaith hospitality
and embrace. She writes:

> Radical welcome is not an invitation to assimilate. . . . We are offering an
> embrace, and that means we have opened ourselves, offered ourselves. The

risk is great, but embrace requires us to gird ourselves with the love of God and to say, "Come, bring who you are. My arms are open to you. Would you open your arms to me?" We will receive one another, not losing our unique identities and histories, but releasing the rigid boundaries so that our stories can connect and a new community might be born.[17]

As members of FCCB shared, a sense of mutual hospitality imbues the metaphor of embrace. Members described their experiences of both offering and receiving hospitality, experiences of advocacy and education toward ending violence and of embrace in kitchens and at candlelight vigils. This work is necessarily a slow and careful dance because it entails vulnerability and must counter a long history of distrust. The reward of this careful work is evoked by Spellers as she reflects upon Volf's words on embrace:

> Because the two have not melted into one, you may once again open your arms. Now you have the chance to look at yourself and rediscover your own identity, "enriched by the traces that the presence of the other has left." And you look again at the other, the one whose identity will continue to change, the one who will continue to be both friend and mystery, the one you may embrace again with your now open arms.[18]

We see here a pathway for Christians to live together with their non-Christian neighbors, not to convert them but to seek with them a mutual embrace, a place of understanding out of which action on behalf of a hurting world might grow. The young people at FCCB have stepped into this radical love-in-action. In this way their lives contribute a signature gift to the ongoing work of embodying the hospitality of Christ.

Convivencia as Emerging Christian Practice

The interfaith movement is largely understood as a worthy venture in a religiously plural culture. But we are on an unmarked road when we claim that interfaith practice can provide formation in Christian identity. How does a robust *living with* people from other religious traditions contribute to the formation of Christian identity, belief, and living, and, as we are further arguing, do so in such a way that strengthens Christian vocational understanding in young adults?

We are using Christian practice here to describe "a form of cooperative and meaningful human endeavor," which inextricably involves both thought and action.[19] At FCCB, convivencia is a shared practice of the congregation, not just an individual choice lived out in the more secular contexts that members inhabit, such as work and school. Living together with their non-Christian neighbors has become part of their common lived Christian response to the real human needs that their context has presented. The interfaith relationships, educational adventures, and acts of Christian witness on campus are responses to the basic human needs that allow the congregation to "reflect God's purposes for humankind" together as a community. This practice is particularly attractive to young adults who struggle with Christian privilege in the U.S. context and with global violence related to religious difference.

For a generation of post-9/11 adolescents and young adults, interfaith practice becomes a key justice issue that demands theological consideration. Living into interfaith friendships and mutual action as a congregation provides the conditions for young people to consider their religious identity and to practice a Christian faith that steps into this contextual reality rather than ignoring it. As practical theologians Craig Dykstra and Dorothy Bass claim, noticing these "God-shaped fundamental human needs and conditions" and living into a response to them is a "crucial theological task" for contemporary young people.[20] Living in right relationship with neighbors of other religious traditions is a crucial human need at this point in history. Likewise, it raises key theological questions as to what a "God-shaped response" might be. This is precisely why congregations that take seriously this challenge are vital places that nurture their young people into mature Christian vocational expressions for love of neighbor.

Intentional convivencia may seem counterintuitive as a Christian formational practice. Resistance to it lies in the fear that it will lead to either the conversion or the dilution of one's Christian belief. On the one hand, the church owns an unfortunate history of learning about people of other religious traditions merely to better convert them. On the other hand, the twentieth-century attempt to manage religious difference by downplaying it and promoting assimilation often resulted in diluting or denigrating the unique beliefs and practices of different traditions. FCCB presents evidence of a third way: through offering hospitality both to people of other religious traditions and to the pressing questions of the young, a vibrant Christian belonging, commitment, and witness can emerge.

Embracing Convivencia
"So the World Might Be a New World"

The Spanish convivencia came to a violent halt as Europeans set out for the "New World." At about the same time that King Ferdinand and Queen Isabella blessed Christopher Columbus's journey to find a trade route to India and prove the world was round, a horrible chapter in Christian history began. The expulsion of Jews and Muslims from southern Spain was bloody and violent. What is left to remember the preceding period of peaceful history has been relegated to museums.

Amid the bloodshed and violence often caused by religious differences today, embracing the current convivencia might contribute to creating a new world through small acts begun close to home. The radically inclusive theology that undergirds FCCB's practice of interfaith friendship may be embraced readily in Berkeley, where the simple act of walking down the street causes one to wonder how so many diverse religious expressions coexist. People who live in more homogenous settings, such as small towns or rural areas, might find it more difficult. If we are not confronted with religious diversity where we live, why should we care? If we care, but don't come in contact with much diversity, where do we start?

We in congregations start by articulating a compelling Christianity that meets young people's desire to create a better world. A young person who is given the opportunity to understand a Buddhist singing bowl while surrounded by a community of meaning-making that encourages questions and conversation is more likely to weather the faith storms of religiously diverse life in college. A college student who is given ample opportunity to consider the historical context and the rhetorical impulse of biblical texts that have been used to argue Christianity as the one true religion may find such intellectually rigorous Bible study invigorating and worthy of her best energy.[21] A young Christian who befriends a Muslim while working side by side in a soup kitchen may come to understand that service is a place where the Bible and the Koran can speak the same language and inspire similar actions. The common denominator in these three examples is a congregation that creates space for young people, in community, to think and reflect on lived experience as it intersects the stories of their faith. In that conversation, new generations get a chance to tweak inherited understandings of God. New theologies emerge—God-shaped responses to particular, contextualized predicaments encourage young people to more deeply question their role in God's dream for the world.

As we learned from the previous chapter, congregations that nurture young leaders provide healthy and robust opportunities for theological reflection. Gifts of leadership among young people today require a congregational culture that intentionally notices, names, and nurtures them. Listening to the voices of parishioners and pastors who have been deeply involved in the convivencia that is FCCB makes clear that interfaith friendships, like most Christian practices when newly embraced, must start small, close to home, where a need presents itself and people respond.

Young people, if left to muddle through on their own, may very well find their church's lack of attention to religious difference in a growing pluralistic world to be a ticket out—a reason for not caring enough about Christianity to stay connected to it into adulthood. What disappears in that gap is both a tragic loss to the church, which needs articulate young leaders to carry its vision of shalom forward, and a loss to the larger human community, which needs leaders whose impulses toward healing the world are sustained by a multitude of complementary yet distinct religious ideals.

Rumi translator, scholar, and poet Fatemeh Keshavarz says, "We speak a new language so the world might be a new world."[22] In the decade since her first visit to a mosque, Shelly Dieterle has become a fluent speaker of a new language. She uses it almost daily. It is the language of many faiths, speaking together, retaining their distinctiveness, and engaging in one another's truths. From the start, she brought others along, and she found friends in her congregation who had begun this quest long before her. Together, they formed a group of conversation partners inviting others into this sometimes risky but deeply rewarding work. The result is a church that has learned to speak a new language "so the world might be a new world." This church is a Greenhouse of Hope where young adults find their imaginations shaped in the form of a Christianity that is already at work creating a new world.

Questions for Refection

ENGAGING VOCATIONCARE PRACTICES

1. *Creating hospitable space* is one of FCCB's signature gifts. Hugs at coffee hour, the intentional inclusion of children in worship, and a banner that reads, "Whoever you are and wherever you are on life's journey, you are welcome here!" all embody hospitality. Indeed, hospitality seems to operate on a continuum—starting with small acts close to home and reaching out to embrace people of other faiths.

   - How does hospitable space at FCCB directly relate to young adults and their quest for meaning, purpose, and vocation?
   - Where on this continuum of hospitable practices does your congregation find itself? Does hospitality in your context extend to welcoming questions, doubts, or non-traditionally held values?

- What are some of the unique features of FCCB's culture that contribute to its particular expression of hospitality as radical welcome? How might the unique features of your church's culture and surroundings create specific expressions of hospitality?

2. *Asking self-awakening questions* provides an opportunity for people to think about their lives in light of their faith. A prompting question can help people hear God's voice in a way they might never have considered before.
   - One example of this at FCCB occurred during worship, when laypeople were asked to share their answers to the question, "How have you experienced God's light shining in your life?" Is this a question that might be asked during your worship? What factors contribute to whether people feel comfortable sharing in this way?
   - Where else do you see self-awakening questions arising at FCCB? How is this like or unlike your context?

3. At FCCB, Shelly Dieterle found companions with whom to *reflect theologically on self and community* following the 9/11 tragedy. When she returned to church after worshiping with her Islamic neighbors, she found folks who were eager to talk with her about the experience. They then joined her in ongoing action and reflection.
   - What are the urgent causes that might open young people in your context to reflecting theologically?
   - Can you imagine your congregation welcoming a young adult's desire to explore the connections between Christianity and other faiths? What infrastructure (such as denominational conversations or particular people who have interfaith experience) is in place to make such welcome possible?
   - What other wriggling life issues might young adults in your congregation be eager to think about through the lens of Christian faith?

4. FCCB has a history of *establishing ministry opportunities for young people* through collaboration with groups on the nearby university campus. Several young adults have found their vocational imaginations enlarged through invitations to take part in interfaith Christian practice.

- What practices does your faith community do beautifully, regularly, and with deep joy? How are young people purposefully invited into these practices?
- Are the young people in your faith community looked upon as having gifts to share with the wider community? How are those gifts supported and nurtured?

PRACTICING ETHNOGRAPHIC LISTENING

"Congregations are thoroughly local. Approaching the holy in their own uniquely incarnated ways, congregations also acknowledge that by definition the holy exceeds their forms and any others."[23]

- How does your congregation's "thoroughly local" way of incarnating the holy become more visible to you after seeing the very distinctively local ministries of FCCB?
- What practices of nurturing young people that you "know by heart" did this congregation's practice call to mind?
- FCCB is set in a vastly diverse neighborhood and has chosen to embrace that diversity. What diversity exists in your context? Is diversity approached as a welcome stranger, a dangerous intrusion, or something in-between?

CHAPTER 5

Converging Streams

AN ISLAND CONGREGATION'S PRACTICES OF VOCATION CARE

Fred P. Edie

> The stream flowing through our lives is from eternity to eternity. It is artesian. It is totally adequate. Everything we need is borne by that stream.[1]
>
> — N. GORDON COSBY

Into the Rapids

For me it was the least likely of scenarios. As a nineteen-year-old college sophomore, my aspirations for the summer of 1980 included heading home to renew a dormant lawn-care business on the island off the Georgia coast where I had grown up, doing a little fishing, then cruising the beach. But through a strange turn of events (in retrospect, God may have been involved), I found myself as the summer youth worker at my home church, the Isle of Hope United Methodist Church (IOHUMC). In fact, I was in the driver's seat of that ministry—literally. One particular morning I was wheeling our congregation's ancient school bus (cleverly dubbed "Old Yellow") away from the coast and through the southern Appalachian foothills, carting most of our youth group toward a whitewater rafting trip on the Ocoee River. Driving the bus was a requisite skill for this unexpected job. Although I had always been a loyal youth groupie, I can honestly say I had *never* thought about ministry before that summer. I imagined myself as too devoted to a career in music, too much the wiseacre, and way less than sufficiently spiritual for *that* kind of calling.

But I did love riding that bus as a kid. On youth group trips, choir tours, and service projects, we had sung every TV-show theme song yet written, horsed around, snoozed sitting up, mooned truckers, and otherwise rollicked our way through much of the Southeast. Old Yellow was a rolling community. Indeed, I first got to know the woman who eventually consented to marry me on one of those all-night bus trips. And, as much as I loved riding in it, I found I loved driving it even more. All that fun was going on behind me now, as I was mostly paying attention to the road and the rhythmic "ching, ching, ching" of the drive train signaling that, for this moment at least, Old Yellow was running well.

On this particular adventure a much newer van (borrowed from the Presbyterians) trailed close behind Old Yellow, driven by a parent and carrying overflow kids. Noticing that it had disappeared from my rearview mirror, this being the era before cell phone calls and quick texts, I slowed down and then pulled over to wait for it to catch up, or if it didn't, to figure out what had happened. As we idled by the side of the road, an ambulance with pulsing lights and piercing siren whipped past in the opposite direction. My stomach flipped with foreboding.

We turned back. Rounding a corner on this still-hazy morning, we came upon what seemed like an apocalyptic scene. The borrowed van had flipped onto its roof and had been flattened to half its normal height. Shattered glass, engine fluids, tire remnants, and pieces of clothing were strewn everywhere. Shaking and bloodied kids who had managed to squeeze out of the mangled vehicle clung to one another by the side of the road. Parking the bus, I ran toward them. "Somebody's still in there," a voice shouted. I felt my lips and then my hands start to go numb.

While paramedics struggled to free the trapped student, I did my best to comfort the others, all the time fighting to control the panic welling up in me. Finally, the last student was extracted, the injured were whisked by ambulance to the nearby hospital, and we followed behind in the bus.

The rest of the day was a blur of phone calls and improvised arrangements. We dealt with medical permissions. We needed to decide whether to call the whole trip off or to continue. We had to find transportation. We tried to figure out how to get the banged-up students home. The whole group required attention—all of them, whether injured or not, were shaken. I found myself repeatedly explaining to highway patrol, paramedics, and hospital officials that *I* was the adult in charge, all the while trying not to break down in front of them.

The picture improved when we learned that even the worst injuries were minor. I went outside the hospital to share the good news with the rest of the group, only to find that it had preceded me. At first they had gathered to pray, but now they were arranged in groups of six in the parking lot *pretending* to raft down the Ocoee River. One of the counselors was barking orders: "Left side reverse paddle . . . Watch that hydraulic! . . . All forward . . . *Paddle, people, paddle!*" They were irrepressible.

When we returned home a few days later, I was astonished to be greeted by parents thanking me for taking such good care of their kids. It was true that, however inadequate I had felt in the midst of it all, we had managed to paddle through it. We got the four most banged-up students home and even salvaged the rest of the trip for most of the group.

Perhaps because we had all glimpsed our finitude on this plunge into the rapids of life, the students and I simply couldn't get enough of one another for the rest of that summer. We loved one another passionately, and we felt joy at any excuse to be together. Though our faith was immature, we rightly sensed that God was in the mix here. God had seen us through this harrowing experience. God had given us one another to love through thick and thin. We did so abundantly, taking nothing for granted. Those three months rank among the most memorable seasons of my life. In retrospect, while I can't in good conscience recommend a near-death experience as a ministry strategy (or as a means to awaken a call to ministry), its effects on the youth group and on my own sense of call are undeniable. God's love and abiding care were powerfully, passionately real to us all. Three years later I was on my way to seminary.

It's in the Water

Thirty years removed from that summer, I am an ordained clergyperson who teaches at a denominational seminary. I recently renewed ties with IOHUMC in an effort to understand anew how that congregation shaped not only my own vocational imagination but also the call of at least eleven other men and women from my generation into professional ministry. I discovered that many of the dynamics of my own story were present in others' as well. Among them are the following:

- Awareness of the unique natural and cultural environment that fosters community identity and spirit in that island community
- Appreciation for the supportive, encouraging, and nurturing *church* community (mostly) free from strife
- A feeling of being cherished as a child and a youth by a congregation that views the young as gifts from God
- An instilled faith that God is present and acting for good in and through the church and its members
- Being vested with significant ministry responsibilities as a young adult
- Receiving informal mentoring from admired clergy and laity

Attempting to capture the cumulative power of these dynamics through which he and so many of his peers had accepted ministry callings, Jack, the present-day youth minister (himself a homegrown clergyperson), chuckled, then put it this way: "It's just in the water."[2]

Perhaps *it is* in the water: *Coastal* waters set this island community apart from others and help form its distinct identity. *Cultural* waters foster an interdependent ecology of attitudes, practices, teachings, institutions, and roles all wrapped in the supportive, nurturing communal relationships that make up IOHUMC. And finally, *baptismal* waters flow, through which God calls all Christians to ministry, lay and ordained alike. Callings to vocations of ministry *do* flow through the waters at Isle of Hope. Tracing these converging streams and their cumulative formative impact on current and would-be clergy carried along by them is the task I will take up in this chapter.

AUTOETHNOG-RAPHY: A practice that self-consciously interweaves the researcher's own story with the context he is studying. Autoethnography acknowledges the writer's status as both an insider (with ties to the community) and an outsider (with critical distance and a wider perspective).

While sharing the ethnographic commitment of other authors in this book, I write from the perspective of *autoethnography*. While I attempt to describe and critically reflect upon the culture of this particular community and congregation as I viewed it through interviews, participant observations, and repeated site visits, I do so as an insider. I grew up here; this church is my mother church, and I am one of the clergy nurtured by its waters. At the same time my insider status is an ambiguous one. I have spent more than half of my life away from the island. I have been immersed in churches, seminaries, graduate schools, and communities that have enlarged my view of the world and challenged some of the assumptions that were sown in my youth. Hence, my perspective on this congregation is different than it would be had I never left.

The Coastal Waters:
How an Island Shapes a Community

If, when you picture Isle of Hope, you are imagining the Outer Banks or Hilton Head or Amelia Island, then you are off course.

First, the island is far smaller than its more famous southeastern U.S. sisters. Even plodding along at a ten-minute mile as I do, you can run around the developed edges of the island in less than an hour. Second, Isle of Hope sports no hotels, restaurants, golf courses, or other tourist amenities. In fact, the only nonresidential buildings include three churches and a chapel easily within shooting distance of one another, an elementary school, and the volunteer fire department. The sole retail businesses are a small, family-owned marina and an interior design studio housed in what was once a general store. Third, there is no beach. Standing on the southeastern bluff of the river, you look over river and marsh to a neighboring island rather than white sand, breaking waves, and sun worshipers.

Even if humble as islands go, Isle of Hope is a place of remarkable natural beauty. From the Google Maps' perspective, you would see a near unbroken canopy of moss-draped live oaks, magnolias, and pines. On the ground looking skyward the effect is more like gazing upon a green firmament through which sunlight is dappled and diffused in ever-changing patterns. The effect of the shade and light penetrating the trees and the languid-looking moss hanging from their limbs is slightly mysterious and conveys a sense of rootedness; as if the place has been around for a long while. Camellias and azaleas light up the landscape in spring. Grasses in the expansive marshes renew themselves annually from dull brown to radiant and then deep green, and the mud they are rooted in oozes the primal stench of death and life. Residents claim that the aroma "gets inside of them," which is surely more than metaphorically correct. Seasonal changes combined with contrasting and ever-changing patterns of sun and shade, themselves stirred together with daily rhythms of ebbing and flowing tides in creeks and rivers, means that the island appears to be changing constantly, and that each revelation of its natural beauty is unique and not to be seen again. One resident, strolling under the live oaks that line Isle of Hope's Bluff Drive and gazing east over the river and marsh, once commented to me: "I walk here every day because I want to see what God will do next."

Homes on the narrow winding streets of Isle of Hope are cozy; no oversized mansions here. Its neighborhoods manage to be at once eclectic, charming, and scruffy. Many residents walk or ride their bikes daily, stopping frequently to chat with neighbors. Children roam freely, often in packs. They get themselves to swim-team practice or vacation Bible school or down to the marina to fish or crab. In these ways, Isle of Hope remains something of a throwback, but it is not unlike rural communities across the United States. The thousand or so families who live here see one another, know one another, and connect and reconnect with one another frequently. Folks meet at church, at T-ball, at swim meets, at the lighting of the Christmas tree, or during their evening walks. Put more abstractly, Isle of Hope is an authentic community where residents who desire it find themselves embedded in a wide matrix of supportive relationships. Indeed, the first person I chatted with at IOHUMC reported that he and his family had just moved back from Atlanta to recover a lost sense of community.

Geography can facilitate relational intimacy. The strong sense of community fostered by the contained geography of this place inevitably shows up in the stories of present-day clergypersons who grew up here. One pastor, Ann, whose ministry emerged out of her musical gifts, tells about the mentoring she received as a teen not only from the music director at IOHUMC, but in equally strong measure from musicians at St. Thomas Episcopal and Isle of Hope Baptist. These musicians lived just down the street from one another. As a result, Ann was invited to play and sing in all three congregations. My own experience is similar. My third grade teacher, perhaps an all-time favorite, was married to the pastor at IOHUMC. Our classroom was approximately one hundred yards from the church sanctuary. My longtime baseball coach (for the Isle of Hope Fiddlers—*crabs* not string players) was a deacon at the Baptist church. The mother of another current clergyperson who grew up at IOHUMC taught me how to swim. I knew where these folks lived, and they knew where I lived. They knew my parents. When I was a child, it seemed to me that everybody knew everybody, and that assessment would still prove accurate today. Once in the midnineties, when visiting in the home of two teenaged boys in my youth group, I watched them begin to salivate as their mom disclosed that she and their dad were going out of town for the weekend. Noticing their reaction as well, she narrowed her gaze and said, "It's a small island, boys, *watch yourselves.*"

Residents of the island generally feel sorry for people who choose to live elsewhere. In the seventies they rose up en masse to protest the possibility of condominiums on their cherished Bluff Drive. The next revolt came over a local government proposal for streetlights. Isle of Hope residents protested loudly that they preferred it to be dark at night. The place seems to breed or at least permit a certain libertarian spirit. For example, the island's hippie dropout can pop into a youth group lock-in at 3:30 in the morning, perform a guitar solo, then pass into the night, and nobody gets too worked up about it. A Vietnam vet who returned from the war with emotional wounds spends his days planting wildflowers in random patterns along ditches and causeways or camping for months at a time on a little hummock across the river, and his lifestyle raises few eyebrows. Residents describe these folks as "local color" and let them be. On the other hand, when a resident slowly succumbing to Alzheimer's becomes confused and disoriented on one of her daily walks, a passerby simply takes her gently by the arm and walks her home. And a twentysomething young woman, victim of a debilitating car crash, is regularly visible to all in her custom-made bicycle/wheelchair. Her presence witnesses to tragedy but says more: Obviously her family feels no compulsion to hide her. We may even surmise that they believe this place and its people to be important to her well-being. Thus, although the cultural veneer of this Deep South community is overwhelmingly, vocally, *stridently* conservative, Isle of Hope's eclectic libertarianism occasionally pokes holes in that veneer, revealing nuances of thinking and living born, in part, out of the community's nonconforming past, its creativity, and also its people's encounters with more than a little suffering. Put differently, the island, because it makes no public pretense of tidiness, seems to grow people capable of acknowledging and responding creatively to life's messiness. This is certainly a factor in the calling of young people into clergy vocations through IOHUMC and its neighboring congregations, and, as we shall see, it is a factor in shaping clergy identities as well.

The Cultural Waters:
Nurturing Christian Life in Worship and Study

At Isle of Hope, worship and study anchor cultural practices of nurturing vocation. In worship, young people step into ever-more-challenging roles of leadership. In study, they are invited into careful and critical investigation of biblical texts. These two very basic practices take on an aura of exploration and discovery set within a context of loving support.

IN WORSHIP

As happens elsewhere on the island, stepping onto the grounds of IOHUMC feels like a step back in time—in this case a step of more than one hundred fifty years. One's attention is drawn immediately toward the simple, white clapboard sanctuary trimmed with large clear-paned windows, themselves flanked by green shutters and a green tin roof—all of it sheltered by huge moss-draped oaks.

Inside, a happy conversational buzz grows to a low roar as the sanctuary fills for worship. Total attendance over three morning services ranges from seven hundred to more than a thousand. Robed clergy casually join in greeting the gathering community. Signaling a transition, a member of the choir tolls the hour, young acolytes process down the center aisle to light the candles on the altar table, and clergy seat themselves in the chancel or front pew. These gathering moments typically include a musical prelude performed by church musicians or instrumental offerings from young people in the congregation. Next comes a musical selection from one of the many choirs (ranging from the very young children's choir, called the Twinklers, to youth, to the adult chancel choir), followed by an informal greeting, a welcome to visitors, and a congregational hymn sung from *The United Methodist Hymnal.*

Music is exceedingly important to this congregation. Hundreds of members participate in its music ministry through singing, playing an instrument, or directing one of the choirs. Music was very important to my own formation at Isle of Hope, as it was to other present-day clergy who grew up there. I was a serious musician in high school and saw myself heading toward a career as a professional musician. Within three months of my becoming a regular attendee at church at age fifteen, Ann, the music director, had invited me to play drums in worship, welcomed me into the chancel choir, and encouraged me to join the new youth choir forming under the name HOPE (Hear Our Praises Evermore). While a youth and later as a leader of youth, untold hours of my life were consumed by HOPE choir rehearsals. Sometimes we spent nearly all of Saturday rehearsing for the next morning or as part of our preparation for a tour. When we sang in worship, the congregation hailed us as if the Mormon Tabernacle Choir had just jetted in.

Other current clergy who grew up in IOHUMC described HOPE as a "place where youth could contribute" or as "providing a role for youth to play" or as demonstrating that youth were granted "responsibility" for corporate worship. One commented that singing in the choir was a practice where he regularly sensed God's presence and where he felt that God could "speak through" him. The youth choir held one more significant formational benefit. One pastor described the following epiphany in a seminary Bible course: "I kept stumbling into Scripture passages I had sung as a kid at church. I *knew* them. They were *part* of me."

Worship at IOHUMC continues to unfold in a nineteenth-century revivalist pattern: preliminaries, then message, then altar call. To be sure, the content and intent of worship are no longer primarily revivalist. Sermons mostly exhort believers, not the lost. The altar call is usually disguised as an invitation for people to walk down to the chancel to join the church, a frequent occurrence nearly always accomplished by a handshake signifying transfer of membership rather than testimony to being slain in the Spirit.

The task of preaching usually falls to the senior pastor. Preaching at Isle of Hope is best described as thematic in content rather than biblical (either expository or narrative) or catechetical. Usually a brief reading from the Bible serves as the premise or launching point for preaching, but sermons rarely trace the chosen passage closely.

Few of the present-day clergy raised here cite the content of preaching as affecting their vocational imaginations. What seemed to matter more for them were invitations to offer their own leadership in public worship along with the affirmation they received for this leadership. While describing her gratitude for the informal mentoring of a pastor, Ann told this story from her college years at the church: "I was asked to sing a solo in worship. I had a serious case of performance anxiety, but I got through it. Then [she names the pastor], I guess he was moved or something, he asked if I would sing it again. Right there. And so I did." Another clergyperson went from seminary to a Christian education job in a church, but, because of a congregational crisis that resulted in the removal of a pastor, she found herself preaching regularly. "I was surprised to find that I loved it," she says, "that I was good at it," and that, as a result, "people began to look to me for pastoral resources." Still another clergyperson displays in his office a framed copy of the worship bulletin listing the first sermon he ever preached—at IOHUMC.

On one of the Sundays I was with the congregation, Jack, the beloved youth minister, having served the church for more than a decade, preached his farewell sermon. It included his recollections of powerful *holy moments*—occasions when the grace and power of God were clearly present to him through the people and situations he encountered there. Deeply significant for his own vocational journey was an invitation to assist one of the other pastors at the baptism of a child. Not yet an ordained elder at the time, he felt the Spirit move him deeply through his close proximity to this sacrament. He said, "I was a basket case for the rest of the service. I sat and cried on the front pew. I couldn't stop." When asked later to clarify the meaning of that event, he added, "I knew this was God calling me to a new step in ministry. I knew I had to be part of this [sacramental ministry]."

As with singing in the youth choir, only now in more personal terms, these pastors' stories testify to the transformative importance of leadership in public worship for shaping their vocational imaginations. The chance to perform the church's "holy things"—interpreting the Scriptures through word or music, attending to the baptismal waters, or, in my case, assisting with serving the communal meal—had deep impact. As we have seen, each pastor testifies to or implies that God was powerfully present and active through them in these practices of worship leadership, a sense confirmed in them by others in the community. Second, they also recounted these events as either awakening or serving in part to confirm their ministry callings.

IN STUDY

After worship, the second major event at IOHUMC on Sunday mornings is Sunday school. Attendance at Sunday school is nearly as robust as worship attendance, typically numbering about five hundred. In addition to graded classes for children and youth, the church provides multiple adult-education offerings on Sundays.

Some adult classes are composed of generational cohorts; others gather around a specific Bible teacher; still others prefer discussion formats. Most classes are lay led. The teaching content in Sunday school classes ranges from biblical-topical to straight biblical; theological perspectives range from Wesleyan to Calvinist and even to dispensationalist. One may pick an approach that feels right simply by sampling the different classes.

In addition to the historically strong adult Sunday school, the United Methodist Bible study program *Disciple Bible Study* has been used here for two decades. *Disciple* requires students to read large chunks of Scripture weekly over the course of thirty weeks, a practice that acquaints them with a salvation-history, narrative approach to the Bible. The class also introduces historical and theological practices of interpreting the Bible. Each weekly meeting gathers around texts and a specific theological theme such as covenant, sin, redemption, and so on. Clergy on staff usually lead such groups. It would be difficult to overstate the importance of *Disciple* and its sister programs to this church. Laity and staff alike agree that, since so many adults and some youth have participated in these studies over the past twenty years, the congregation's level of biblical literacy has been raised and people's imaginations have been opened to discerning their own ministries here and in the wider community.

"It was a safe space to ask questions . . . and not be given answers. I was invited to use the mind God gave me. To go exploring."

One Isle of Hope-raised clergyperson explained that his involvement in a *Disciple* group as a young adult helped to awaken his present love for careful biblical study. Remarkably, another intimate *Disciple* class of three in the 1990s yielded two theology professors and a pastor. Said one member of the class about her youthful experiences there and in other teaching contexts at the church: "It was a safe space to ask questions . . . and not be given answers. I was invited to use the mind God gave me. To go exploring."

Since the mid-1990s, the church has been blessed with a passionate and disciplined full-time minister of Christian education. In addition to leading worship regularly and carrying an enormous administrative load that makes her "frantic" at times, Liz maintains a steady practice of teaching children, youth, and adults. One of her favorite projects is preparing older children for confirmation each year. Partly because of her commitments to teaching, more than one adult member credited her with helping to create an "expectation for spiritual growth" in the congregation that is also emblematic of the church's vitality. Asked to reflect on this compliment, Liz volunteers modestly only that *she* has grown in her time at the church: "My theology is so different than it was eight years ago." She says it is challenging to integrate continuing education classes at a regional seminary, study with biblical scholars, and personal reading into her ministry; but this challenge is part of living out her call to teach and her Christian call to grow.

Her own transformation occasionally creates conflict with students: "I mean, some people don't even want to hear that God's not a male," Liz says as an example of the tension she sometimes feels between her transforming theological convictions and the understandings of those she is teaching. Yet she also believes that her long tenure at the church has provided her "the gift to connect with people" plus the credibility and authority to lovingly challenge them in their faith.

Growth would seem to be a self-evident goal for Christians. Jesus's disciples called him "teacher," and Jesus himself is said to have grown in wisdom and truth. The Christian tradition is everywhere peppered with the language of growth: *holiness, sanctification*, even *divinization*. Yet educators recognize that growth can also be deeply threatening. Demands for too rapid or radical growth may destabilize or deconstruct the self. Threatened people tend to dig in their heels. Key to growth, therefore, is a community capable of holding its members in love over sustained periods of time as they undertake the risks of transformation. IOHUMC manages this tension well. Most members of the church staff have served the church for more than a decade. Hence, unlike a person's experience in more tenuous educational contexts, the threats to the self that correspond with maturing in faith are, in the case of IOHUMC, mitigated by the cultural waters that buoy people up and bear them along in loving support.

The Water Is Wide (Enough):
Youth Ministry as Community of Practice

Dating back at least to the 1970s when church membership numbered only a few hundred, youth workers at IOHUMC have served as paid members of the church staff. Commitment to youth ministry only deepened as years passed and the church grew; youth ministry exists not separate and apart from the larger congregation, but as lively tributaries that flow into and express themselves through the wider community. Presently, youth ministry is part of the portfolios of two full-time staff associates plus several college-aged interns and numerous adult volunteers. From an institutional perspective, this youth ministry takes the form of wide and varied programmatic offerings for youth from middle school through college. In addition to participating in choirs and Sunday school classes, youth may join Bible studies, guitar classes, age-level youth groups, and Scouts. They are also encouraged to participate in mission activities, both locally and to more (and less) exotic locations. Youth are also everywhere at vacation Bible school, serving as teaching assistants, music leaders, gofers, and so on. As with HOPE Choir, the latter is an example of how youth, while often participating in their own age-specific ministries, nonetheless also find themselves in the midst of the significant events of the congregation's life. In the spring of 2009, the youth ministry moved into an extraordinary three-million-dollar facility complete with state-of-the-art classrooms and technology, plus spaces for worship, recreation, and dining. This facility was built around an old house that happened to be painted green and christened (appropriately enough for this volume) the "Green House Project." It is safe to say that youth ministry historically and presently is a *central* commitment of the congregation.

YOUTH MINISTRY PROVIDES COMMUNITY

The pastors I interviewed repeatedly testified to a powerful sense of community in the church's youth ministry when they were teens, a community within which they found a home. Recalling his struggles through a "tough freshman year" in a new town and high school, Jack described his surprise and delight at "fitting in quickly with a group that was welcoming." His "fondest youth group memory" involved the group coping with a broken-down bus (yes, Old Yellow again) at a scenic overlook on a mountain road. Though they were on the way to go tubing at a creek as part of their annual mountain camping trip, to his recollection no one cared about the blown day. "What mattered was the people. . . . [We had the feeling that] whatever happens, we're in this together." He recalls them playing Frisbee, then sitting around singing to guitar music. "It was almost a sacramental moment," he recalled with deep feeling. For Jack, who had been active as a child at church but who had taken on the persona of "river rat" as a young teen and dropped out of church life, trying out the youth group was "like coming home." Another recalls feeling "loved and supported through the whole body of the church but also particularly through the youth group." Another described the first time he set foot on church grounds: "A football came sailing over the church office building. I picked it up, and out of nowhere fifteen people piled on top of me. Welcome to UMYF!"

I was curious whether this hospitable spirit and inclusive community continues in the church's youth ministry today. One tenth grader described her senior high youth group as "a tight-knit community," quickly adding, "the church is, too!" She continued, "Nobody pressures you, but for me they are a strong support group."

My observations mostly affirm her claims. Currently the church hosts two separate youth groups, one for middle schoolers and one for high schoolers. Each group follows a similar pattern for its weekly meetings. As young people arrive they participate in some form of recreation. Next, they sit down together for dinner at round tables on one of the Green House's porches. The "program time" that follows includes communal praise singing with guitar accompaniment; some form of "lesson," which varies from guest speakers to participative Bible studies; and concludes with announcements and prayer. Each group of students is shepherded by adult lay volunteers and staff members that participate with students in the evening's events.

The sense of community was palpable in the senior high group of fifteen to twenty students. Members not only knew one another but also clearly shared a common body of experience. Overt tension and conflict were absent. Gatherings felt relaxed and comfortable.

If the senior high group gave off a mellow and positive vibe, the middle school fellowship shook the entire building. Student attendance ranged from forty to fifty on the nights I was present, and, as a group, these students were far more boisterous than their older peers. They yelled, screamed, sweated, groaned, laughed, ran, stomped, gulped, giggled—all apparently without any felt need to effect or embody public decorum. Yet, even in this group, hospitality abounds. I credit Liz, the Christian educator, and her close-knit team of adult volunteers. They repeatedly demonstrated patience, good humor, and gentle discipline with the students. They obviously care about and know students individually. A culture of care and inclusivity permeates the group. For example, one of the striking features of this community is that students in it are often openly, publicly spiritual. Boys volunteer to pray, doing so unabashedly for others without risk of being massacred by enforcers of the macho "boy code." Girls speak up willingly, even to a stranger bearing questions and notepad. The group's dynamics are not perfect, Liz professes. "Every time we go on a trip together we have drama," but "we talk about this [welcoming community] all the time."

YOUTH MINISTRY TRANSFORMS, PERSONALLY AND SOCIALLY

Because adolescence is, developmentally, the season when capacities for self-reflection begin to blossom, it is not surprising to hear clergy speak of their teen years as important to their faith maturation and vocational directions. One pastor described a conversion experience in the church's broom closet while the youth group was simulating worship in the Roman catacombs. Another was powerfully moved as a teen by the joy evident in the testimonies of a lay witness team and by encountering "the deep personal element to their relationship with the Lord." For still another, reflection upon the experience of community into which he had been welcomed unconditionally became the means by which he came to trust the authenticity of Christian faith.

Not only was the youth ministry a setting where God seemed powerfully present and active in the shaping of individuals and the community, it also offered youth roles and responsibilities for ministry. Past members of the youth ministry recall local and distant mission initiatives where they found themselves way beyond their comfort zones but with a powerful sense that they were engaged in God's work. One clergyperson shared that this commitment to justice and to society taught her the importance of the social alongside the personal dimensions of Christian faith. Another recalls his and other youth group members' serving as "security guards" the night before the annual church bazaar as evidence of the church's trust and willingness to vest them with responsibility.

YOUTH MINISTRY IMMERSES IN MISSION

At the time of my interviews, many of the same youth ministry practices and programmatic events from a generation ago are still on the youth ministry schedule. Students continue to camp in the mountains each summer, the choir still tours, and Youth Week comes round every July. One practice that seems to have grown in importance is a commitment to mission. Youth at Isle of Hope frequently are invited to participate in mission-related ministries both locally and further afield. Indeed, all of the church staff I interviewed stressed mission as critical to the church's present identity. The congregation has set lofty (if still unmet) goals for mission giving and participation. Nowadays it also employs part time a director of mission. Middle-school students gain exposure to mission through a summer trip to South Carolina and senior high students participate annually in the weeklong Appalachian Service Project. College students have begun to journey outside the country, most recently to Haiti. Even the youth choir is shaped by a missional commitment—singing in shelters or hospices or serving for a day at one of the denomination's crisis-relief centers. According to at least one present-day clergyperson, early mission ventures with the church's youth fifteen years ago catalyzed the current congregation-wide commitment to mission.

Asking why mission matters and what it accomplishes prompts a variety of responses. The straight-talking director of mission at IOHUMC says bluntly, "God calls us to do it. The Bible says to seek justice for the poor." Most church staff also share the opinion that mission activities open members to the realities of poverty and its causes. As the director of mission put it, "If you've grown up where things are organized and happy, it's hard to understand [situations] where things are not." Hence, staff, at least, intend for mission to sensitize participants to the "real world." Adds Jack, the youth minister, "skewed reality" of life on the island means that ministers have "a responsibility to jar [the students'] world. To make it bigger." But there is more. The mission experience is one where Christ may "break kids' hearts" by "creating opportunities where God can use whatever they have to give." Hence, from the perspective of current church leaders, mission activities are intended to transform those who participate as much as they are intended to help those being served. Those serving gain critical insight, learn compassion, become reconciled to difference, and discover true Christian vocation.

Student perspectives seem less developed. Some student missioners do gain insight—for example, one described the ability to discern the signs of poverty locally as a result of traveling to West Virginia. Yet most I spoke with were more conventional in their reflections. "It made me more appreciative of what I have," said one. "I came and brought happiness to people's lives," offered another.

In the group of current clergy, those who participated in mission trips earlier in life do seem to have been transformed by that participation. "Mission trips taught me the importance of service alongside the personal relationship with Jesus," said one. Jack discovered mission through his own youth director, a "radical" who told him to "give everything to the poor," and who did so himself by leaving IOHUMC to serve as a missionary in the inner city and later in Peru and Cuba. Mission was also critical to the evolving sense of calling for Ann, the music director turned pastor. She described being challenged early in her ministry by a curmudgeonly yet loving chair of the mission committee (herself the mother of another Isle of Hope-raised pastor) with this question: "How is choir missional?" That question stayed with Ann as she continued in music ministry at the church and as she began to pursue studies leading toward certification as a diaconal minister. Under her maturing leadership, the youth choir ventured into inner cities locally and regionally. In addition to singing, youth taught and served with people in poverty and in prison. The choir's increasingly missional practices were supported by what Ann was learning in school, including, memorably, a powerful challenge from liberation theologian Gustavo Gutiérrez "calling us to the margins." Continuing mission and education led to deepening convictions about the need to connect Christian life with justice. As a result, Ann also reported discovering that "I had something to say. A voice within me needed to be let go." She embraced a calling to pastoral ministry even though it meant going through the "wrenching" experience of leaving music ministry behind.

As we have already seen, transformation (including vocational transformation) does not go on in isolation at IOHUMC rather, it occurs in the context of a hopeful and expectant communal spirituality and with the support of caring and encouraging leaders and friends. In the case above, Ann recalled that her own vocational clarity emerged over years of conversation and prayer with other members of the community. It is significant that three of her conversation partners included the woman who is today director of mission at the church (and who credits Ann with helping her to discern her own call) and two (then) teenaged women, one who has become a pastor and the other a professor of theology. It appears that where pursuing Christian vocation is a vital, growing concern, the Spirit's harvest is even more abundant than we might predict.

In the effort to sum up the long-term success of the church's youth ministry, Jack offered these thoughts: "These people will do anything for the kids. They are always making a place for kids both institutionally and relationally. And people are looking for and seeing giftedness in the young." Moreover, "if you're a kid hoping to connect with God, this is the place to be." The church's long-term "investment" in youth ministry has borne tangible fruit, not the least of which are numbers of people devoting their lives to ministry. Strength builds upon strength, creating an environment in which the shared expectation is for God to continue to do great things for and with the youth of the church.

YOUTH MINISTRY SHAPES VOCATIONAL IMAGINATIONS

IOHUMC has long employed young adults as ministry interns, particularly in relation to its youth ministry. As a college student, I served the church as a youth worker because I was asked, not because I felt at all fit, called, or prepared. I recall that it also made a difference to me that the position paid the equivalent of a summer job, thus also enabling me to continue to cover some of my college expenses. To my surprise, I discovered gifts that summer I never knew I had. I came back to serve in the same position for the next two summers. Those experiences fueled in me the desire to continue in service to God through the church. Upon returning to the congregation a decade later as an associate for Christian education and youth ministry, I recruited college students and young adults to work alongside me over the summers. Aware of the powerful formation an introduction to ministry had been for me, I hoped it could do the same for others.

My successors continued and expanded this practice over the years. In the summer of 2009, five young adults served the church. Three worked primarily in youth ministry, the fourth also in youth ministry but with responsibilities for children as well, and the fifth with college students and young adults. The total salary paid to all interns each year would no doubt go a long way toward filling a full-time staff ministry position. Yet the church persists in this practice of investing in the young. At least four present-day clergy have participated in this informal internship program.

I met all of the current interns and watched most of them in action. That vocation is a live issue, at least for some of the interns, was evident in a teaching series two of them planned for the senior high

youth group. The series, which they called "*Kaleo*," was "something
God put on our hearts to challenge youth with the question 'What
would it look like to follow God in their lives?'" To that end, they
invited a number of past and present church members whom they
judged to be living out their callings faithfully to share their stories.
In the two sessions I attended, the speakers were, indeed, remarkable
for the power of their testimonies.

One twenty-five-year-old guest and church member described
his struggle for vocation during and after college. Acting upon advice gleaned from a college vocations program that he should major
in what he loved, he chose art. Upon graduation he was determined
to try to make it as an artist, and soon discovered that "starving artist" is not just a cliché. Poverty of money was not the real issue for
him, however; it was the isolation from past communities of support. Loneliness and depression drove him to seek out community
in a local church in the city where he was living. There he met a pastor visiting from Haiti who invited him to join that church's mission
to the country. He accepted. Being fluent in French he immediately
found himself teaching art classes to Haitian children as part of the
mission. He went on, "I found all my interests colliding—art, teaching, French, travel, Christian community. It felt like a divine two-
by-four to the head: 'Come live with the poor in Haiti and I [God]
will heal you.'" He wound up staying for seven months. During
this time it gradually became clear to him that he would not only
follow his father into medicine but he would also return to Haiti to
practice. Defining the word *vocation* for himself, he said, "Pastor and
artist come together in medicine for me. Art testifies to what's on my
heart and pastor is one who creates a space to exchange vulnerability
for healing."

Following the hunch that vocation was a compelling subject for
the youth interns as much as or more than for the youth themselves,
I explored with them the relationship between their ministry internships and the vocational paths they were imagining. An earnest male
intern professed to have "no clue what I wanted to do" before his
first summer internship. But after a summer spent serving alongside
the youth minister, the picture became clearer. Central to his emerg-

ing sense of vocation was a conversation at the end of the summer when the youth minister told him, "I think this could be a calling for you." Still not certain about the future, he nonetheless now believes that "this [ministry] is exactly what I am supposed to do in this season of my life."

Another intern, Matt, works for a church member at her non-profit mediation center in addition to his ministry at church. He also described the importance of mentoring. He characterized the mediating attorney as an "amazing edifier." Talking about debriefing sessions she conducted with him after he had begun to do some mediation on his own, Matt said, "Those were my favorite part. She challenges you [to see more options for reconciliation between disputing parties] and affirms you through [the process]."

Clearly, these young interns are paying attention to the adults with whom they are working in close tandem. The interns are drawn to them by the combination of skills, practical wisdom, and character that these adults display, plus the encouragement and training they receive from them. They also reflect upon the example these adults set when attempting to describe what motivates their own ministries or when struggling to describe the emerging trajectories of their life paths.

A key ingredient to these internships seems to be the mentors' investments of significant trust and responsibility in their interns. Quizzed about the highlights of their ministry internships, all of the young adults described ministry activities for which they were given primary or sole leadership responsibility. In each case, entrusting responsibility seemed to beget competence and confidence: "I was in a room alone mediating cases between *grown-ups*." Or, "We did this [whole youth trip] on our own from start to finish!"

Whether any of these interns will take up ordained ministry remains an open question. Nonetheless, their stories provide glimpses into the process of vocational imagination as it is presently unfolding in their own lives. Within this group, none entered into his or her respective ministry internship having already discerned a calling to professional ministry or even necessarily the broad contours of his or her anticipated future. But some did possess a language of calling and vocation that they were using to make sense of their current situations. For example, one articulate young woman described a calling as something about which you are "passionate," that "meets a need," and that "terrifies you." Asked later in the conversation to reflect upon her own vocational plans she said, "This [ministry internship] experience has taught me to be open [to God's call]." Though headed on to graduate training in social work, she would be "going into school open-minded" about ordained ministry even if "still terrified" of the prospect.

Matt spoke of being drawn to meet hopelessness in its many forms with the "authentic hope of Jesus." He sees himself doing this through both church and nonchurch positions; as he works as a youth minister, he helps students find healing from doubt and self-hatred through Christ; his work mediating personal and geopolitical reconciliation in the secular arena is likewise a way of bringing Christ's hope to the world. Indeed, he believed the Spirit was prompting him to be personally present to perpetrators of political violence in order to offer them the hope of authentic reconciliation through Jesus. For him God was "far more creative and capable than we give him credit for," hence this bold statement: "Where God's name is perverted and justice is at stake, I want to be there." Asked, however, whether he considered this work of reconciliation to be a form of ministry, Matt replied that he found *ministry* too "churchy" a word. Ministers, in his view, are "clean" and "proper" and they mostly avoid talking about "the broken stuff." Such avoidance prevents the possibility of "forging real faith." I will return to his evocative comments below. Suffice it to reiterate at this point that, as these stories indicate, the experience of ministry internships at Isle of Hope offers young men and women a crucial context for imagining and refining vocational possibilities for their lives.

The Baptismal Waters: Invisible or Transparent?

IOHUMC is a community of faith in action. Empowered by the conviction that God is present and working in the community, many members claim multiple forms of ministry. Yet, for all its vitality, the church does not possess the language to adequately describe or interpret its robust ministry practice. Said one present-day pastor, "I wish the church had been more intentional about the belief that God is calling people into ministry. . . . I didn't know that vocabulary . . . [as a youth], or talk it." As if to illustrate this point, when asked if she could imagine herself as an ordained minister, a thoughtful senior high student replied, "Ministry? I'm not sure about ministry. But *community work* like what [here she names the director of mission] does . . . I could maybe see myself doing *that*." Perhaps that lack of ministry vocabulary also explains why high school students appeared to be rendered mute after listening to powerful vocational testimonies in the *Kaleo* series. When invited to ask questions of the approachable young man who found his calling in Haiti, the best they could muster was, "What is it like to speak French all day?" I dare say theirs wasn't just a case of being awed by displays of moral courage; their silence demonstrated their lack of practice interpreting the meaning of these testimonies in the language of call and vocation.

Strangely, when it comes to vocational imagination, including imagining ministry callings, IOHUMC seems to have difficulty *talking* its *walk*. To be sure, this problem is one that many congregations would love to have. After all, Christians are to be known by how they live, not by what they say. Whether the congregation talks about the theological significance of baptism may be beside the point; the community is definitely *living* into that significance. Baptisms and the rite of Confirmation are regular and frequent practices in this growing congregation. And whatever folks want to call it, members do regularly take up lay and ordained ministry vocations. So does the language matter?

Scholars debate whether a community's deepest convictions are embedded in its practices or its ideas. I think it is both.

IOHUMC has regularly and enthusiastically invited young people to grow with them into the practices of Christian life and ministry that have sprung up in their context. In this way, they embody the kind of churches the contributors to this volume are calling Greenhouses of Hope: it is a lively, vibrant church actively noticing and nurturing its young people—in worship, in study, in music, in mission. It then gives them plenty of opportunity to make these practices their own through designated youth ministry radically connected to the larger community's life. In exemplary fashion, these practices have propelled young people into lives of meaning and purpose, several through ordained ministry.

This greenhouse didn't need a lot of renovation—its practices of nurturing have been consistent across the past two decades. But faithful formation also requires that Christians learn a language with which to interpret their experiences. That means coming to recognize that, by virtue of our baptism, our lives do not belong to us but belong to Christ (Rom. 6). A community blessed with robust baptismal grammar will also understand that to be baptized is to be, like Jesus, called and commissioned for ministry in church and world (Matt. 3–4, 28). Moreover, when an entire faith community comes to understand itself as called to ministry by virtue of baptism, it will interpret and encourage individual members' decisions for ordained ministry not as exotic, mystifying, or exceptional but simply as a specific kind of response to Christ's universal call to all of the baptized. With this kind of vocational language and imagination in place, Matt the reconciler would feel no need to disavow ministry; he would, instead, recognize reconciliation to be at the very heart of ministry (2 Cor. 5). Developing a robust language of baptismal ministry and inviting people to reflect on their Christian lives by using this language can only support and strengthen Isle of Hope's profound ministry practices. Perspective on the baptismal waters would shift from invisible to transparently life-shaping.

Converging Waters: Swimming toward God's Reign

Not every congregation enjoys its own island, surrounded by the life-giving waters of God's good creation. In what ways might this glimpse of IOHUMC's cultural waters converging with Christ's baptismal waters speak to other contexts? Raising up ministers at

IOHUMC is not the result of a complex strategy. Engendered by God's creative Spirit, it is the harvest of significant and sustained ministry with the young; of myriad invitations for young people to practice ministry; of an embracing, communal love and support; of a willingness to receive young people as bearers of the gospel; and of the commensurate invitation for all members to grow in their faith. In my view, this harvest will only multiply as this church and churches in other contexts claim that such ministry is not optional; rather, it is the heart of Christian identity and purpose. To be sure, each congregation has its own cultural waters—ways in which it is uniquely suited to invite young people into fuller expressions of faith and people of all ages into lives that respond to the gospel. Indeed, the baptismal waters are already flowing, waiting for us to wade in and grow in hope.

Questions for Reflection

ENGAGING VOCATIONCARE PRACTICES

1. *Creating hospitable space* includes actual physical space—places where people can be comfortable spending long stretches of time, either in focused activities such as choir practice or in more relaxed settings, such as hanging out in the youth room. In addition to physical space, Fred Edie points to a "culture of care and inclusivity" permeating the middle high youth group at IOHUMC and making it possible for members to feel safe praying or speaking openly about their spiritual lives.
   - What are some of the factors you think may contribute to the safe space young people experience at Isle of Hope? What are other markers that tell you such space exists?
   - The nicknames "Old Yeller" and the "Green House" convey an emotional attachment between the actual physical space of church property and the peak spiritual experiences members associate with them. Does your church

have nicknames or terms of endearment that might hint at similar emotional connections?
- What times and places in your congregation's life (mission trips, choir practice, Bible study, and so forth) require long stretches of young people's presence? What are the challenges you face in creating hospitable space? What helps you overcome those challenges?

2. *Asking self-awakening questions* can help people hear God's call or listen more attentively to the presence of God within them. A great example of such a question occurs in this chapter when young adult interns ask youth, "What would it look like to follow God in your life?"
   - When in the life of your faith community do you ask people to imagine a future in which they faithfully follow God?
   - One approach to self-awakening questions arises from imagining the world if we were to choose not to follow our calling. What would your family and your neighborhood look like five or ten years from now if you say no to a particular voice calling you forward? Or, you might ask, what would disappear from this neighborhood or community if our church ceased to exist?

3. *Reflecting theologically on self and community* occurs in formal and informal settings. It happens any time people wonder how their image of God is changing or even how such images differ from person to person. Isle of Hope seems to expect people to grow and change over time. But growth can be threatening.
   - How does your congregation deal with growth and change? Is there freedom to challenge one another? Is there an "expectation for spiritual growth" implicit in the congregation's teaching, preaching, praying, and mission?

- How might leaders give people permission to risk changing in light of their growing familiarity with the gospel?
- A primary place IOHUMC members grow in familiarity with the gospel is in *Disciple Bible Study*. How does your culture or context specifically engage people in deeper and deeper knowledge of God's story in relation to their own?

4. As a young adult, Fred Edie was nudged to *explore opportunities for ministry* during a summer internship. Through the years, a steady stream of paid summer interns have also reflected on their call with trusted mentors who serve alongside them on the church staff. Sometimes, as was the case for Fred and others he interviewed, the internship became an entree to imagining possibilities for a life of ministry or mission that had not been considered before.
   - What kinds of regularly established ministry opportunities—such as internships for high school or college students—does your congregation offer?
   - If you noticed a young person who clearly showed signs of promise for ministry, social work, or another caring profession, would your congregation be equipped to help him explore the nuances and discern more closely his call?

PRACTICING ETHNOGRAPHIC LISTENING

"To cultivate the arts of paying attention means to watch deliberately, make notes, conduct interviews structured around questions planned in advance, in short, to push through the facile gloss that comes so readily to us."[3]
- How might you—as an insider to your congregation—learn from the different ways Fred Edie saw his congregation through the "arts of paying attention"?
- What practices of nurturing young people (perhaps rather invisible because they occur so naturally) did this congregation's practices call to mind? How might your congregation be

creating space where visionary questions about the purpose of human life arise?

- Fred Edie is writing about an island congregation, rather remote and somewhat isolated from urban centers of diversity and rapid change. Given the racial, ethnic, geographic, and economic background of your context, how did any "juxtaposition of opposites of collisions of difference" (Thomas E. Frank's phrase) spark your imagination?

CHAPTER 6

Embodying *Sankofa*

WHEN ANCIENT WAYS INFORM THE CHURCH'S FUTURE

Jeffery Tribble

> There is no calling without recalling, no vocation without invocation. Christian vocation begins with questions in the face of tears.[1]
>
> —CORNEL WEST

One Pastor Looks Back to Look Forward

In my late twenties, I found myself in a congregation perfectly poised to help me hear and respond to God's call. During the summer between graduating from Howard University with a mechanical engineering degree and entering a graduate program at the Massachusetts Institute of Technology, I heard an inner voice say, "Give this degree over to me." I went on to graduate school, pondering along the way how God might use my engineering career or whether maybe God wanted something altogether different of me. Would I one day be called to "[suffer] the loss" of my career aspirations and "count them but dung, that I may win Christ"? (Phil. 3:8 KJV). When I joined the Cross Street African Methodist Episcopal Zion (AME Zion) Church in Middletown, Connecticut, I was, like Jacob, wrestling. Meanwhile, I poured myself into the ministries of the church.

Cross Street, one of the earliest churches in the AME Zion family, was a place where my spiritual gifts were needed and welcomed. I had previously been at a larger church with a staff leading a variety of excellent ministries, a church where I could simply express myself in my comfort zone of music ministry. Here in this smaller congregation staffed only by the pastor, I drew close to Rev. Douglas Lawrence, who took a keen interest in a small group of women and men that he sensed had some type of ministry call on their lives. With his encouragement, I began to stretch beyond music ministry. I incorporated Bible studies into my choir rehearsals and began to lead prayers with a new depth and intentionality. After being invited by a friend to enroll in Hartford Seminary's Black Ministries Certificate Program, the call to preach grew clear. Being in a community of people yearning to be equipped for ministry helped me recognize and respond to God's call. When I approached the pastor to confess my own sense of call, he said with a smile, "I know. I was just waiting for *you* to know."

Rev. Lawrence was my father in the ministry—an Elijah figure to whom I drew near so that I might receive a portion of his spirit and the power to do as he had done: pursue full-time ordained ministry (2 Kings 2:8–10). I had come to Cross Street as a young adult with vocational questions. The pastor and the practices of the congregation allowed me to try on ministry. In that setting, I solidified my course toward ordained ministry. The congregation gathered in a circle of prayer to send my family and me forth as we moved to the Midwest for me to attend seminary.

My personal history resounds with the truth that congregations have a role in helping a person respond to God's call. My journey from mechanical engineer to pastor and scholar of the church is pervaded with gratitude for a congregation that noticed, named, and nurtured the latent gifts in me. When asked to think about a Greenhouse of Hope—a contemporary congregation engaged in such practices—I remembered my journey at Cross Street and began to wonder where a person like myself would receive similar nurture today. I was drawn to the First Afrikan Presbyterian Church

(USA) in Lithonia, Georgia. In its fifteen years, this church has nurtured sixty people as they explored their inner promptings toward ministry.[2] They came to this church, says Rev. Mark Lomax, not only for personal mentoring but also to gain experience in Christian ministry and companionship as they discerned God's call. Today, many are serving in a variety of ministry roles as pastors, counselors, and parish leaders. The church's first vision statement expressed the goal of being a teaching congregation—like a teaching hospital—for preaching and worship leadership. This vision continues in the present-day ministers' council, a space where about fifteen people gather regularly for discernment, theological reflection, mentoring, and trying on the practices of ministry. Much like the circle I experienced at Cross Street, this practice has roots in larger circles of African American church and community life. Rev. Lomax says:

> Very early in this ministry, I started following Jeremiah Wright's model called ministers-in-training.[3] [Those interested] didn't have to be Presbyterian, or related to the Reformed theological tradition. [Their calling] didn't have to be pastoral ministry or preaching ministry. They just had to be women and men interested in some form of ministry. Most have come for pastoral care, but they felt this was a place they could be nurtured in their seeking as they sought God's will for their lives.

In this chapter, I will share the story of First Afrikan Church (FAC) as it came into view as a "living human document" through my research of the activities, accounts, and artifacts of the congregation.[4] Though I have been intimately related as insider to black congregations as a member, ordained pastor, presiding elder, and researcher, I entered FAC as an outsider. I had no experiential knowledge of the philosophies, histories, cultures, and spiritualities that shape the unique African expression of Christianity. So I worshiped, studied, ate, and talked with members over the course of a year with this guiding question in mind: What are the signature practices of this community that help people—especially the young—to discern and respond to God's call?

As I immersed myself in worship, meetings, interviews, archives, teaching moments, and other gatherings in this Greenhouse of Hope, I discovered a faith community whose distinctive interpretation of Africentric Christianity is inextricably linked to its ability to nurture people who respond to God's call in their lives. A cluster of worship, teaching, and youth ministry practices feed a narrative consciousness of African people's cultures, spiritualities, and communal contributions. Over time, this cluster of practices came into sharper focus as what I am calling *sankofa* practices, after a Ghanaian image and proverb very familiar to the people of this congregation. *Sankofa* is an Akan term meaning, "Go back and get it." It is depicted as a mythical bird flying forward with its head turned backward and an egg in its mouth; the egg represents the treasured knowledge of the past upon which wisdom is based and also the generation to come, who may benefit from that wisdom. The sankofa symbol is often accompanied by a proverb translated as, "It is not wrong to go back for that which we have forgotten."[5]

THE *SANKOFA* BIRD OF GHANA: A reminder of the need to look back in order to move forward.

Interweaving the past with present and future occurs naturally. This chapter began with a reflection on my own past as it informs my current task: this movement becomes a "sankofa moment" when it is tied to the communal and ancestral memories of people of African descent as they move ahead into the present and future. When interwoven repeatedly into the worship, study, and community life of this congregation, sankofa moments form a distinctive Christian practice. Dorothy Bass reminds us that

> practices are borne by social groups over time and are constantly negotiated in the midst of changing circumstances. As clusters of activities in which meaning and doing are inextricably woven, practices shape behavior while also fostering a practice—specific knowledge, capacities, dispositions and virtues. Those who participate in practices are formed in particular ways of thinking about and living in the world.[6]

Ndugu T'Ofori-Atta, scholar of African religious heritage, describes the way sankofa imagery functions for people who were disconnected from their native land, languages, cultures, and family ties: we *re*-member those things that were *dis*-membered through the African slave trade and its legacy of denigration and exploitation of African peoples. "Securing our present in this way makes it possible to secure our future,"[7] he says.

A distinctive part of African American Christianity, this practice relates to the sacramental practices of the global church. When Jesus commanded his disciples to "remember me," he was saying more than to "look backwards" at his life, suffering, death, and resurrection. The looking backwards we do in the Eucharist sustains us as we move forward into the fray of life as Christian disciples where we, too, experience suffering, death, and resurrection. African and African American Christians see this as affirming a need to go back to put together connections that have been disconnected—from God, from one another, and from our calling to participate in God's work in all of creation. In sankofa, as in the Eucharist, we attend to the possibility of God transforming suffering into life.

In this chapter, I will describe the embodiment of sankofa as the signature calling practice of First Afrikan through its

- worship that integrates traditional elements of word, sacrament, and order with nontraditional elements growing out of African religious heritage;
- privileging the agency of young people by providing meaningful leadership and mentoring opportunities;
- community-wide education and Christian formation around African American identity that inspires action on behalf of the world.

By looking for useful and recognizable categories for these activities, I seek to faithfully represent one particular ministry in a manner that assists congregational leaders elsewhere to imagine what they might learn from, see anew, adapt, or replicate in their own settings.

Sankofa Moments in Preaching

Rev. Lomax provided one of my first glimpses of a sankofa moment in his preaching as he reflected on the seeds of his call, planted in his childhood. He told about sneaking into a downtown department store with a few of his friends at age seven or eight:

> We went and put our dirty fingers on the counter, white folk looking at us and all that. That was 1964, maybe earlier. . . . We crammed on the elevator, stinking from playing outside, knobby kneed, making noise, just as conspicuous as can be. There were three nuns in the elevator. Three white nuns, with their white habits, black skirts. . . . Each of us were asked by the nuns, "What's your name?" Those of us with biblical names, they made remarks. But, when they got to me . . . I said, "Rusty." . . . They said, "Rusty? For real?" No, my real name is Mark. One of the nuns—I had never seen her before or since, but what she did was unusual even for "up south"—she grabbed my face in her hands. I hadn't ever been touched like that. *She said, "You're supposed to make a point with your life. Your name is Mark and you're supposed to make a mark." There is a sense in which she was conferring heaviness, weight, a responsibility.* There were times in our community when adults looked at the children and said . . . "You have a purpose for your existence in a world in which they say you are the last, the lowest, and the least."[8]

In a world that says to blacks, "You are the last, the lowest, and the least," Lomax, the pastoral staff, and other congregational leaders here have created a congregational culture that not only is a site of resistance to the negative interpretation of Africans and people of African descent but also communicates, "You have a purpose for your existence in this world"—a way of being in relationship to God, self, family, and community.

This church came to be around kitchen tables, as friends dreamed of a new kind of community of faith. But rather than start an independent church, its founders decided to stay within the structure of the Presbyterian Church (USA) congregation that gave it birth.

Lomax, in another sankofa moment, reminded the congregation of its past as he set a vision for its future on the occasion of its fifteenth anniversary. In pastoral remarks following the sermon, he reflected:

> When we sat round those first kitchen tables, we asked, "Who do we know?" . . . In the first eight months, 140 people joined us beginning with our first worship service. . . . When we were asked at the presbytery what we would name ourselves, we said "First Afrikan." After this, a decision was made to cut off our funding. We persisted with the vision of a church embracing African cultures and spiritualities, blending both African and Christian consciousness. We said, "Our people knew God *before* the missionaries. They had their own ways of understanding." We married African cosmology with Christianity. For some, we are just too black! Somehow to honor our culture, spiritualities, history, hairstyles, and loudness is supposed to be wrong? Excellence comes from being who you are!

AFRICENTRICITY: A perspective asserting that people of African descent have a right and responsibility to interpret the world through their own analysis and to study and teach world history from the viewpoint of subjects and not objects.

As Rev. Lomax remembered the community's origin and founding as a living out of "excellence," he simultaneously cast a vision forward for the church to continue hearing and responding to God calling the people by their names—their authentic African Christian selves. In this sankofa moment, Lomax cast a glance backward in order to move forward.

Sankofa moments, while present in isolated fragments of preaching like those just described, are hardly owned by the preacher alone. They are pervasive throughout the worship service, as I will point out as we walk through the Sunday liturgy.

Sankofa Moments in Liturgy

A significant part of looking back and moving forward at FAC involves careful attention to inviting the young people to climb into these practices along with the adults. Every Sunday, the children, youth, and adults recite by heart this mission statement: "First Afrikan Church is an Africentric Christian ministry that empowers women, men, youth, and children to move from membership to leadership in the church, community, and the world."

The rest of the liturgy is an intentional combination of traditional Protestant elements of worship with nontraditional African-based language, customs, and practice. Some traditional elements include the use of the Bible as the primary sacred text, singing of spirituals and hymns, communal prayer, preaching of God's word, and worship leaders who serve as liturgists, ushers, acolytes, musicians, and choirs. Some of the elements received from previous generations of African people are honoring the ancestors, pouring of libations, African dance, and drumming. I describe these in detail here because they lie at the heart of sankofa practices.

HONORING THE ANCESTORS

The First Afrikan Church credo, recited at every service of baptism, provides a helpful understanding of honoring the ancestors. Part of the credo says:

> We believe that those people who have gone before us and who, while alive on the physical plane of existence, were loving, nurturing, committed to the welfare of younger generations, lived just lives, spoke the truth in love, and worked to make their own villages, tribes, nations, and world better than . . . when they were born, are ancestors. We believe that the ancestors are with us and should be honored and respected by us; and that we should invoke their names and honor their memories frequently.[9]

Lomax explained this ancestral emphasis biblically, saying:

> Go to the Old Testament in particular. In the first five books, we are the descendants of Abraham, Isaac, and Jacob. There was the constant recognition and remembrance of the ancestors. The Passover meal was rec-

ognition of what God had done for the ancestors. In the Gospels, Jesus reinterpreted this. When Africans talk about their ancestors, people call that demonic, but in the book of Hebrews in the eleventh chapter we see ourselves as surrounded by a great cloud of witnesses, whom we call ancestors. We don't perceive this life as ultimate. There is a resurrection of the dead. But, in the meantime, we believe that there are those who are aware of what we are doing on earth. We believe that is a way to honor them, to venerate them, if you will, for without them we could not exist. There are those that take it even further—I have done it myself—that appeal to the ancestors, because there are times that we need the kind of wisdom, vision, and strength that they had. The first thing we do in worship is to pay homage to our cosmic sky. We use those names to call on God, names unique to the African language world, as the language world of our people was not English or German. It reminds them that we have not forgotten them, and it is our hope that that they have not forgotten us.[10]

Clearly, the ancestors are a part of the worshiping community at FAC.

AFRICAN DRUMMING

Next to the pulpit is a large African drum. This drum, given to the church by members who'd made a pilgrimage to Africa, was especially created for FAC and was dedicated four years ago. According to Mehib Holmes, teacher and leader of the African drumming ministry here, drums and dance are "integral to all facets of African society." Holmes says, "Drums and dance open up the way to God and ancestors." African drumming is taught in FAC's youth rite-of-passage programs as a way of "returning to the tradition of our ancestors." Africans of the diaspora have not only been disconnected from their ancestral home and language, they were also disconnected from the implements of the culture, such as the drums.

Holmes was instrumental in introducing African drumming to the congregation's culture. When he joined the church, he asked, "How can you have an Africentric church without African drums?"

Introducing them was not easy, even at FAC. Reflecting on internalized racism, Holmes frankly shares the perspective that "a lot of us have been conditioned to hate and resist anything that is African. We do not understand and appreciate what ancestors have left to us." African drumming is complex, filled with polyphonic rhythms. In his classes, drummers learn that every rhythm has a cultural context, a song, and several accompaniments.

AFRICAN DANCE

After the call to community, the acolytes lead the processional, bearing the light of God into the darkened sanctuary. A liturgist processes, carrying the Bible. Following the elders and deacons are the *Tamba Issa* Dancers. Projection of visual imagery on a screen adjacent to the pulpit area is one way congregational teaching is integrated into the worship service. While dancers take to the aisle, on the screen appear these words: "When the chief of the village or important elders or priests come before the people on the important occasions such as at harvest or planting time or ceremonies celebrating births, marriages, or death, the people dance *lamba* in honor of God and their ancestors." Dancing is choreographed and performed by women dressed in brightly colored African dresses and head wraps. As they dance, pictures of African women dancing appear on the screen, creating in me a sense of identification between the dancers before me and the images of African women on the screen. As dancers and drummers become more energetic and rhythmic, worshipers join in the rhythmic movement with swaying and hand clapping. Elementary school girls in the first row mimic their mothers' and aunties' dance moves in perfect step and rhythm.

POURING OUT LIBATIONS

Worshipers next join in an ancestral invocation and memory verse, led by the liturgist of the day, a passionate worship leader named Charlotte Caldwell. Caldwell prays, invoking God and pouring out libation to the ancestors: "We call the names of the Creator, using some of the names spoken in the language of African people . . ."

The word *invocation* means to summon or call forth. Liturgists symbolically invoke the presence of God using the names ancestors used in their native languages. Taking seriously the histories, cultures, spiritualities, and values of African peoples requires attention to language, for language is the means by which people think and communicate in a culture. To limit one's God talk to terms commonly used in English-speaking parts of the world would be an acceptance of the theological, political, and cultural hegemony of historic oppressors (that is, missionaries) who devalued African cultures. The Divine Creator is known by many names: Nana Buluku, Nyame, Oludamare, Mawu-Lisa, Ausar, Heru, and Auset are derived from African languages and are used in services of worship and education at FAC. Transforming the language of worship to include African names for God is a way of exercising freedom to think and talk about divine reality from an Africentric Christian perspective. This perspective is uniquely honed at FAC, where theologians, pastors, and ministers are steeped in both African history and philosophy as well as the black liberation theology movement.

As Caldwell invokes God's presence by calling some of these names of God, the congregation responds robustly with the word *ashe*. Ashe is a Yoruba term meaning "energy or essence" and is used as a word of affirmation. It is similar to the word *amen*; however, a more nuanced meaning is something like, "I affirm with my all of my energy, with all of my essence that which is taking place."[11] For the ancestral invocation, the liturgist then calls the names of African heroes and "sheroes." After each name—Harriet Tubman, Sojourner Truth, Nanny, Marcus Garvey, Nat Turner—the congregation shouts, "Ashe!" Though this particular service closes Black History Month, the celebration and teaching of black history is a year-round project here.

Next, a contemporary praise chorus begins, "Don't you feel his presence? Don't you feel his presence? Hallelujah!" A mix of the African drummers and a band consisting of synthesizer, drum set, organ, and guitars leads the varied rhythms of this part of the service. Rhythms—drumming, hand clapping, foot patting, and use of other instruments—are a means of summoning the Spirit of God and inviting celebration among the people of God.[12] African polyphonic rhythms, up-beat tempos of contemporary praise and worship music, various gospel rhythms, and the "shouting music" rooted in Black Pentecostalism all occur during worship.

WORSHIP AS CULTURAL PRODUCTION

In a portion of the liturgy called "inviting God's pleasure," members of FAC enact *harambee*, a Swahili word meaning "unity in the community." A church officer comes forward saying, "We take time to welcome each other and our visitors." The traditional phrases of passing the peace are shared, but in keeping with the service's African tone, this celebration occurs against a backdrop of African drumming, providing an atmosphere of warmth and joy. First-time visitors are asked to stand, while people greet them and the ushers distribute a welcome booklet. This small booklet provides a field guide to FAC, carefully describing to the uninitiated what Africentric worship is and why it is important here. As the service progresses to the choir's singing of a special selection, a map of the world with Africa shown at the center appears on the screen.

The preacher of the morning, Matthew Williams, is in his early thirties. A graduate of International Theological Center in Atlanta, he came to FAC about ten years ago and now leads sessions of the ministers' council and teaches in the church's Center for African Biblical Studies. Before preaching, he prays, "The way that we walk does not come by chance. It comes by your ordering our steps. We thank you for those who have gone before us who have shown us how to walk in the Word. We ask that you will show us how to walk in that same Word. Here we are, hearts hungry and minds thirsty. We pray in the name of the North African from Nazareth, even Jesus, Yeshua the Christ."

Jesus Christ is known as "our African Messiah" for two reasons: First, members of the congregation believe he was a descendant of African peoples, the ancient children of Israel who migrated out of Egypt and came to occupy a geographic location on the northeast peninsula of Africa, now called the Middle East. Second, Jesus (Jeheshua or Yeshua in Hebrew) is understood to be African because, while present in human form, "he occupied the same social, political and economic location of most Afrikan peoples in the world—oppressed, colonized, financially and materially poor."[13]

The sermon, portions of which follow, is consistent with the sankofa practice embodied thus far in worship. Williams preaches:

> No, if you want to know what faith is, look at your forebears. . . . When I look at the ancestors, I see them acting in faith in the face of bondage, in the face of lynching, in the face of Jim Crow segregation. I see them acting in the face of downsizing, infant mortality, HIV/AIDS, heart attacks, and I could go on. . . . Can I invoke the words of James Weldon Johnson here? "We have come over a way that with tears have been watered. We have come treading our path through the blood of the slaughtered." Can I invoke Grandmaster Flash here?

Williams begins to rap: "It's like a jungle sometimes. It makes me wonder how I keep from goin' under. It's like a jungle sometimes. It makes me wonder how I keep from goin' under."[14] When Williams got to the refrain, members of the congregation spontaneously joined him. The lyrics of this hip-hop classic, "The Message" by Grandmaster Flash, describe the plight of the underclass trapped in conditions of poverty and violence. It is a contemporary counterpoint to the traditional lyrics of Johnson's hymn, sung during the civil rights movement and well known by church folks as the Black National Anthem: death and destruction are realities in both contexts. Here, the preacher uses secular rap music and its message about traumatizing conditions to engage this generationally diverse congregation, keeping focused on his point of "acting in faith in the face of challenging circumstances." Williams then emphasizes that we are more like our ancestors in faith than we are different from them:

> Our ancestors acted in faith in spite of being complicated characters. Most of us have been duped and hoodwinked: we've been made to think that you've got to be flawless to be faithful. But, look at the stories of the folk inducted in the Hall of Fame of faith! When you want to see faith, look at Jacob, whose very name means trickster. When you want to see faith, check out Rahab, a madam in a whorehouse. When you want to see faith, check out Abraham, a wandering man who used the women in his life to achieve his aspirations. When you want to see faith, check out Moses, a murderer with a stutter. . . .
>
> I have no use for a hero who doesn't know what it means to be human. I need a Harriet Tubman who freed her people despite some brain damage. I need a Malcolm X who was a leader despite a background as a street hustler and ex-con. . . . I need a Jesus who in the garden said, "Take this cup from me. . . . I don't want to go through the suffering of dying on a cross."

This practice of lifting up of biblical ancestors of faith alongside ancestors of the African diaspora is commonplace practice here: biblical ancestors and African ancestors are equally revered for their faith in the struggle for freedom and justice. Indeed, I sensed some people in this congregation seemed to celebrate more noticeably during Williams's recitation of African ancestors' contributions than his celebration of Jesus Christ's struggle, passion, and death.

I considered this in light of what Lomax describes as the "incredibly complex" makeup of the congregation. First Afrikan has a special niche in the region, drawing people from beyond the immediate neighborhood, though Lomax estimates that 80 percent of the membership lives in the community directly around the church. However, the educational arm of the church sponsors more than a dozen major programs each year that intentionally focus on reaching out to the larger African American community. Itihari Toure (known affectionately as Mama Itihari) leads First Afrikan's Center for African Biblical Studies (CFABS), which is at the heart of all formal educational instruction at FAC. CFABS sponsors congregational teaching and community experiences, which include new member classes, leadership education, rites-of-passage programs to transition girls and boys into African adulthood, and classes for all ages on Wednesday nights. These programs draw what Lomax calls a "conscious crowd" of people who may or may not be Christians but are interested in gaining an African-centered perspective. One example is a group of Hebrew Israelites who regularly attend FAC as a part of their spiritual journey. Mama Itihari—one of the congregational leaders I spoke with frequently—described the spiritual journeys of some of the members as ranging from those who settle in and stay to those who leave in one, two, or three years. Further, FAC is an open-door ministry that does not require membership. The religious diversity present in the pews includes cultural nationalists who study Rasta, African traditional religions, and Islam. Thus, on any given Sunday, people come to FAC to have deeply varied needs met. Acknowledging this complexity helped me see nuances that I might otherwise not have noticed; the complexity also helped me view FAC's Africentric Christianity as a form of hospitable ministry to people of non-Christian traditions.

As the sermon continued, Williams reflected upon Africentric teaching from his home church, Trinity United Church of Christ in Chicago. He asserts a connection between the African continent and the peoples whose stories we find in Scripture, recasting the so-called Middle East (before the building of the Suez canal) as the northernmost tip of the continent. Thus, he illustrates how socialization shapes our view of the world in such a way that in naming reality we ignore the obvious. Williams says:

> We must remember that we don't start telling the story [of black history] in captivity. It began in the beginning. Jeremiah Wright, in his teaching, would ask, "What is a continent?" We would answer, "One of the main, large land areas of the earth, usually surrounded by water." He then would say, "Name them." We would answer: Africa, Asia, Australia, Europe, North America, South America, and sometimes Antarctica. He then would ask, "When did the Middle East become a continent?" It's not. It's

a region that spans Africa and Asia, which originally were connected. The modern Middle East was created in 1945 with the establishment of the state of Israel and the Suez Canal, which now separates the land mass of Africa from the land mass of Asia. You have some deeper origins!

But what God began in your ancestors must continue in you. Their work is not complete. The writer of the Hebrews says: These, though well tested in faith, did not receive what was promised, since God had foreseen something better for us, that apart from us they would not be made perfect (Heb. 11:39). *Their work is not complete. It must be completed in what we do!*

He concluded the sermon by describing the race depicted in Hebrews 12 as a relay race. As he did so, he came out of the pulpit, mimicking the act of running.

When the second, third, or final leg of the relay prepares to receive the baton, the runner looks back. As the person finishing their leg approaches, [the next runner begins] running. Now, there is a space of time when the two runners run together. Then, the one behind shouts, "Stick!" they put the baton in the hand of the next runner. Today, we receive the baton from Mary McLeod Bethune who shouts, "Stick!" Today, we receive the baton from Fannie Lou Hamer who shouts, "Stick!" We receive the baton from Malcolm X who shouts, "Stick!" . . .

He continued this pattern, rhythmically naming figures whose spirituality was infused with the fight for justice.

I describe the sermon in such length because it so aptly illustrates the sankofa practice—liberally included in all portions of the liturgy—but quite explicitly embodied here. When Williams left the pulpit to be the runner, he embodied an image of FAC as a space that explicitly contributes to vocational inspiration and aspiration by "looking back to lead forward." As I watched and listened to Williams, I could imagine the generations "running together for a space of time" and making the critical transfer of the accumulated wisdom of the past to a new generation. Indeed, the image illuminates so much of FAC's various ministries: ministers-to-be running together alongside the senior pastor in council discussions; young adults working alongside the seasoned Mama Itihari in teaching programs; big brothers and big sisters becoming a cadre of caring mentors in rites-of-passage programs; youth choir members singing alongside mature choir members; and children and youth serving in meaningful roles as ushers, audiovisual technicians, drummers, and dancers.

After the sermon, worship concludes with a portion called "implementing our purpose." It includes receiving gifts, called the *zwadi*, a Kiswahili word implying that time, talent, and money together create the gift worth giving. After the offering, a closing hymn, the recitation of the mission statement, and the benediction, the service closes with a recessional of the worship leaders punctuated by drumming. People join in the rhythm, greeting one another joyfully, and some literally dancing their way out of the sanctuary.

This full, vibrant, dynamic worship service is unlike any I have ever attended, reminding me that worship is a central manifestation of a congregation's culture. In his book, *Congregations in America*, Mark Chaves asserts that congregations' primary work is cultural production, as "congregations mainly gather people to engage in the cultural activity of expressing and transmitting religious meanings."[15] Jackson W. Carroll, who focuses much of his work on congregational studies, builds on this idea in describing the work of clergy as producers of culture. Developing the metaphor of clergy as God's potters interacting with other leaders to shape a congregation's particular way of being a congregation, Carroll writes:

> As clergy preach, lead worship, teach, and counsel, they draw on beliefs, symbols, stories, and practices from the Christian tradition to construct narratives and interpretive frameworks that help members to locate themselves and find meaning and perspective for dealing with issues in their daily lives. Through their leadership and support of congregational gatherings, programs, and organizations pastors help to build community and supportive relationships—social capital—among members. In turn,

members are helped to engage in their own ministry beyond the congregation in their family, work, and community life.[16] Worship is a dynamic cultural production in which pastoral leaders interact with God's people in the communal experience of responding to God's call. Meanings of the "cultural creators" are actively received and resisted to construct new meanings for the concrete situations of the worshipers.[17] Indeed, says Itihari Toure, "aspects of the Sunday worship including the preaching, liturgy and flow of service will reflect serious consideration of listening, waiting for God."[18]

Privileging the Agency of Young People

"Youth and young adults—what part of our community needs more attention? If we don't take care of our young people, we have no legacy," says Lomax. FAC's commitment to entrusting young people to lead and supporting them as they learn in these roles is exemplified in the story of Roberto Young, who is twenty-nine years old.

Young is presently chairman of the board of trustees. Lomax invited him to "bring his skills to the table" after he joined the congregation a little over a year ago. An investor, business owner, and wealth manager, Young is learning how his business skills relate to his Christian calling in church and society. In the church, he helps FAC to tighten its financial belt in a difficult economy, to develop financial structures, and "to grow in a very smart way." Young talks about his role as helping the church "from a finance and leadership perspective—to continue to press the envelope on financial awareness, at least understanding business and how our collective genius, our collective dollars work."

What does it mean for him to be a member of an Africentric Christian ministry that embraces the cultures and heritages of African people? Young says,

It's a liberating experience. Growing up in the Baptist church . . . when you look at the black church, one missing link is there's no emphasis put on African legacy and culture. I think this is a tremendous disconnect. Late nineteenth century to twentieth century, when you look at the black church, it was sacred ground, a refuge, an economic engine. It was a marketplace. It touched every aspect of a person's life, from playing basketball, cooking, or business. It all touched on the church. But, now in the twenty-first century, a lot of that is gone. Now, people have made the focus the economic piece and made it prosperity preaching only. You have black nationalists that focus on Africentricity only. I look at FAC as a place that brings together each one of those segments, incorporating it into one. I see the core competencies of FAC as being unapologetically black, but not being offensive, but also the teaching, the intellectual experience, the Christian community, and the warmth.

Young recently took a spiritual gifts inventory that caused him to mull over having the apostolic gift. He sees the apostles as having been courageous in founding the church. He says that this courage is needed for change in the world of business. He says:

I'm very outspoken, but respectful. In the business, civic community, I stand up for what I believe to be righteous. When I think about the financial services industry, I think differently from most in industry. I think God is calling me to transform how business is done in the industry. It becomes the standard. When people see you doing good and making money at the same time, they see that it's possible to do that and some people will follow. . . . In the business world that I work in and live in, I can show people that you can make money while doing good. Most folk in the business community are just focused on making a dollar.

One way Young lives out his faith involves buying distressed housing and making it available for single-mother families. He sees it as benefiting the community, benefiting these families, while at the same time bringing economic benefit to his own family.

Alexis Wells, twenty-six, is another young adult active in leadership at FAC. A seminary graduate who is now in her second year of a PhD program in American History at Emory University, Wells serves as secretary of the youth and young adult initiative, a mentor in the rites-of-passage program, and a teacher of liberation theology in the CFABS. She talks about the ways FAC supports her spiritual life and her work in the world:

> It means a connection with certain theological commitments that resonate with me. On an ancestral level, my family is rooted in the Caribbean Anglican Church in the British West Indies. First Afrikan is a kind of reclamation of roots. Another part of my family is Baptist. So, First Afrikan brings both of these together for me. It reconceptualizes a kind of new and old. Also, I appreciate its commitment to honoring the ancestors and what it means to be Christian. In some churches, the African experience is almost denigrated or neglected. I like the way that the African experience is foregrounded. Other ministries degrade our previous spiritual experiences prior to Christianity. . . . The biggest way that I experience this is in the question, "What constitutes the community?" It's not just those sitting in the pews, but those who have preceded us and those who will come after us. We build on and honor their legacy. Along the lines of Christian responsibility, we are building a legacy of what it means to serve our community. . . . In our most well-intentioned moments, we can become inwardly focused. We have a larger responsibility beyond the church walls. It is an expansion and deepening of theological ideas.

Wells describes a particular kind of space created for youth and young adults here. This space honors young people's presence, shares information and decision making with them, and creates a dialogical model that serves as a corrective to hierarchical models prevalent in wider society. She describes this space:

> For youth and young adults, we take seriously that they have something to contribute to the community, not in a trivial sense or simply for display, but an important contribution. . . . It goes with belief [in] the creativity of God and your own unique creativity. Bible study classes transcend teaching the Bible, doing things like spiritual inventories. First Afrikan is the most information-centered church that I've been at, but another part

of nurturing leaders is giving a space for dialogue. In most churches, it is hierarchical. Also, there is an atmosphere of full disclosure—I think the atmosphere, the ecology of the church makes it comfortable for people to ask questions. They emphasize the decision-making aspect of everything. A part of the church's role is to help people to make good decisions and give them tools to do this. What we do with youth, we say that at every age you have agency.

Though individual mentors may be important, Wells emphasizes the role the entire faith community has played in creating space for her to explore vocation. She says:

Ministry is a heavy call to answer. . . . I see it as a spiritual process, being in spaces that resonate with you, having a community of people that I can talk to makes a difference. . . . The pastor is our leader, but he is not the end-all and be-all in the community. I tend not to be one that connects with the one that is ultimately in power. Sometimes it's just people that you talk with in a space after church and it ends up being a conversation about vocation. For me, it's about the community. Even me teaching a class has helped to nurture who I am in ministry—not the top-down approach, just me functioning in community. Sometimes you recognize things that don't fit.

When asked, "How has FAC noticed and nurtured your gifts in leadership?" Wells responded, "It's something basic: they ask." She went on to explain:

When I first came to FAC, they knew I was a minister, but didn't push me into the role. But, then they began to ask me to do things. I'm not the kind to go in and take the reins. A church like FAC, where it seems to function like clockwork, you don't know how to fit in because it looks like they don't need anything. The first steps to nurturing me were giving me opportunity to teach a Bible study class and work with youth, also having a group of people that are identified with ministry, the ministers' council. We talk about things important to ministers at FAC. We get a lot of feedback . . . on preaching and liturgical leadership that becomes a clinic. . . . On a personal note, people check on me. People help me to do self-care—helping me not to burn out. All those things have been helpful in nurturing me.

Wells feels called to teach in the academy as well as providing preaching and pastoral ministry. As Wells grows into her vocation as a scholar and pastor, she finds FAC an exceptional climate:

INCLUSIVE LANGUAGE: The disciplined practice of avoiding exclusively masculine language for God and humanity. It reflects an understanding that scripture uses various imagery—both male and female and gender neutral—for God.

The church's orientation toward the academic pursuit of religion has been helpful to people like me. Sometimes you are so transformed by your seminary experience, you don't fit in many churches. Something like inclusive language, I have a commitment to it as a womanist—it's practiced at First Afrikan. It's difficult to find a worship place to [which you can] bring all of those commitments with you, not to censor yourself in what you think about God. It's a questioning church. It's constantly evolving. The leaders are constantly asking questions about themselves and about the congregation. This is always helpful coming out of a traditional church context. It is not common for churches to allow this space of questioning. . . . It gives me a place to worship and not be in conflict.

Community-wide Education and Christian Formation That Inspires Action

After participating in the regular Wednesday night dinner in the fellowship hall one evening, I joined the adults in the sanctuary, where a woman skillfully played the harp. Destiny, a self-described "harpist from the hood," used her skills "to sculpt a harmonious environment."[19] Destiny played the harp while telling the biblical story of the call of Samuel. (Meanwhile, downstairs, master puppeteer and storyteller Akbar Imhotep engaged the youth and children in a dramatic retelling of Jonah's call.) Destiny concluded her narration of Samuel's call story with the admonition: "If you allow that voice to guide you, open your heart and say 'Speak, Lord!'" After this experience of the biblical narrative, she rendered a special selection. The lyrics illuminate the calling practices at First Afrikan:

> *I can hear the voice of God calling my name.*
> *Say my name, Lord. Say my name.*
> *What do you want me to do?*
> *What do you want me to say?*
> *How do you want me to be?*
> *You called me by name.*
> *I can hear the presence of God calling me by name.*
> *I am listening. I am praying.*
> *I am willing if you call me by name.*

These lyrics mirror some of the key themes of the community conversations around call I heard at First Afrikan. First, we need to develop our "inner ear" to hear the voice of God calling in our life. ("I can hear the voice of God calling my name.") Second, our name is our authentic self; it represents our life purpose and role, our vocation. ("Say my name, Lord. Say my name.") Third, our calling is marked by the desire to pursue *our own* particular creative path, despite family and societal pressures to conform to other voices. This concept is developed in the book, *You Are the Jewel in the Stone*, which was used as the text for a community-wide Bible study on discerning God's purpose.[20] In the authors' view of vocation, the inner voice directing one's path is inspired and supported by an ongoing dialogue with the Creator. Fourth, we must demonstrate our desire to hear and act on the voice of God by getting into the presence of God by practicing spiritual disciplines. ("I am listening, I am praying. I am willing if you call me by name.")

Being in harmony is a collective calling of this faith community. Harmony, not only in a variety of sounds working together but also as a principle, was embodied in the music, performance, and teaching of Destiny. Creating a hospitable environment for people of all ages to remember and envision together marked this sankofa moment. The moment, though brief, does not occur in isolation. It reverberates throughout the community, connecting with other sankofa moments offered at other times and in other spaces.

One last example of community-wide education and Christian formation that enables people to discern and respond to God's call occurred in the church's focus for 2009. The year was devoted to a congregational capacity building on the theme "People Get Ready to Do a Good Work." The goal was to discern and plan selected program initiatives that would empower this congregation to faithfully live out their identity and purpose as African people. The bivocational members of the pastoral staff as well as church members—comprised largely of busy professionals situated in an affluent community—are on a journey of discerning God's call. At First Afrikan, this means taking seriously the histories, cultures, and spiritualities of African people.

"Getting ready" is shorthand for this faith community's response to God's call. Answering their collective call requires each member of the community to pray and critically reflect on what God has called each one to do in his or her lifetime. The pastoral staff hopes that churchwide program initiatives relating to African and African American identities will be firmly grounded in individuals' responses to their God-given purpose. Specific initiatives, such as HIV/AIDS ministries, enhancing children and youth programs, mission work in Haiti, strengthening African American congregations in the Greater Atlanta area, partnering to enhance land and economic development for the poor in the Black Belt, and sustaining rites-of-passage programs for young people, will grow out of each member's own process of discerning God's call.

Leaders who envision hope and embody courage are needed in society. However, quality leaders who live out their vocations to contribute to the broader social good are at risk among all races and ethnicities. They will not likely emerge or survive without a community. Cornel West, a scholar of race in America, frames the dilemma:

> Quality leadership is neither the product of one great individual nor the result of odd historical accident. Rather, it comes from deeply bred traditions and communities that shape and mold talented and gifted persons. Without a vibrant tradition of resistance passed on to new generations, there can be no nurturing of a collective and critical consciousness—only professional conscientiousness survives. Where there is no vital community to hold up precious ethical and religious ideals, there can be no coming to a moral commitment—only personal accomplishment is applauded.[21]

FAC could hardly be more intentional about providing a greenhouse environment in which people of all ages, but particularly youth and young adults, are inspired to think about how their dreams for the world intersect God's dream for the world. In its unique practices that bring African cosmology to life in a decidedly Christian setting, this church creates a nutrient-rich environment. From it, teachers, preachers, pastors, and caregivers move on to a wider world where this distinctive form of Christian practice surely will contribute to the work of God's Spirit.

Questions for Reflection

ENGAGING VOCATIONCARE PRACTICES

1. One way First Afrikan Presbyterian Church (USA) *creates hospitable space* for vocational discernment is through a ministers' council—a regular gathering of people who are exploring a call to pastoral ministry. This kind of space can be carefully constructed to observe confidentiality and hold people during times of clarity as well as times of unknowing.
   - What benefits might you imagine coming from a trusted circle of conversation partners who explicitly care for one

another's emerging vocational calls? How might this help young adults who have not yet discerned a particular call?

- Is there a tradition that resembles this in your cultural context?
- What people in your congregation, in addition to pastoral leaders, are particularly good conversation partners for people who long to discover how to use their particular gifts?

2. *Self-awakening questions* are implicit in the icon of the sankofa bird, the Ghanian proverb to which it points, and the congregational practices guided by this metaphor.
   - When you look back at your individual or familial past, what are some of the ways you see that history directing your future?
   - When you think about your congregation's past, either its local expression or its role as part of a larger cultural movement or denominational body, how do you see the past providing resources for building a meaningful future?
   - What does your congregation need to "go back and get"?

3. *Reflecting theologically* occurs on many levels in this chapter. The author mentions having an "Elijah figure" in his own ministry. In a sermon, Pastor Lomax puts his own life story in the context of the biblical narrative when he tells about his childhood encounter with a group of nuns.
   - In your leadership of Bible study, prayer groups, worship, or music, do you help people name parallels between the biblical stories and the lives of people around you? What might prompt you to do so more regularly?
   - Thinking of our life stories theologically or biblically can be intimidating. Some of us do not even see ourselves as having a story to tell. The sermon quoted in this chapter makes the point that biblical characters were often less-than-perfect people. What are some of the ways of

bringing biblical and theological reflection into ordinary, everyday conversation? How might your congregation's ministries help people see their life stories as meaningful, valuable, and part of God's story?

4. This congregation *establishes ministry opportunities* by allowing young people meaningful roles in leading both worship and administration. This creates an atmosphere in which young people come to believe their entrepreneurial ideas might be welcomed rather than disregarded.
   - This form of nonhierarchical leadership could feel threatening to some institutions. Can you envision your congregation investing newer members and younger people with meaningful leadership opportunities?
   - What are some of the biblical and theological mandates to listen to the voices and to encourage the gifts of young people? What biblical themes inspire shared leadership?

PRACTICING ETHNOGRAPHIC LISTENING

"A deep river of images feeds the roots of congregations; the collective imagination expresses itself in a profusion of symbols, stories, rituals and activities. Thus congregations themselves are springs of theological imagination."[22]

- *Sankofa* practices embody the "deep river of images" that feeds the theological imagination of First Afrikan. The deep river is accessed through worship practices that have been creatively woven into the liturgy over the fifteen years the church has been in existence. What is the deep river that feeds your congregation? How do you access it?
- Preachers and teachers at First Afrikan intentionally include representations of youth culture in their ministry. Does your congregation find ways to affirm what is positive in the subcultures your youth represent?

- Jeffery Tribble writes about a highly educated and intentionally Africentric community in a suburb. Given the racial, ethnic, geographic, and economic background of your context,
  how did any "juxtaposition of opposites of collisions of difference" (Thomas E. Frank's phrase) spark your imagination?

CHAPTER 7

Calling amid Conflict

WHAT HAPPENS TO THE VOCATIONS OF YOUTH WHEN CONGREGATIONS FIGHT?

Joyce Ann Mercer

Everywhere there are churches, there is fighting.

—ELLIE, AGE FOURTEEN

To tend the garden well is to direct people's attention to their own broken-ness. In their broken soil, they may be blessed with new shoots of green.[1]

—THOMAS E. FRANK

"Fighting. . . . That's what church has been about lately, fighting with each other. I really wish it would stop," began Ellie, a four-teen-year-old member of All Saints Episcopal Church, as we talked in the living room of her suburban split-level home in Northern Virginia. "I know people in our church have different views about gay priests or bishops, and now they have different ideas about how the priest should do things in our church, but why can't we just get along?"

Ellie has seen more than her share of church fights lately. In 2007 her parish split over the denomination's earlier decision to allow the election of a gay priest as a bishop. Ellie and her fam-ily stayed at All Saints, while their priest and a sizable number of church members left to form a new Anglican congregation not af-filiated with the Episcopal Church. Among the members remaining at All Saints, many still express a deep woundedness from the long, costly fight. Others in the parish say they have put the experience behind them and are now focused only on their desire to move on and rebuild.

Already strained by its recent schism, Ellie's parish continues to be embroiled in internal conflict. Most members blame the current conflict on disagreements with their new priest and say it has "nothing to do with the split." Ellie speaks of All Saints as "a wonderful, close family" and reminds us that "all families have problems from time to time." But, she notes,

> It gets really hard to make sense of all this fighting . . . and they are all people who matter to me. They all love God. I don't mean to say anything bad about the adults here—I love them all—but why can't they get over their disagreements in a more mature way? I see that it's happening in lots of other places too, though. I hear on the news about the churches fighting over who gets to keep the buildings when there is a split. It's not just us.

For Ellie, the confluence of the national church struggle and her own local parish's fights causes church conflict to seem "kind of ordinary, like I just expect people to be fighting over something now. You hear about it on the news, and then you go to church on Sunday and live it. Everywhere there are churches, there is fighting. That's sad. When it happens in our church, it really hurts."

What happens to a young person's faith when they see churches fighting? Can a church in constant conflict still be a source of nurture and care for young people and their emerging sense of purpose? Congregational studies on church conflict seldom consider the experiences of youth. And yet, as Ellie's story makes clear, young people are deeply affected by church conflict. In this chapter I will explore church conflict and the call of youth through the experiences of young people in two congregations in the southeastern United States that have been in conflict with their denominations over issues of human sexuality: All Saints Episcopal Church in Northern Virginia, and St. John's Lutheran Church in Atlanta, Georgia.[2]

Not Your Typical Greenhouse of Hope

Like the rest of this book, this chapter is based on ethnographic re-search with young people in the church. And like the other authors in this volume, I too engaged in practices such as interviewing, par-ticipant observation, oral history taking, and demographic studies to learn about congregational life and the calling of youth. Unlike the other authors, however, I did not set out to find an exemplary church where young people are apt to discern a call to vocations of leadership or service. Instead, I wondered about young people in churches that are fighting. Churches in conflict are not hard to find. Over the past decade, almost all major mainline denominations have debated the inclusion of gays and lesbians in leadership positions. Some churches struggle with whether to perform rituals of union for gay and lesbian members. And others have taken sides in larger political debates about gay marriage. Some of the conflict happens at large denominational gatherings, and only later becomes an issue to local churches. But often, as is the case at Ellie's church, disagree-ment ends up ripping apart local congregations, tearing asunder communities that have together baptized, married, and buried their loved ones for generations.

Denominations at war might create one more reason for young people to walk away from church altogether or to choose a different path if called to ministry themselves. For these reasons, I thought it important to wonder: What happens to the vocations of youth when the church they love feels more like a messy battleground than a fertile greenhouse? Is it possible that fighting with passion about justice, inclusion, and human dignity becomes, in itself, a practice that teaches and forms young people in particular ways?

This chapter is part of a larger study on congregations in con-flict with denominations that I conducted in 2009.[3] I initially began learning about these congregations not because they stood out as Greenhouses of Hope, but because each had an interesting story to tell about conflict. As I began to immerse myself in these churches, however, I quickly learned that young people were part of that story, and I realized that even in such conflict situations it might be possible to nurture hope.

I selected these churches based in part upon their willingness to partner with me in the research to learn about congregations in tension with their own denominations. Vulnerability arises in addressing conflict, whether current or in the past. Not every congregation dealing with discord is willing to have a researcher come into their community to learn about what are surely some of the most painful and difficult aspects of their life together. Each of the churches I studied had experienced a different form of conflict with its denomination but over a common issue, namely, policies regarding sexual orientation of professional church leaders. Only one, All Saints, was in a state of acute conflict at the time of my study. The other churches had been through some significant controversies in their recent past and by 2009, at the time of my research, were working through the issues and consequences of those conflicts for their congregations and members. I include congregations such as St. John's—which is now relatively free of conflict—in a study on churches in conflict, because it illustrates my understanding that conflict is an ongoing process incorporating multiple phases across time. In this chapter, due to space limitations, I will report on only two of the churches in my larger research project. One limitation of this study is that both congregations are primarily European American, although neither is exclusively so. (I am also of European American heritage, a factor that shaped my access to congregations within the time frame of the research.) This does not mean that the churches partnering with me contain no diversity within them. Many forms of diversity, including race and ethnicity, class, gender and sexual orientation, and generational diversity, find expression in each of the three faith communities.

The story these churches tell does not apply to every congregation; rather each is deeply particular and confined to its context. Other churches may experience similar patterns of conflict or may struggle with similar issues as the congregations in my study. As such, these particular stories add to the existing knowledge about congregations, conflict, and the calling of young people to lives of faith. I have altered the names of both youth and adults, and some identifying information, in order to protect the anonymity of individuals.

Chosen because of their narratives about conflict, St. John's and All Saints constitute somewhat atypical sites for learning about youth. Only one of them, St. John's, had a paid youth minister and a developed youth program. All Saints has only a handful of adolescents among their membership. And in the past two years both churches have been far more focused on their struggles than on their young people. But as I began to explore how young people in these churches experienced their congregations' conflicts, I soon learned that even when congregations fight and even if a church has few specific programmatic activities for youth, congregations can continue to nurture the faith commitments and vocations of their young people. At the same time, though, listening to young people in these churches also reveals that church fights can take a heavy toll on youth and can have a decidedly negative effect on their participation in the church and their personal experiences of Christian faith. After telling the stories and listening to the voices of young people in each of these two congregations, I will conclude by considering what these narratives can teach about the intersections of church conflict, faith formation, and youth. This chapter began with a glimpse into Ellie's church, All Saints Episcopal. Here is more of their story.

All Saints Episcopal

On a chilly Sunday morning in March 2009, I met Ellie sitting on the floor outside the sanctuary of All Saints Episcopal Church. She held a large container filled with aluminum tabs from soft drink cans and appeared to be counting them. "The youth have been collecting these as a mission project to support the Ronald McDonald House so that families have a place to stay if their children are in the hospital. I'm kind of in charge of the project," she told me. I complimented her on her cello playing during the service that morning.

"Thanks. I was nervous. But people here are all like family to me, so I got through it."

Ellie is a young person whose religious commitments and practices have been formed through her lifelong participation in Episcopal parishes, most recently and significantly including All Saints. She frequently referred to it as being "like a family," not just because it is the church attended by three generations of her relatives. Ellie quickly and easily named eight adults from the congregation whom she knows well and believes know her well. She can tell several of the central stories from the congregation's past, including some that happened before she was born. And she identified herself religiously as "Christian, Episcopalian, and a member of All Saints." Much of her emerging sense of meaning and selfhood take shape in relation to her understanding of the Christian faith; a faith she says she learned from her grandfather, her parents, and other adults at the church, including its former priest. Ellie also is a young person in a congregation wracked by conflict.

All Saints Episcopal Church is a relatively young faith community: It began in 1958 with twenty-five families meeting in a local elementary school in this rapidly growing Northern Virginia suburb known for its historic homes, beautiful rivers, and proximity to the nation's capital. From this modest beginning, the parish grew. All Saints' simple, single-story building sits on a wooded lot close to several large military bases. This proximity is reflected in the membership of the church, large numbers of which either have some direct association with the military (active duty or retired army, coast guard, air force, and an occasional member of the navy or marines) or indirect associations through their work in a defense-related industry or in government jobs.

Ellie comes from such a family. Her father is an officer in a branch of the military whose base is located near the church. "All Saints is good for people who move a lot," she said, "because it's such a welcoming place." The congregation has an active outreach mission to support families of deployed soldiers from the nearby bases. Military culture infuses the congregation in a number of ways.

They follow their singing of the Doxology every Sunday with a verse from "America the Beautiful." They pray for the congregation's deployed military personnel by name. They place a high value on tradition and orderly procedures and have written procedural manuals for most church operations. The brass gets shined regularly and the church kitchen is tidy, everything in its place as if ready for inspection. Folks at All Saints like their church community as it has been and are somewhat suspicious of change.

The congregation is largely, though not exclusively, white. The mixture of middle- and upper-middle-class people includes college graduates and a few adults with PhD's alongside others who are high school and trade school graduates. Some members pride themselves on being the last church in the diocese to stop using the 1928 edition of the *Book of Common Prayer*. They continue to hold one of their two weekly Sunday services using the older Rite 1 liturgy from the 1979 revision of the Episcopal Church's prayer book. Ellie prefers the more contemporary language of Rite 2. She almost never looks at the prayer book during the Sunday service because she has committed most of the liturgy to memory. "I love the prayer book," she told me. "I know that some people think it sounds boring, but I think the prayers are beautiful." Like others at All Saints, Ellie values the sense of tradition embedded in the Episcopal prayer book.

That sense of tradition came under threat in the eyes of many All Saints members in 2003 when the national Episcopal Church authorized the consecration of Gene Robinson, the first openly gay and partnered man to be elected a bishop by his diocese. Initially, All Saints responded in a way similar to several neighboring Episcopal parishes in Northern Virginia: they expressed outrage toward those who voted in favor of this consecration by sending a letter of concern to the bishop from the vestry. Walt Tinsdale, a founding member of the congregation who believed that the denomination was "making a wrong turn," recalled later that "After the 2006 General Convention reaffirmed its earlier decision to elect a gay bishop and approve same-sex marriage, quite a few Virginia Episcopalians including some at All Saints became agitated and began to act on the plans they had been making to take their parishes out of the [Episcopal] church." That was clearly the desire for All Saints' former priest, Father Henry.

When the bishop came to All Saints to meet with concerned congregation members, youth did not participate in the meeting. Adults who were present recall it with chagrin. "It was awful," one vestry member recounted. "People were screaming at each other and even at the bishop. There was name calling and shouting. And Father Henry, our priest, was one of the loudest!" A few lay leaders spoke of getting caught up in the fervor of this meeting, finding themselves participating in actions and behaviors for which they later apologized to the bishop.

When members of All Saints reflect on this time in their congregation's recent history, many recall that their priest had become increasingly concerned about what he considered the "godless" directions of the denomination. He had begun to explore through the Internet various networks of Episcopalians who disagreed with what they perceived as their denomination's turn away from biblical fidelity and orthodox Christian faith. Some members grew upset with Father Henry's frequent focus on homosexuality and with the amount of time the issue and the new networking took from other pastoral ministries at All Saints. They believed Father Henry's priorities and vision for ministry had become quite different from those held by many congregation members. Others, however, saw Father Henry's concerns echoing their own about the Episcopal Church as a denomination. The seeds for congregational conflict were sewn, fed, and watered by the growing influence of networks of disaffected priests and lay leaders who were priming their congregations to leave the Diocese of Virginia and the denomination.[4] Ellie, in a sad voice, remembered this time of conflict:

> I was about eleven or twelve so I didn't really get in the loop like I am now, knowing things. But I remember my dad was on the vestry, and I knew that things weren't going well with Father Henry, that people were upset . . . and I didn't really understand why until he was actually gone. Leading up to that, I didn't know that anything was wrong, but just that suddenly

there were all these cranky people and sometimes things got out of control. I didn't see it very much, but I knew there was yelling going on and people were not being very kind.

"What did you come to understand the trouble being about?" I asked her.

Well, when [Father Henry] finally declared that he was resigning, . . . I found out about the gay bishop and, of course being influenced the way I am with my family and my grandfather, that upsets me too. But [my mother] explained that Father Henry was very involved with that situation instead of pastoral care for the members of the church. And he wanted us to leave the Episcopal Church and he wanted All Saints to start off in a new direction and in a new denomination. And All Saints didn't want to do that. . . . Well, I look at that and I understand that people would be upset that he would kind of, in a way, make people feel neglected by paying attention to that situation instead of maybe being there for us a little bit more. But at the time I had no clue.

In the fall of 2006, All Saints' vestry rejected the efforts of Father Henry and some church members to have the church leave the Diocese of Virginia and the Episcopal Church. Father Henry abruptly announced his resignation in November, after ten years of ministry at All Saints. He left in December, in the midst of the Advent season, along with some thirty to forty church members. Among the continuing Episcopal congregation that is All Saints were those who disagreed with the departing group's views on homosexuality and scriptural interpretation. Also remaining at All Saints were church members who, while being in broad agreement with Father Henry, had loyalties to the Diocese of Virginia or otherwise sufficiently strong ties to the All Saints parish that, as one woman put it, they "wouldn't leave our church over something like that."

For Ellie, the effect of her relative ignorance about the divisions in the parish was that Father Henry's departure seemed "out of the blue, just all of a sudden . . . and people were mad for a while and then they just stopped talking about it." While she knew from listening to her parents and other adults in the congregation that there was tension in the church, she was not aware that the differences in the church were great enough for their priest to leave.

Ellie told me that she "personally agrees" with Father Henry's stance about homosexuality, understanding it as "not righteous. It's a sin." That is what her family believes too, although she indicated that her mother leans toward a more tolerant view than does her father. "Our church is like my family—there are some differences in the way people think about it [homosexuality], even though most people at All Saints probably think it's wrong." At school, however, she said she finds herself alone in that viewpoint, amidst other students voicing support for gay rights. Emerging from her own experience of being a lone voice standing up for a value she holds, Ellie expressed admiration for Father Henry's choice to press an issue he felt strongly about even though it brought conflict:

> But I really look at it in the sense that when he wanted us to leave the Episcopal Church, he must have really had faith in what he was saying. That he wanted to leave and he wanted to start off in a new direction, and I really admire that he had so much faith in what he thought God was telling him, that he would want to bring All Saints with him and go off in this new direction. He must really have faith to do that and I admire that.
>
> And I think about what he did as if he was saying, "Hey, come with me. Why don't we all do this together and go off and leave the Episcopal Church for this?" I think he had strong faith in that respect. In the sense that you wouldn't impose that on other people unless you really believed that.

When I asked Ellie how it affected her that the members of her church argued with their priest and fought with one another, she began to cry as she spoke:

> Father Henry was very close to me, like, just as a role model in general. I know that a lot of people were upset with him but he taught me a lot of

things, and people are mad at him and some people probably still are. But I don't see any reason to be mad at him the way some people are. And he was just a very important person to me. Like, in general, just as a priest but also the way he taught me. When my grandpa died, that day he was with us. Like after school I went to my grandma's house and he was there, and he sat and talked with us and it really helped me. . . . My grandfather had the strongest faith. I miss him.

Father Henry did not conduct her grandfather's funeral, because, as Ellie noted, his death happened after Father Henry's departure from All Saints, and "he [Father Henry] said it was up to us, but he probably shouldn't do it because some people would be really upset if he did."

After Father Henry's departure, All Saints got by with help of a part-time interim priest until a new priest-in-charge, Father Keith, arrived. Father Keith inherited a church still wounded from long months of rancorous conflict, the loss of their priest, and the division of the congregation. In addition, the church faced a huge financial debt from a building project undertaken prior to the denomination's actions and the congregation's split. In the face of all of this, church leadership expressed high hopes that their new priest would help them bring in new, young families. But after a brief honeymoon with Father Keith, various quarrels began to be voiced. Discontent surfaced. Over time these escalated into a significant conflict of their own, which continues into the present life of the parish.

As noted earlier, All Saints is a parish with relatively few youth. With Father Keith's arrival, they experienced an influx of new families with younger children, and eventually a small youth class, led by a vivacious newer adult member of the vestry, began to meet on Sunday mornings. A member of the vestry holds responsibility for children's and youth ministries, and youth can participate in various activities for fellowship and service led by lay leaders or the priest. As is often the case with smaller churches, these arrangements appear somewhat episodic and lack the feel of a coordinated youth program, but often have a hidden benefit: Instead of segregating young people into their own activities, the entire life of the church becomes ground for young people's participation, leadership, and formation. Such is the case at All Saints. The primary ways in which young people participate is through involvement in various parish activities. A young person is almost always involved in an "up front" role in the liturgy, for example.

A few weeks after my conversation with Ellie in her living room, she was serving as an acolyte for one of All Saints' Sunday morning liturgies. Dressed in a white alb, and lined up in preparation for the procession into the sanctuary with the priest, choir, and other participants in the liturgy, Ellie smiled as she adjusted the Velcro closure of her alb and pushed a wisp of blonde hair away from her eyes. As usual, she appeared calm and poised that morning, seeming entirely comfortable in her public role as she processed into the service carrying the candle that she told me symbolizes the light of Christ. "Sometimes I get upset too," she confessed in our conversation. "But I try not to take that into the service with me. I try to focus on Christ and why we are there."

Instead of segregating young people into their own activities, the entire life of the church becomes ground for young people's participation, leadership, and formation. . . . The primary ways in which young people participate is through involvement in various parish activities. A young person is almost always involved in an "up front" role in the liturgy, for example.

That particular Sunday morning, however, Ellie's calm demeanor was not widely shared by those around her. Some in the mostly adult processional lineup smiled briefly and offered greetings to those visitors and children weaving their way around the sea of white albs and silver grey choir robes to enter the sanctuary. But most of the faces in this line of choir members and liturgical leaders for the day had no smiles for anyone. They instead displayed irritation and distress, betraying the conflict besetting this congregation. When the time came to process for the start of the liturgy, their flushed faces, pulsing veins, and tension-creased foreheads continued to speak of conflict even while they sang a spritely processional hymn.

By the end of the liturgy, manifestations of conflict managed to disrupt even Ellie's poise and calm. One upset choir member, apparently inflamed by something in the sermon, stormed out of the service. A few other members made obvious their displeasure with the priest by refusing to participate in the Eucharist, as still others moved toward the altar throwing shocked and upset glances at others. Even Ellie's normally sanguine facial expression began to take on tension as the drama of conflict played out in largely unspoken but visible ways throughout worship. As she attempted to fulfill her role assisting the priest in preparing the altar for the sacrament, she could not ignore the rising tensions all around her.

During the coffee hour afterwards, the usually welcoming and friendly time for sharing food and conversation among the congregation and its guests had been replaced by a palpable sense of disease throughout the room. I observed that a visiting couple and a few people who were newer to the congregation left the coffee hour more hastily than usual that day, perhaps picking up the unspoken tensions in the air.

Among All Saints' longer term members, little groups stood in clumps of twos and threes around the long room, holding their steaming cups of coffee close as they whispered with faces turned away from the sight and hearing of others. Some stood with arms crossed protectively against their bodies. A few women exchanged what appeared to be knowing glances across the room when certain others entered the fellowship hall. Father Keith did not come to coffee hour that morning.

One did not need to hear the content of the various hushed conversational huddles to recognize the thick bile of dispute leaking out through such irritated gestures, closed body positions, and various offended or inflamed tones of voice present in the room. "My mom is crying, and my stomach is in knots," said Ellie. "I know some people disagree about things, and I am probably not aware of all the details because I'm a teenager—but why can't they at least try to solve the problems in some other way? Why are people yelling at each other and getting mad? . . . I think I understand why people are upset and I just wish people would handle it differently."

"What do you wish they would do? " I asked her later in an interview as she talked about the unfolding conflicts over Father Keith's leadership. She replied:

> Well, I see people are getting upset, and we're not really sitting down and talking with each other about things. So, I think I wish people would just quit bickering and try to come together in this situation. I think that people really . . . I'm not going to say that people are acting immaturely. I'm just saying that as adults I think that people could try a little bit harder to get along, but I look at the adult world now and I think I know that people aren't going to get along. There will always be disagreements, but we love each other so much at All Saints. I think it's kind of like those family fights. Like me and my brother . . . (*laughter*). I love him to death, but I want to strangle him sometimes. I think we're kind of like that at All Saints. We love each other. We're all close to each other, but you're always going to have your disagreements and you're always going to have your rival brothers, sisters. Like there are rivals at All Saints. And we all love each other. We can all get along. It's just sometimes you have that sibling that you're having a fight with.

St. John's Lutheran Church

St. John's Lutheran Church is a long way from All Saints in many respects. Geographically, St. John's is in a different state; and it is affiliated with a different denomination. Located in Atlanta, Georgia, in a neighborhood near the campus of Emory University, St. John's is a congregation of the Southeastern Synod of the Evangelical Lutheran Church in America (ELCA). In contrast to the relatively short congregational life of All Saints Episcopal, St. John's is Atlanta's oldest Lutheran congregation, organized in 1869 to serve German immigrants moving into the city. All Saints faces declining membership, while St. John's is one of a handful of churches in its synod that continues to grow. But the greatest distance between these two congregations can best be told through the story of one of my research visits during which I spent some time with youth.

On a cool, wet spring day in 2009, St. John's Lutheran Church was all grey, except for the bright red sanctuary doors characteristic of Lutheran churches. A sign proclaims, "God Welcomes Everyone—So Do We." Inside this mansion-turned-church-building, three girls and the adult teacher of the middle school Sunday school class engage in an activity that talks back to the drab, rainy day: they paint tiny clay pots with bright colors, planting seeds that promise to bring more color in due time.

"What does that sign outside mean?" I asked these middle school girls. "It means anyone can come here and hear that God loves them," Birgette responds, her straw-colored blond braids and name betraying her Scandinavian heritage. "It means that we try to treat people the way God treats them," interrupted a second girl with dark hair and a Norwegian-sounding last name. A third girl of Asian heritage, who looked about twelve years old, listened to all this without comment. Walking out of the room at the end of the class, though, she too spoke to me about the message on the church signboard. "It means everybody is welcome here, but at our church you are especially welcome if you are gay. Like our pastor. Our church is a little bit famous for that," she said.

St. John's is indeed "a little bit famous for that." In 2000 they called a noncloseted gay man to be their pastor. At the time Bradley Schmeling was called to St. John's a few families left the congregation, unable to accept a gay man as their pastor. Most people at St. John's say that although six members left at that time, a few others drifted away over the course of the next few years. The overwhelming majority of members enthusiastically supported the call, and the congregation quickly experienced an overall sense of internal unity in its acceptance of and appreciation for Pastor Brad's ministry.

But a second wave of controversy soon followed. When the congregation called Schmeling as their pastor in 2000, he had been single. A few years into his ministry at St. John's, Pastor Brad informed the congregation and his bishop that he had entered into a committed partnership with Rev. Darin Easler. At that point, the ELCA's rules allowed only married—and, therefore, heterosexual—clergy to be in intimate relationships. The bishop filed charges against Schmeling. The congregation mobilized to fight for change in the church and to keep their pastor as a rostered ELCA pastor. The situation propelled them into the national spotlight.[5]

The congregation went into action. They hired an attorney to represent Schmeling and St. John's at the trial. They developed formal processes for dealing with the media attention the case drew. They wrote letters and mobilized a network of supporters from across the United States, deepening ties to other groups working to change ELCA policy. Congregational leaders created a series of special liturgies for the week before the trial, preparing both for the large numbers of people drawn to St. John's in the heat of the conflict and for the possibility of disruptions from hecklers, threats, or actual violence. And they created prayer weavings, a unique and artistic means of weaving the prayers sent by supporters from around the nation on small colorful strips of cloth into one mass of color, a piece that now rests on the wall outside the main entrance to St. John's sanctuary.

Among the members of St. John's testifying at the Chicago trial were various congregational leaders and members, including a couple of youth. The trial did not go in favor of Pastor Brad, and appeals were unsuccessful. Schmeling was removed from the list of rostered ELCA clergy in July 2007.

Ben Aims, a high school student at the time of the trial, calls it his least favorite memory of his lifetime in the church. Ben and his family have been active at St. John's for as long as he can recall. "It's a rule in our family that you have to go to church every Sunday until you graduate," he said candidly. "So I have been here pretty much every Sunday for twenty years." He calls the times in which the church was exploring whether to call a gay pastor and then the two years the congregation was "dealing with the whole 'Pastor Brad being gay and in a relationship thing'" conflicted, stressful times, although not so much within the congregation as in relation to the wider church:

How did it affect me personally, him being gay? I didn't really care. I feel, like, my reaction was if he was dating a woman and he was getting married, it's the same thing to me. It's not that big of a deal. But then for some people it was. I don't know. I guess that's just how I was raised. It's not that big of a deal. Yeah. It wasn't. I didn't understand, I guess, why everybody else had a problem with it. It just seems strange that in this time, like, I don't know. It's 2009. I thought people would be over it by now, but I guess not. That was an interesting time for the church. . .

Ben recalled the time during which the congregation prepared for the event that would come to be known among them simply as "The Trial" as especially difficult.

It gave me a bad taste of religion in general. That it was so silly, all of the rules and stuff like that. It wasn't a good experience going through all of that, basically. I wouldn't say it was good at all. After the whole trial here and that sort of stuff, I guess I just really didn't feel connected to the denomination. I kind of felt, like, instead of working with us they kind of worked *against* us. . . . I don't know everything that's happened with it, so there's a lot I don't understand. But I feel like, I don't know, it feels like there's a little bit of, I guess, stress between our church and the denomination. . . . I feel like it would hurt the church, just wouldn't be good for them to say, "You have to kick Pastor Brad out or we're gonna drop you" sort of deal. Have we been dropped? I'm not even sure.

A further reason Ben experienced this time as such a stress-filled one was that participation in these processes involved a huge time commitment, with many hours spent in meetings at the church—understandably not a felicitous situation for a high school student. But in addition, when he did participate, Ben did not always feel that his contributions to the process were valued because of his youth:

It's interesting. I know when the whole situation was going on even though I was a confirmed member of the church, I felt like I didn't have as much say as other people in the congregation, but I felt like we all felt pretty much the same way, but I don't know. I was still seventeen, eighteen, nineteen at the time, so I was still—I mean, I'm still young. But it's hard to really say how you feel when there are other people that have been in the church for, like, thirty years. But that's just what happens when you're young. . . . But when the church disagrees, it's hard to be taken seriously when you're a youth, I guess. . . . Like, there were a ton of meetings. So many meetings. But I felt like if I said something it would just kind of be, like, "Yeah, okay, let's talk about something more serious." I just felt like, "Oh, that's cute and we're glad he likes Pastor Brad" or whatever. I felt like I just wasn't taken very seriously so much.

In a meeting between the congregation and then-Southeastern Synod Bishop Ronald Warren about the decision to file charges, Ben was an active participant, speaking up in the meeting along with other St. John's members. But Ben experienced frustration over what he perceived to be tokenism on the part of the bishop toward him as a young person:

I spoke up when the bishop was here. He was, like, "Okay, whatever. I'll call on the younger person." I don't know, I felt like I was just saying basically, "We really care for Pastor Brad here, and I think it would upset us a lot if you had him removed." [The bishop] was, like, "Yeah, next person." It's just—I don't know. I didn't feel like I was given as much consideration as older members. That may be wrong, but I just don't feel like I was treated the same, I guess, for being younger. But that happens with everything when you're younger.

In the time following the ecclesiastical trial that resulted in Schmeling's removal from the ELCA rostered clergy list, the congregation stayed in the ELCA while continuing to work for change in the ELCA policies. Schmeling remained on, as their denominationally unaffiliated pastor.[6]

In Ben's senior year of high school and shortly after the trial's conclusion, St. John's hired a youth minister. Ben graduated from high school and went on to college. The congregation went on with its ministry in the city of Atlanta, reaching out to its neighbors and educating its youth in confirmation classes and Sunday school and nurturing their faith through the experiences of their youth group. St. John's youth regularly engage in ministries of service, such as their work with Central Presbyterian Church's night shelter.

Ben credits practices of ministry such as this with shaping his identity and forming him into the kind of young adult he is becoming:

> I feel like being a part of this church, there are a lot of different people in this church from a lot of different backgrounds. So I feel like the church has taught me to be really accepting of other people, and I feel like I'll go out and be really accepting of other people. As far as life goes, I guess, I would be a completely different person if I didn't go to this church. . . . I feel like I would be very narrow-minded. I'd be kind of, like, I don't know. Let's say homosexuality for example. I'd just feel like homosexuality is bad . . . like, it's bad. I wouldn't really care for a reason.
>
>   I feel like the church has really given me an opportunity to think about what I believe in. And I feel like, without the church, I would be very stuck in my ways sort of. . . . I guess not everybody has this sort of openness about their church, about things in general, as our church does. So I feel like I'm called to, when I meet other people, I guess, show them how to be more accepting.

Ben credits St. John's for forming him as a person with an open, accepting attitude toward other people, something he now says he believes he is called to share with the world. In fact, he cites specific practices of ministry, in which the youth group of St. John's participated, for shaping this sense of compassion for the well-being of people who are different from himself and who are disadvantaged by their differences:

> There was one youth group event that I helped organize with [an adult who worked with the youth] that was, like, a Thanksgiving meal thing. Then we stayed up all night, well, not all night, but we stayed up and

helped cook meals for homeless people and then we went out the next morning and distributed a bunch of . . . meals to homeless people. Like Thanksgiving meals. There were sweet potatoes and stuff. Nobody is gonna feel comfortable when you're seventeen going out and, I guess, sharing with homeless people. It feels really awkward when you're that young. But, like, when I told my friends they were, like, "What did you do this weekend?" I was, like, "I went out and distributed meals to homeless people." A lot of them were, like, "What? Like why would you do that?" . . . a lot of kids at that age hadn't done stuff like that. I guess the church has offered a lot of things to me that other kids haven't been offered.

In the course of their time in the youth group at St. John's, adolescents encounter some of Atlanta's most down-and-out, suffering people as they engage in regular service at church night shelters and other ministries. Such experiences may seem far from the concerns of their pastor's ecclesiastical trial over sexuality and the congregation's fight with its denomination to change policies about gay clergy. But, as one young person at St. John's simply stated, "In our church, somehow it's all connected. I think we are just trying to live by our faith."

Youth, Calling, and the Practice of Conflict

In spite of their many differences, the two congregations whose partial stories I tell here display several significant commonalities. Both congregations, trying to be faithful to the Christian gospel as they understand it, have been caught up in larger, national social and religious turmoil. Through this turmoil not only denominational sexuality policies but also the very nature of the relationships between congregations and their denominations are being refashioned. Both All Saints and St. John's went through experiences of conflict that were difficult and painful for them at communal and individual levels, and that continue to be played out in the lives of the two churches. And in both of these congregations, youth participate in—and are formed by—congregational life and practices, including practices of conflict.

Church folk do not regularly mention conflict as a Christian practice. When asked about practices that shape them as Christians in their everyday life, folks are more likely to name practices such as prayer, hospitality, service, hymn singing, right giving, or care for the earth. But how communities deal with contentious differences is also a faith practice. As practical theologians Craig Dykstra and Dorothy Bass note, "Practices are those shared activities that address fundamental human needs and that, woven together, form a way of life,"[7] and "Christian practices are things Christian people do together over time in response to and in the light of God's active presence for the life of the world."[8] The stories of St. John's and All Saints show that conflict easily fits this definition of practices. The implication of such a claim is that congregations continue to form their members in faith by the ways they fight as well as the ways they love, because participation in practices shapes faith even while embodying it.

Listening to Ellie, Ben, and other young people from the congregations in my study of church conflict and sexuality makes clear that youth experience the costs of conflict in church fights along with adults. They lose people who matter to them and feel grief that the conflict situation often leaves little room to process. They suffer being discounted, overlooked, or tokenized in the seriousness of conflict exchanges among adults. They struggle to make sense of what it means to claim an identity within a denominational heritage with which their congregation is at odds. They can feel pressured unfairly to choose sides in the fight. The need to have their particular gifts noticed, named, and nurtured by the congregation may well be placed on the back burner as conflict takes up much of the available energy of adults and congregational leadership.

Conflicted congregations have different patterns for involving youth in their practices and processes of conflict. In the name of being protected from conflict, youth who are nonparticipants in congregational processes related to controversies may be isolated and marginalized. This can leave them vulnerable to misunderstandings or taken by surprise at the turn of events, as happened for Ellie. On the other hand, in the name of being included as full participants, youth like Ben may experience stress from a sense of overexposure to a conflict they feel relatively helpless to affect.

At the same time that conflict brings costs, the stories of Ellie, Ben, and other young people at All Saints and St. John's also show that congregations can find ways to continue to affirm and nurture their young people amid conflict. The congregations continued to "be church" for and with their youth. Adults accompanied Ben and other youth group members in serving Thanksgiving meals to homeless people. Ellie played her cello in the eleven o'clock worship service and experienced the support and positive regard of other worshipers for her musical leadership. Confirmation classes, baptisms, ice skating trips, and mission activities still took place. Young people served as ushers and acolytes. Perhaps these stories might serve as reminders to congregational leaders that youth are watching, listening, and being shaped by all that goes on in church. Perhaps it's not too much of a stretch to understand conflict as an opportunity to learn the importance of maintaining relationship and continuing to be church even, maybe especially, when that gets difficult.

These two congregations remind me of the neglected greenhouses described in chapter 1. For many years, scholars and practitioners have been rethinking Christian teaching about sexuality, especially in light of new scientific and psychological conversations about gender, gender fluidity, and the ways culture shapes our expression of being male or female. Gay men and lesbian woman who feel called into professional ministry have found ways to answer their call, causing the church to look within itself, its interpretation of Scripture, and its ethos of love to discern the best way forward. In many ways, the conflict Ben and Ellie witnessed is the pain that comes as the church discerns its own vocation, its own way of being church in and for the world. Refashioning the abandoned greenhouse is backbreaking work as we pull out the debris to make room for new soil and new kinds of flourishing. The conflict these churches experienced is part of that backbreaking work.

These two congregations, each in its own way, invited young people to recognize that something important was at stake, important enough that members were willing to become passionately engaged in difficult fights for its sake. Kenda Creasy Dean, professor of youth ministry, writing on the generally passionless state of many mainline churches, contends that young people are in search of a "faith to die for"—a faith that involves passion for which people are willing to risk or even suffer, as they surely do when there is a conflict. Ellie speaks to this in her affirmation of Father Henry's decision to leave.

Certainly, some church conflict is unhealthy and destructive. It should not be baptized as good by virtue of its ability to engender the passions of the congregation and its young people. Nor need we romanticize conflict: it is always hard, and people often experience real harm. What can be affirmed, though, is the power of conflict to mobilize energies and bring clarity about what matters most. As Laura Crawley, a lay leader at St. John's at the time of their pastor's trial, said, "There is something about the work of the Spirit that is worth fighting for; there is something about faith that is worth fighting for; and there is something about a community that is inclusive and welcoming that is worth fighting for."[9]

In greenhouses where conditions are less than ideal, some plants wither. But others can flourish, developing a certain resilience out of the difficulties they faced. At All Saints and St. John's I saw young people shaped by these faith communities into resilient young adults. Seeing them, I find a sense of hope emerging in me—hope that perhaps, if young people are privy to adults fighting with passion about issues that matter, they will come away with a sense of Christianity not as a crowd of bickering rabble-rousers, but as a living, changing, growing entity, ever renewing itself to better reflect the image of God. Maybe one could find—in this kind of greenhouse—exactly the tools necessary to answer one's own call, to engage oneself in the hard work of changing the world by embodying hope in action.

Questions for Reflection

ENGAGING VOCATIONCARE PRACTICES

1. A church's capacity to *create hospitable space* can come under threat when conflict arises. Young people at both St. John's and All Saints told about moments when they felt uncomfortable; Ben when he felt his voice was tokenized and Amy when she experienced the anger of warring factions during worship. But both of these young people were also learning that churches, like families, are sometimes places of struggle instead of easy peacefulness.

   • In what ways can you imagine your congregation continuing to be authentically welcoming of young people and their gifts, even if they are distracted by energy-consuming disagreement over important matters?

   • The question of including gays and lesbians in church leadership and in rituals of union often seems trivial to younger generations, who have experienced diversity of gender orientation and are not troubled by it. How does your church find ways to hold a space for both older and younger people's voices around these issues?

2. In this chapter, the researcher is often the one *asking self-awakening questions*. For instance, she asks youth what the sign "God Welcomes Everyone—and So Do We" means to them. She also asks a series of questions that evoke painful stories from Ellie about the fighting at her church and its effect on her. Frequently, during ethnographic listening, interviewees

find themselves speaking newly recognized truths because of the presence of an attentive listener.

- Although the purpose of ethnography here was to learn from Ellie, not to help her, do you see the careful interactions between the researcher and Ellie serving as a form of care or ministry?
- If so, how would you translate this into your context? Are there places of hurt, conflict, or pain around which a time set apart for asking self-awakening questions might be a form of ministry?

3. Fighting about interpretations of Scripture is one way people *reflect theologically on self and community*. In spite of being difficult, this can also be a sign that something important is at stake. In the midst of doing so, young people in the congregation learn from adults who see the story of their lives overlapping with what God is doing in the world.

- When might you invite young people to reflect on how their dreams for the world intersects God's dream for the world?
- How does your culture or context specifically practice theological reflection? In Bible study? Through testimony? In what other ways does it do so?

4. Both of these churches continued *establishing and enacting ministry opportunities for young people* during their seasons of conflict. Ellie was active in leading worship and music. Ben helped serve Thanksgiving meals to the homeless. In this way, the church continues being the church, despite its visible division and even schism.

- If a young person in your congregation seems particularly gifted for leadership, who, in addition to pastoral staff, may be likely to notice?
- Think of a time when a young person discovered a gift through participation in the life of your faith community. What support or encouragement was given?

PRACTICING ETHNOGRAPHIC LISTENING

"There is no church apart from local congregations gathering in certain places. This means that when we say 'church' we should not imagine a static structure frozen in eternity, a timeless ideal to which actual congregations feebly aspire. Nor should we simply call to mind all the embarrassing and exasperating features of congregations we know, and give up on church altogether."[10]

- It is refreshing to remember that churches are dynamic, living, never-finished beings. How do the stories shared by Ellie and Ben remind you of your own congregation's "embarrassing and exasperating features"?
- How do the stories of these two congregations inspire you not to "give up on church altogether"?
- Who are the Bens and Ellies in your congregation who may need a listening ear because of conflict or disagreement they have witnessed?

What on Earth Are We Doing?

YOUNG LIVES EMERGING TO CHANGE THE WORLD

Melissa Wiginton

> God now calls the next generation of church leaders to grow the germinating seed of idealism by advocating the formation of radically inclusive communities.
>
> —2010 FUND FOR THEOLOGICAL EDUCATION MINISTRY FELLOW

I pointed to the empty window seat on row 11 of my flight homebound for Austin and the young man on the aisle stood up. Squeezing past him, I couldn't help but notice that he was reading *A New Earth: Awakening to Your Life's Purpose* by Eckhart Tolle. That's one of those books I feel I should read. I sat down and as I pushed my laptop case under the seat in front of me, I pulled out the book I was reading, *Emerging Adulthood: The Winding Road from the Late Teens through the Twenties* by Jeffrey Arnett. Before long my companion struck up a conversation.

This young man was on the last leg of a yearlong spiritual quest. From a wealthy family in Palm Beach, he had traveled all around the world in his search. He was planning to meet his guru,

EMERGING ADULTHOOD: A stage of life following adolescence but preceding adulthood. Ranging from the late teens to the midtwenties, this newly identified developmental stage is now widely recognized among scholars.[1]

Leslie, in Austin. They had only worked together online, so he was looking forward to meeting Leslie in person. I hoped for this young seeker's sake that his guru didn't turn out to be our town's infamous Leslie—a tall, skinny older man with long bushy hair who wears a thong, sometimes with a feather boa, as he roller skates on South Congress Avenue.

I asked my new friend about Eckhart Tolle. He said the book was very helpful, but he couldn't quite express what he was taking from it. He was clear, though, that he constructs his spirituality, his meaning in life, from all kinds of religions, choosing the parts that he thinks are true. What, he asked, are the morals and values of your religion?

As I pondered his question, I thought about the congregations we have come to know in this book. They are each communities of people sharing a way of life growing from, leading into, and moving forth from the love of God who became human. The members of these communities are deeply formed as individuals by values enacted through the practices—the morality—of Christianity. Somehow the categories of "morals" and "values" didn't seem robust enough to describe being Christian.

The nineteen-year-old sitting beside me in row 11 seemed to fit a popular profile of his generation: seekers of meaningful lives only loosely tethered to religious tradition and certainly not limited by it in their spirituality. His mother was Catholic, he told me, but he had not been reared in the Church because his mom didn't want to force religion on him. She supported his effort to make up his own mind now. I thought of Ben from St. John's ELCA in Atlanta whose family rule was going to church on Sunday morning. Unlike Ben, my airplane companion didn't really come from anywhere or belong to anyone.

What Greenhouses of Hope Are Doing

Congregations we might call Greenhouses of Hope are places where people belong to God and to one another for the sake of the world;

we have seen many examples in this book. Each one is unique, some more alike than others. All would be categorized as mainline Protestant and somewhere within the broad spectrum of middle class. Many kinds of congregations don't show up in this picture at all. Our conclusions about Greenhouses of Hope in this chapter are drawn from the congregations in the admittedly limited view of the pictures here, knowing that Greenhouses of Hope abound within Roman Catholic, Orthodox, evangelical, ethnic, rich, poor, multi-racial, and all other kinds of congregations who have ways of life that result in young people hearing, responding to, and serving God's call.

Greenhouses of Hope foster relationships among people of all ages and with people outside one's own family. A middle-aged pastor and several teenagers have each other in their cell phones' contact lists at First United Methodist Church, Evanston. At St. John's Evangelical Lutheran Church, youth plan and lead a service project together with adults. At Choongsuh Korean Presbyterian Church (USA), teenagers are known well by a cadre of others five years older. Similarly, at Isle of Hope United Methodist Church, college students return to serve in formal roles, relating to both the younger members to whom they minister and the older ones who mentor them and their work. Life at First Afrikan Presbyterian Church (USA) includes relationships with the ancestors, living and dead. Ellie at All Saints Episcopal Church knew and was known by Father Henry. She could talk to him and he shared meals in her home. Over and over, people in these congregations spoke of church as family: people who care about you just because you are who you are.

Greenhouses of Hope also provide youth and young adults authentic roles in congregational life, not simply symbolic ones or solely the roles

> Greenhouses of Hope foster relationships among people of all ages and with people outside one's own family.

> Greenhouses of Hope also provide youth and young adults authentic roles in congregational life, not simply symbolic ones or solely the roles youth are typically expected to play.

youth are typically expected to play. The leadership of youth in worship is significant, whether they be acolytes, readers, musicians, or members of a choir. Those roles engender investment in the corporate life of the gathered people. But youth in these communities show up in lots of other places as well.

One of the points of pain for Ben was being invited to participate in congregational meetings at St. John's and then being patronized when he spoke. Yet he remained a member of the community. He was hurt but not alienated by the experience of what he called "tokenism" because it occurred in the context of many meaningful roles he had in church life. Adults entrusted the youth at Choongsuh with leadership of their group in the absence of pastors, and the youth trusted each other as the leaders. Decision making at First Afrikan relies on community-wide dialogue, which includes young people rather than hierarchy. The youth of Isle of Hope catalyzed and continue to stoke the congregation's commitment to mission, now part of the whole congregation's core identity. In Evanston, teenagers teach older members how to cross cultures as they plan a trip together into Appalachia.

Finally, Greenhouses of Hope are more than sites for doing service or social justice, for friendship and play. They are safe places to be spiritual. People in these congregations act with confidence that God is real and moving among them. They practice liturgy that is truly the work of the people to connect with the holy—through prayer, music making, teaching, and serving. Youth and young adults are not observers but are taught these practices by example and instruction and given agency to claim them for themselves. At First Congregational Church of Berkeley, the young adults began their relationship with the mosque by being in worship, and the connection continues to include sharing in each other's prayer and worship. Choongsuh's passionate prayer and rites of reconciliation

exemplify spiritual practice as powerful. First Afrikan's worship includes liturgical dance, pouring of libations, and prayers that connect their African heritage, their lives as African Americans, and the
life of God. God moments are regularly and unhesitatingly named
at First United Methodist Church (FUMC) in Evanston. Boys unabashedly volunteer to pray out loud at Isle of Hope. In the midst of
a culture that holds the material to be all that is real, these churches
hold a space in which it is normative to point to another reality in
which to find oneself—again and again—to be a child of God.

These three common themes—intergenerational relationships,
authentic roles in congregational life, and embodied spiritual practices that connect lived experience with the holy—do not exhaust all
that echoes across the seven congregations presented in this book.
Readers who have worked through the questions
at the end of each chapter should have a healthy
outline of practices that resonate in their own
congregations.

Within Greenhouses of Hope lies a seed of
the capacity for vocation—that is, responding to
God with the whole of one's life, including what
one does to make a living, but also what one
does to make a life. The question now becomes
how Greenhouses of Hope will keep those young
people alive once the seed is planted and takes
root. These congregations form young Christians in particular ways, and because they are
living communities, they hold the potential to
provide for ongoing nourishment and constant
re-formation in response to changing, challenging, and sometimes
hostile environments. In the introduction Dori Baker described
Greenhouses of Hope as congregations who are creating space for
the dreams of young people to be grafted onto God's dream for the
world. If these grafts are to take, if the plant is to be enlarged and
made stronger, more beautiful, or more fruitful, there is tending,
pruning, and fertilizing yet to do.

> Within Greenhouses
> of Hope lies a seed
> of the capacity for
> vocation—that is, re-
> sponding to God with
> the whole of one's
> life, including what
> one does to make a
> living, but also what
> one does to make
> a life.

The Environment Outside the Greenhouse

Greenhouses—and we are surely now nearing the end of the usefulness of this metaphor—serve a particular function: to help a plant survive that would not make it on its own in its unmediated environment. It is worth taking a close look at the outside environment in which youth and young adults are formed to understand what is needed from congregations.

Robert Wuthnow, a sociologist of religion, describes the generation of people who have completed their formal education, of whatever level, and yet have not achieved the traditional signs of adulthood (marriage, home, financial independence, career, children) as bricoleurs or tinkerers.[2] That is, they use ideas and activities to create a pastiche that is their identity. (Remember my companion in row 11?) Traditional adulthood comes at a later age than ever before. Some argue that this new life stage of young adulthood is a good thing, that it gives people a time of freedom to explore and enjoy life; others interpret it as a time of increasing inability to make commitments to relationship, location, or work life that is often marked by depression and hopelessness.[3]

Young adults also confront economic realities that limit their choices. Because older people stay in their jobs longer, fewer opportunities come open for entry into work that can grow in significance. For young people in rural and stressed urban areas, jobs that pay a living wage are practically nonexistent, particularly as employers jockey to avoid paying for health care. People of this generation know they will probably never have the economic opportunity or stability that their parents likely had; they are downwardly mobile. Most young adults worry about money.

A first year graduate student in psychology, Erika, shared with me four profiles of young adulthood based on her assessment of the trajectories of herself and her friends two years postcollege. Erika's typology captures what I too have heard from young pastors and others.

The first group of Erika's friends got jobs working for state or county public welfare agencies because they wanted to help people who did not have the advantages they had been given. They wanted to change the world. Her friend Dylan's experience was typical: He began as a caseworker for children in abusive homes. He quickly learned to recognize what was happening, assess needs, and create a plan of action. He also quickly learned that the rules, regulations, and systems of the bureaucracy made it extremely difficult to implement the plans fully or successfully. Within two years, he was burned out, looking for other work outside the helping professions. Dylan had no mentors in the system and no community of support, other than friends in the same dilemma. I hear lots of stories of people who pour themselves into a cause, see nothing change, and quit to get a job at a coffee shop.

Erika described her friend Kristen and Kristen's boyfriend, Jake, to present the second profile: People who cannot get off the merry-go-round. These are young adults who went to college, with their parents' explicit or implicit encouragement, to find out what they liked through a variety of classes and experiences. Once college ended, however, they had neither discovered a path for their lives nor gained any skills to help them do so. They now move from city to city and relationship to relationship to look for a place of belonging, but most often those in the second profile tend to move in and out of their parents' homes, start something and drop out, and become increasingly anxious and depressed under a carefree veneer.

The third profile in Erika's diagnostic portfolio is epitomized in Amelia's story. For as long as she could remember, Amelia wanted to be a lawyer. Her high school and college plans were all geared toward preparation for law school and positioning for admittance to a good school. She moved to Washington DC after graduation and worked for a year as an intern in a political think tank. She then got a job as a paralegal in a prestigious firm, planning to apply to law school while she was there. It only took three months for Amelia to realize: *I hate this. I do not want to work in a place like this. In fact, I don't even want to be a lawyer.* And now she is paralyzed. She has never developed any other interests or capacities. By her own admission, she does not even know who she is. Amelia is moving to the town where Erika lives to get some kind of job and start to figure out her life.

Finally, Erika described the profile that fits her: Through difficult childhood circumstances, Erika came to know at an early age that she had a responsibility for her own life and had learned to be resourceful, hardworking, and grateful. She looked for and found adult sponsors and supporters, and she paid attention to where in her life she felt most alive, what she had the potential to be really good at, and what the world might need—and be willing to pay for—that she could do. Other young adults who have a similar sense of purpose and selfhood talk about the role of parents in setting examples of integrity and giving back to the community, and often about the faith commitments that shape how they live.

Looking at the outer lives of young adults from theory and from experience, I wonder about what they are carrying around inside. Their parents and teachers have formed them to believe certain things about who they are, what they deserve, and what is expected of them. Everyone who studies young adults agrees that this generation has been raised to believe that they are special. They have been protected from failure and promoted to build up self-esteem. Social commentator David Brooks says they are a generation with closets full of trophies yet one that has never actually won anything.

But many young adults of conscience carry a burden that comes along with the specialness: They feel a lot of pressure to make the right decision, and they believe there is only one right decision. Inundated with vast amounts of information about what is wrong with the world, they feel a moral imperative to choose to do something that makes a difference. Often they believe that every decision they make is very important, so, of course, choosing what to do with their life is heavily freighted. Tim Clydesdale, a sociologist from the College of New Jersey who studies young adults two to five years postcollege, calls their plight the occupational equivalent of finding a soul mate.[4]

What Greenhouses of Hope Can Be

Congregations who nurture hope have gifts to offer young adults nearly paralyzed by the burdens of too many choices or not enough good choices; it is, in Evelyn Parker's phrase, indeed emancipatory hope. Scrutinizing the Greenhouses of Hope represented in this volume with the situation of young adults in mind, we find some clues about how congregations may develop their gifts, capacities, and practices to answer the call to emancipatory hope in action for young adults seeking vocation.

I earlier named the frequency with which the image of family surfaced in the self-descriptions given by people in the congregations; the word *community* also rang out with clarity and consistency. Community is theological language that connects the life of a particular congregation to God's covenant with the people of Israel, to Jesus and his friends traveling together, to the first Christians who shared everything in common, and to all those Christians practicing the way of Jesus Christ in particular places and times since then. This robust symbol as manifest in local, living bodies holds what is needed for young adults to move toward freedom from the fear of making a commitment and toward courage to pour out their lives in love—whether the social and environmental problems get solved or not.

From Sinai Chung's depiction of mozying at Choongsuh, we learn about mutuality in community—mutuality, not transaction; sibling love beyond mentoring; intimate connection not between individuals but between groups. The moziers invest significant time, both inside and outside of church, taking care of the moziees, talking about serious questions, studying the Bible, showing them how to live the Christian life. They enter into relationships without expecting any reward; yet, through the practice, both groups benefit. Moziees benefit from the close relationships with slightly older people who help them grow in faith. Moziers share a community with one another as shepherds, experience deep satisfaction and gratitude when they see the younger ones develop, and grow in faith themselves through their sacrifices for and attention to the moziees. For the young adults at Choongsuh, the inescapable burden is not to choose the right work but rather to love people; the unexpected fruit is finding oneself in a community of mutual blessing and ongoing transformation.

We see pictures of challenges to community in All Saints and St. John's churches and feel the pain of uninvited, unwelcome, and perhaps unhealed conflict. As Joyce Mercer points out, young people are watching, listening, and being shaped by what goes on in church, for better or worse. What do they see? One person—Pastor Brad or Father Henry—can make choices, for lots of good reasons, which cause conflict and hurt to people in the community. But, in these two examples of congregations, one person did not have the power to destroy the community. People come and people go, but the life of God is not shut down by their arrival and departure. For young adults overwrought with the significance of what they might do, making relative the power of one may be a gift.

In a similar way, First Afrikan's Sankofa community reminds us that the community existed before us and will go on after us and is the source of identity. Jeffery Tribble describes the community as enacting another world through worship, reinforced in practices outside of worship, by acknowledging the actions of the ancestors in the past and celebrating their presence now. When people enter into this other world, they learn who they are to be and what they are to do in the present day-to-day world outside the community. If the core of the question, What am I do with my life? is Who am I? then the practices of Africentric Christianity at First Afrikan provide a powerful beginning answer: Who you are is part of who we were before you were born and who we are now; what you do influences who we are becoming.

Emily, at FUMC-Evanston, holds community as core to Christianity itself. She says she has come to understand following Jesus to mean helping others and learning how to do this through Christian community. Her pastors are candid about their own practice of community as central to Christianity; that through one another, congregants learn the Christian way of life and young adults discover a map for their futures. They uncover resources beyond their own self-understandings that are reliable for finding a way forward, for creating a meaningful life.

Community in these Greenhouses of Hope—as mutuality, as resilient and durable, as a source of identity, as instructive—could offer the place of nourishment and the conditions for liveliness young adults rarely find in the environment of their culture.

Community in these Greenhouses of Hope—as mutuality, as resilient and durable, as a source of identity, as instructive—could offer the place of nourishment and the conditions for liveliness young adults rarely find in the environment of their culture.

What Greenhouses of Hope Can Do

The Calling Congregations team at The Fund for Theological Education suggests that four central practices undertaken within communities such as those described above help young adults—like those in Erika's profiles—discover and claim the vocations calling to them from the life and love of God. The VocationCARE approach rests on creating a certain kind of space, asking self-awakening questions, reflecting together theologically, and establishing opportunities to enact who you are called to be.

Creating space to listen to one's life is critical for vocational discernment, especially for hearing and responding to God's call to ministry. Frederick Buechner, in his essay "The Calling of Voices," says that it is at least as accurate to talk about a vocation choosing us as of us choosing a vocation, of a call being given and of us hearing or not hearing, listening or not listening, responding or not responding. And he cautions that the call is hard to hear:

> The danger is that there are so many voices, and they all in their ways
> sound so promising. The danger is that you will not listen to the voice
> that speaks to you through the seagull mounting the gray wind, say, or
> the vision in the temple, that you do not listen to the voice inside you

or to the voice that speaks from outside but specifically to you out of the specific events of your life, but that instead you listen to the great blaring, boring, banal voice of our mass culture, which threatens to deafen us all by blasting forth that the only thing that really matters about your work is how much it will get you in the way of salary and status.[5]

Buechner wrote this in 1969 while he was chaplain at an elite boarding school in the Northeast. The environment now is polluted with the effluviums of many more sophisticated and more persistent voices, endangering young people in 2010 beyond what Buechner could have imagined.

Christians have a long, rich tradition from which to draw practices for creating space. We often think of silence first. A priest at an Episcopal retreat center in Minnesota told me that a youth group came to visit and he invited them to practice silence. Reluctantly, they agreed. He led them in what seemed to them a long, long time of silence. As the group was leaving, one fourteen-year-old boy pulled on his sleeve. "Could I come back and do this again some time?" They had driven two hours to the center; silence had lasted eight minutes. In congregations where boys can pray unabashedly and teenagers can raise their hands in praise, the ground has been laid for trying new, perhaps initially odd, adventures in Christian practices for creating a different kind of space.

To create space for vulnerability in which the shy soul can speak, congregations are invited to enter into a covenant of presence through which members of the community agree to practice, attention, suspension of judgment in favor of wonder, generosity in hearing, kindness in speaking, and gentleness in attitude.[6] This covenant makes possible holy listening, a phrase that denotes listening to another wholly so that the speaker comes to know his or her own truth in its telling; the listener, as theologian Nelle Morton says, hears "me to my own story."[7]

Our own Greenhouses of Hope show us still other practices for creating space in which to hear God. In Margaret Ann Crain's rendering, the quality of the time spent by young people among the people living in poverty in West Virginia was palpable: they were in a time out of time, taken there by ground-touching connection to harsh realities and real people. At the risk of overstatement, the young people seemed to experience *kairos*. Isn't this what God moments point to? These moments of kairos—creating a different kind of space—feed Christians hope for God's dream of shalom.

But simply creating space does not provide ample nourishment for young adults who are longing for an alternative to the blaring, boring, banal voices of mass culture. Clydesdale confirms that the salient question for young adults is how to make a meaningful life. But, he wonders, without a faith tradition, where one can dig below the surface.[8] Without that, the quest for meaning becomes only a sentimental journey. Greenhouses of Hope must practice asking provocative questions—the *A* in VocationCARE represents asking self-awakening questions—that not only lead young adults more deeply into their own stories but also connect them to the stories of our faith: Scripture, the history of the church, the lives of the saints and the people around them.

Young people all over the world are mobilizing to take action for healing the planet, for housing the homeless, for educating the oppressed. We can see this as the work of the Holy Spirit loose in the world. Congregations join that movement in all kinds of ways, from Appalachian Service Projects to CROP walks and all manner of social justice action. Further, young adults today not only can pursue helping professions and not-for-profit leadership but also have an abundance of opportunities for salaried jobs in the burgeoning sector of social entrepreneurship, working for companies with the mission of solving social and environmental problems and contributing to the public good. These may all be good choices. But to find vocation, and to enter into intimacy with God, young adults deserve more than the chance to do good works. They deserve to connect their lives with the life of God. This is the purpose of the *R* in VocationCARE—reflecting theologically together—and in the congregational profiles here it appears mostly implicitly. Without opportunities for explicit theological reflection, young people might miss the sacred connection between their longing to serve and a long history of service inspired and sustained by the Christian story. Finding one's story reflected in God's story is powerful; learning to do so in community may be one of the most important gifts the church can offer young people today.[9]

Remember Ryan, burned-out by a system he can't change; Kristen and her boyfriend, Jake, who can't get off the merry-go-round; Amelia, who does not know herself; and Erika, trying to put together a life of integrity on her own? Imagine what it might mean for them to come into relationship with the salvific gifts given through Christian theology that liberate us from the tyranny of our own individualism. Consider what it would be like for them to discover the prayer prayed by Archbishop Oscar Romero at the funeral of martyred priests, which says in part:

> That is what we are about: We plant seeds that one day will grow. We water seeds already planted, knowing that they hold future promise.
>
> We lay foundations that will need further development. We provide yeast that produces effects beyond our capabilities.
>
> We cannot do everything, and there is a sense of liberation in realizing that. This enables us to do something, and to do it very well.
>
> It may be incomplete, but it is a beginning, a step along the way, an opportunity for God's grace to enter and do the rest.
>
> We may never see the end results, but that is the difference between the master builder and the worker.
>
> We are workers, not Master Builders, ministers, not Messiahs. We are prophets of a future not our own.[10]

Isn't this foundational truth—that we are prophets of a future not our own—the particular charism that congregations can offer to young adults who would seek to change the world?

Finally, as we consider the potential within Greenhouses of Hope to extend themselves to young adults of faith seeking to live meaningful lives, two specific examples of the *E*—enacting opportunities for ministry—in VocationCARE practices in congregations we have studied deserve to be underlined: the intern program at Isle of Hope and the role of pastor as attentive guide at First Congregational Church of Berkeley (FCCB). These practices engage young adults in ministry at critical moments of their own vocational development. But also, and of equal importance, they create mentoring communities of peers and older adults. That congregations can be mentoring communities is a gift of our faith practices; it makes the difference between an internship in any nonprofit and one in ministry.

Sharon Parks, a long-time astute and wise observer of young adults, strongly advocates such mentoring communities due to the absence within our culture of mediating structures to hold and support young adults as they navigate developmental tasks during the extended transition from adolescence to mature adulthood. Mentoring communities, Parks argues, should offer young adults recognition, challenge, support, and inspiration.[11]

Fred P. Edie tells us that Isle of Hope hosted five paid interns during the summer of his study. The interns were mentors and were mentored. They taught a senior high series to explore the question, What would it look like to follow God in your life?—a question they were also asking themselves. They were given the agency to create a space in which to ask self-awakening questions and to reflect theologically, and to do so in dialogue with peers and slightly younger people. The interns were not only trusted to lead the process of probing their own questions but were also given resources and support: past and present church members who were living out their callings and close, easy access to the more seasoned practitioners on the pastoral staff.

The mentors' investment of significant trust and responsibility proved to be as important as the actual experiences of doing ministry. One young man recalled his mentor's comment at the end of the summer, "I think this could be a calling for you," as a turning point in knowing that youth ministry is where he belongs "in this season of [my] life." The mentors both challenged and affirmed the interns, offering instruction, advice, practical wisdom, and windows into their character. Edie writes in chapter 5, "They also reflect upon the example these adults set when attempting to describe what motivates their own ministries or when struggling to describe the emerging trajectories of their life paths."

Shelly Dieterle at FCCB operates on a smaller scale and less formally than Isle of Hope. Because she is adjacent to a college campus in Berkeley, she has the opportunity to walk beside the younger adults in her congregation over the entire school year. Through the congregation's practices of hospitality, nurture, and interfaith action, young people with many different motivations and varying faith formation walk through their doors. Dieterle breaks bread with them, literally inviting them for dinner, listens to their lives, and makes a path to connect faith and service as a way into God's call. Coronado Morse names a process in which she felt led by her own longings and by Dieterle's care into work that fit her and led her to discover more of her own gifts and her place of belonging. It was an iterative process of recognition, challenge, support, and inspiration.

Where Are We Going?

About eight years ago, I was a part of a conversation in which an African American pastor from Northern California began talking about how his congregation involves young people in its life. He described many familiar practices. They had a cohort of ministers-in-training who studied and served. Every fifth Sunday was Youth Sunday where young people led worship. They had rites-of-passage programs, one for girls and one for boys. After a while he paused. He looked around the room and he said, "We do this for the greening of the church. We've got to green the church."

We know that in many denominations and many places in this country, demographics and economics are forcing change in church structure and raising significant questions about how congregations will operate going forward. We also know that most young adults are not part of congregational life; most do not engage in religious practice at all. Those who are in church are not interested in business as usual. They want change.

Greening of the church puts me in the mind of how the whole neighborhood looked different after rain broke the drought last summer. Greening of the church might be the change we thirst for. Might it happen now as the young people raised in the congregations here, and in hundreds of other congregations not visible in this collection, come of age? Where will the young adults, pastors, and laypeople together, lead their congregations? What is God doing with the church?

Jürgen Moltmann, a German Protestant theologian, wrestles with this question. Moltmann became a Christian while a prisoner of war during World War II as he read a Bible given him by an American chaplain. He spent his academic career as a professor of theology at the University in Tübingen where one of his colleagues was then-Cardinal Ratzinger, now Pope Benedict XVI. Steeped in tremendous knowledge and expertise, he nevertheless begins to answer the question of what God is doing with the church through a kind of ethnographic study of his own home congregation, St. Jakob's, in an old section of Tübingen, Germany.[12]

Moltmann begins by looking back as he seeks to move forward. In the sixteenth century, the government in power established St. Jakob's as a regional Protestant parish church. For hundreds of years, people simply belonged to the church where they lived; they did not choose a church to join. Their theology was the theology of the ruler of their region. The church was present in the minds of people only at key life events. The church was for taking care of people; it was not a church in which the people participated or took care of one another.

In 1934 "so-called German Christians," as Moltmann calls them, occupied the regional churches to resist the Nazi Party, and they organized themselves as the Confessing Church. Congregations joined councils as alternatives to the dictatorship of the State, and congregations became voluntary communities that took care of vicars and pastors by themselves rather than institutions supported by the state. For the first time, Protestant Christians created their own constitution separate from the state. By their very existence, Moltmann claims, these independent and resisting congregations were signs of the church's future.

When Moltmann came to St Jakob's in old Tubingen, attendance on Sunday morning was only twenty people. When a new priest came, they made a decision to become an inviting community. They agreed on three regulations for the life of their congregation:

1. Every person is an expert on his or her life, talents, and gifts.
2. What doesn't go simply doesn't go.
3. What we can't do regularly we should not try, and when we try the first step we must also go the second step.

St. Jakob's had become a missionary church—reaching out and opening its arms to all comers. It now has many members. Almost all are between the ages of twenty and forty-five. Moltmann, in his eighties, is the oldest member. The secret of this congregation, according to Moltmann, is community, and the secret of community lies in more than twenty house circles where people know one another and are known. Now, worship is not for the people, it is by the people. They present themselves and what they are doing or what they need in the worship. In all they do, they trust in the gifts of each member rather than orienting themselves to the tasks that should be done or limiting themselves by saying what they cannot do.

The greening of St. Jakob's began with a charismatic pastor, but its life is not dependent on him: what is not done by the members themselves is not done at all. When the pastor retired, the congregation carried on and the worship services were as packed as ever. In sum, Moltmann says, we live in exciting times. Old forms of the church are fading away and new things are coming to life. The new things emerge from below, he says, where people stand up and say, *we are the church.*

Forming Communities of Radical Inclusion

I quoted a young woman in the epigraph for this chapter: "God now calls the next generation of church leaders to grow the germinating seed of idealism by advocating the formation of radically inclusive communities." She is a first-year seminary student preparing to be a pastor, and she wrote this sentence as part of an essay responding to the question, How do your gifts fit into what God is calling the church to be and do at this time and place? It is a hard question, but an important one for young adults discerning a call to ministry. I remember a conversation with a young adult who had spent a volunteer year of service with a faith-based organization at the U.S.-Mexico border. The experience birthed in her a passion for working with immigrants. She was agonizing over whether to go to law school and be an advocate for immigrants within the legal system or to go to seminary and become a pastor who helped immigrants by building up the body of Christ, the church. Was she called to pour her life out for immigrants or to pour her life out in equipping the saints to minister to all kinds of strangers and immigrants, the weak and wounded, the blind, the lame, and the poor in spirit?

The young pastor quoted above and the one in the borderlands were most likely raised in Greenhouses of Hope. Among a random sample of students entering seminaries who received Fund for Theological Education fellowships in recognition of their exceptional capacities for ministry, 100 percent indicated that they participated in church as children. It does matter for the future of the church that congregations are Greenhouses of Hope. The vision for what that church is becoming and where young pastors are called to lead it is beautiful.

This young woman speaks of growing the germinating seed of idealism. Looking at young adults, we can see idealism in action. Barack Obama's presidential campaign slogan—"Yes, we can! *Si se puente!*"—galvanized a generation thought to be lost to politics. The young people who came alive for a cause of hope are now spread

across countless organizations working for the common good. Teach
For America draws thousands more applicants than can possibly be
placed to serve in the neediest, most desperate schools in America;
more than 60 percent of Teach For America alumni continue in the
educational system to work for systemic change that will lead to
schools where every child can learn. By the year 2014, an estimated
two hundred fifty thousand young people will have participated in
a voluntary year of service through AmeriCorps, VISTA, and hundreds of other placements. What are the germinating seeds of idealism in your community? In your congregation?

Our seminarian also calls for advocating the formation of radically inclusive communities. For many middle-class people in mainline churches, the phrase "radically inclusive communities" evokes
an image of congregations in which not all members are of the same
race, ethnicity, social class, able-bodiedness, education, income, or,
perhaps, sexual orientation. That is certainly a different picture than
we see in most congregations. However, radical inclusion bespeaks
something more.

The pastor of a congregation in the state of Washington who is
developing the doctrine and practices of vocation in the congregation he leads recently wrote, "For the people in their 20s and 30s
in our congregation, the language of vocation is a 'language of acceptance' of them and their condition, their questions, their suspicion of overchurched agendas that are not curious about their lives."
Radical inclusion means that everyone is not only accepted as he or
she is but also that we are the experts of our own lives, our individual
callings, and the energies and experiences we can contribute to the
community. However, radical inclusion in this fundamental sense—
that each person must include him- or herself in the community
and has the authority to claim and bring his or her own gifts into
life together—does not belie the unity of the church. The unity of
the church lies in the one divine Spirit that gives rise to this amazing multiplicity of diverse gifts, desires, and stories. In this Spirit, in
what Moltmann calls the nonhierarchical community of friends, we

are bound together by mutual love and mutual respect in the power of the Holy Spirit. What practices will enact this radical inclusion?

Further, as young leaders advocate the formation of communities of radical inclusion, we should not be surprised that the power of denominations as sources of identity will continue to wane. This is the movement of radical inclusion: We are members of the church of Jesus Christ, not members of St. Jakob's parish. We are not counted as a visitor if we attend worship in a different denomination, and we are not guests at the Eucharist of another. Radical inclusion? The importance of difference between Christians recedes even as the need to commit to community with a particular people over time and circumstance becomes more significant.

Trying to envision a community of radical inclusion, I remember the young man in row 11 of the inbound flight to Austin. He was tall and skinny like young men can be, with gray eyes, wavy sandy hair, and freckles enough to keep him boyish for years to come. I felt in him something vulnerable and yet awkwardly strong and wild, like an unborn colt stretching, kicking, and dying to be born, even as his posture conveyed the studied cool demeanor of someone made sophisticated before his time. I couldn't call which way he would go. He had a lot of privilege, but that seemed part of what would keep him from becoming fully alive. I think he wanted to be part of a community so radically inclusive that it could make room for even him and give him the permission to be free to include others. The odds were against him. The last question he asked me was whether I knew the best way from the airport to the Ritz Carlton—an icon of radical exclusion.

> The way of Jesus Christ is the way down . . . deeply into the heart of God and closer to the neighbor. But no one can follow this call alone. Each of the young people whose lives we have glimpsed moving in the life of the Spirit has been graced with companions.

The way of Jesus Christ is the way down, away from the Ritz Carlton and toward the poor and the poor in spirit, deeply into the heart of God and closer to the neighbor. But no one can follow this call alone. Each of the young people whose lives we have glimpsed moving in the life of the Spirit has been graced with companions. As we stepped out of row 11, I could have given the young man seeking his guru some answers from Christian faith and walked away never to see him again. That is not what he was looking for. If the words cannot take root, be watered, and grow in the soil of a community, in authentic relationship, they are like clanging cymbals. And relationships of love take time, attention, and risk. They are sometimes hard and often they fail. Yet love known through relationships is the signature gift of life found in Greenhouses of Hope, and the ground of growth into vocation. Jesus told us so in Matthew 13:3–8, the parable of the seeds scattered: some are eaten by birds; some fall on rocky ground; only a few fall on good soil, but there they bear fruit and multiply. The soil holds the gift of life's growth. God's blessing of the world—of young adults—through the people of God "starts small, grows silently, faces setbacks, but nevertheless permeates the world with love."[13]

Notes

INTRODUCTION

1.　Elizabeth O'Connor, *Cry Pain, Cry Hope: Thresholds to Purpose* (Waco, TX: Word Books, 1987), 14.

2.　The Calling Congregations Initiative of The Fund for Theological Education (FTE) sponsored the research for this book. Calling Congregations works to support the next generation of excellent and diverse young leaders for the church by helping congregations notice, name, and nurture the vocations of youth and young adults. See www.fteleaders.org.

3.　Unless otherwise noted, quotations from youth and adult members of the congregation come from interviews or field notes. Some of the authors use pseudonyms for the people they interviewed or the churches they studied. All interviewees gave written permission to take part in the research and be quoted in this book.

4.　Mary Clark Moschella, *Ethnography as a Pastoral Practice: An Introduction* (Cleveland: Pilgrim Press, 2008), 4.

5.　The phrase "good enough home" is adapted from psychologist D. W. Winnicott's phrase "good enough mothering" and is used to describe a church that is not perfect, but provides a stable enough environment to enable the growth and development of its members over time and life circumstances. I am grateful to Melissa Wiginton for the use of this phrase in her work with Calling Congregations.

CHAPTER 1: GREENHOUSES OF HOPE

1.　Shane Claiborne, interview by Krista Tippett, "A Monastic Revolution," *Speaking of Faith,* American Public Radio, July 1, 2010, http://speakingoffaith. publicradio.org/programs/2010/monastic-revolution/. The phrase "We reclaim abandoned spaces" is recast as "Relocation to the abandoned places of Empire" and listed as the first of twelve marks of a new monasticism in The Rutba House, ed., *School(s) for Conversion: 12 Marks of a New Monasticism* (Eugene, OR; Cascade Books, 2005), xii.

2.   You can see photographs at the Lynchburg Grows website, www.lynch-burggrows.org.

3.   See Dori Baker and Joyce A. Mercer, *Lives to Offer: Accompanying Youth on Their Vocational Quests* (Cleveland: Pilgrim Press, 2007) for a fuller description of this idea.

4.   Numerous scholars have attempted to define vocation. See FTE Calling Congregations, "Vocation Care Curriculum: Glossary of Terms," http://bit.ly/vocare-glossary.

5.   Learn more at Broad Street Ministry website, www.broadstreetministry.org and Mount Vernon Place United Methodist Church website, www.mvpumc.org.

6.   See Tony Jones, *The New Christians: Dispatches from the Emergent Frontier* (San Francisco: Jossey-Bass, 2008), xix. The Emergent Church refers to a varied and widespread reform is birthing new churches—outside denominational structures—during the last two decades. Many mainline denominations have joined the conversation and are attempting to incorporate learnings from the Emergent Church into their new church growth and development. Tony Jones makes a helpful distinction. The proper noun *Emergent* refers specifically to a relational network of church leaders that formed in 1997 and is associated with a network called Emergent Village. When not used as a proper noun, the word *emergent* refers more broadly to new forms of Christianity arising from the American church of the twentieth century, including those emerging within established denominations that are the focus of this book.

7.   Tony Jones (keynote lecture at "The Blaze: A Formative Gathering for Youth Leaders," Montreat Conference Center, Montreat, North Carolina, January 8, 2010). In this lecture, Jones says that the structure of denominational churches mitigates against entrepreneurialism in young people. Jones empathizes with "cultural creatives"—leading-edge Christians who feel called by God to begin professional ministry—who would skip the traditional three-year seminary education and accompanying ordination requirements of many mainline denominations, choosing instead the quicker route of beginning a nondenominational ministry.

8.   See Phyllis Tickle, *The Great Emergence: How Christianity Is Changing and Why* (Grand Rapids: Baker Books, 2008).

9.   Barbara Kingsolver, "How to Be Hopeful" (commencement address, Duke University, Durham, NC, 2008), http://news.duke.edu/2008/05/kingsolver.html.

10.   Evelyn L. Parker, *Trouble Don't Last Always: Emancipatory Hope among African American Adolescents* (Cleveland: Pilgrim Press, 2003), 3–4.

11.   Ibid., 16 (emphasis added). In a later essay, Parker includes gender oppression as part of that against which emancipatory hope is activated. See Evelyn

Parker, "Emancipatory Hope Reloaded," a paper presented to the Religious Education Association, November 2009.

12. Parker, *Trouble Don't Last Always*, 15–16.

13. Ibid., 14.

14. Ibid., 17.

15. Ibid., 17, quoting James Cone, *God of the Oppressed*, rev. ed. (Maryknoll, NY: Orbis Books, 1997), 129.

16. Parker, "Emancipatory Hope Reloaded," 19. Her language here is reminiscent of liberation theologian Nancy Bedford who writes of "small acts against destructiveness" as an appropriate response to the failure of some monumental movements to achieve justice in one's lifetime.

17. Walter Brueggemann, *Hope for the World: Mission in a Global Context* (Louisville, KY: Westminster John Knox Press, 2001), 17 (emphasis added).

18. Walter Brueggemann, "The City in the Biblical Perspective: Failed and Possible," *Word & World* 19, no. 3 (Summer 1999): 243 (emphasis added).

19. Ibid.

20. Brueggemann, *Hope for the World*, 19.

21. Kingsolver, "How to Be Hopeful."

22. In fact, one of the churches in this book, First United Methodist Church of Evanston, Illinois, nurtured a young woman by the name of Francis Willard, who helped form the Women's Christian Temperance Union (WCTU) in the late nineteenth century. At first focused solely on the link between poverty and intemperance, the WCTU later widened its reform agenda to provide primary mobilization and leadership for the women's suffrage movement. See Carolyn DeSwarte Gifford, "Nineteenth and Twentieth-Century Protestant Reform Movements in the United States," *Encyclopedia of Women and Religion in North America,* ed. Rosemary Skinner Keller and Rosemary Radford Ruether (Bloomington, IN: Indiana University Press, 2006), 1029.

23. Christian Smith, with Melinda Lundquist Denton, *Soul Searching: The Religious and Spiritual Lives of American Teenagers* (New York: Oxford University Press, 2005), and Christian Smith, with Patricia Snell, *Souls in Transition: The Religious and Spiritual Lives of Emerging Adults* (New York: Oxford University Press, 2009).

24. Kenda Creasy Dean, "After Youth Group," *The Christian Century*, February 9, 2010, www.christiancentury.org.

25. Ethnography is a form of qualitative research that uses postmodern sensibilities to attempt to tell one version of reality amid many competing and often conflicting versions. Qualitative research differs from quantitative research in many significant ways. For a good summary of the differences, see Norman K. Denzin and Yvonna S. Lincoln, *Strategies of Qualitative Inquiry*, 3rd ed. (Thousand Oaks, CA: Sage Publications, 2008), 14–16.

26. S. Steve Kang, "Reflections upon Methodology: Research on Themes of Self Construction and Self Integration in the Narrative of Second Generation Korean American Young Adults," *Religious Education* 96, no. 3 (Summer 2001).

27.   Because of deeply embedded scholarly traditions that privileged quanti-tative research over qualitative methods, scholars at first had to rationalize methods that varied from the norm of the unbiased observer. With the dawn of postmo-dernity and its accompanying ideas, such as more widespread acceptance of mul-tiple views of reality, ethnography has been more resoundingly embraced and is, therefore, coming to be more freely adapted to wider purposes. See Margaret Ann Crain and Jack L. Seymour, "The Ethnographer as Minister: Ethnographic Re-search in Ministry," *Religious Education* 91, no. 3 (Summer 1996): 312; Mary Clark Moschella, *Ethnography as a Pastoral Practice: An Introduction* (Cleveland: Pilgrim Press, 2008); and Thomas Edward Frank, *The Soul of the Congregation: An Invitation to Congregational Reflection* (Nashville: Abingdon, 2000).

28.   Frank, *Soul of a Congregation*, 36, 65.

29.   Ibid., 24, 177.

30.   Ibid., 55.

31.   Dorothy C. Bass, "Ways of Life Abundant," in *For Life Abundant: Practi-cal Theology, Theological Education, and Christian Ministry*, ed. Dorothy C. Bass and Craig Dykstra (Grand Rapids: William B. Eerdmans, 2008), 29.

32.   For a more in-depth description of these practices and information about becoming a VocationCARE congregation, go to www.fteleaders.org/pages/calling-congregations. See also Dori Baker, *Kick Off Your Flip Flops: A Barefoot Guide to Finding Our Purpose* (Westminster John Knox Press, forthcoming July 2011) for a guide that can be used by congregations, campus ministries, and individuals on the particular practice of reflecting theologically on self and community.

33.   Frank, *Soul of a Congregation*, 73.

34.   These definitions come from working documents of the VocationCARE approach.

35.   Patricia O'Connell Killen and John De Beer, *The Art of Theological Re-flection* (New York, Crossroad, 1997), viii.

CHAPTER 2: STAYING AWAKE

1.   Patricia O'Connell Killen and John De Beer, *The Art of Theological Re-flection* (New York: Crossroad, 1997), 2.

2.   Killen and De Beer, *Art of Theological Reflection*.

3.   Thomas Edward Frank, *The Soul of the Congregation: An Invitation to Congregational Reflection* (Nashville: Abingdon, 2000).

4.   Mark Chaves, Shawna Anderson, and Jason Byassee, "American Congre-gations at the Beginning of the 21st Century: A Report from the National Con-gregations Study" (Durham, NC: Duke University, 2009), 9; www.soc.duke.edu/natcont/docs/NCS11_report_final.pdf (accessed August 13, 2010).

5.   Carolyn DeSwarte Gifford, "Nineteenth- and Twentieth-Century Prot-estant Social Reform Movements in the United States," in *Encyclopedia of Women*

and Religion in North America, eds. Rosemary Skinner Keller and Rosemary Radford Ruether (Bloomington, IN: Indiana University Press, 2006), 1029.

6. Christian Smith, with Patricia Snell, *Souls in Transition: The Religious and Spiritual Lives of Emerging Adults* (New York: Oxford University Press, 2009), 254.

7. G. Alan Smith, "Because You Are God's Chosen Ones" (Carol Stream, IL: Hope Publishing, 1978).

8. Brian Wren, "Carry the Flame" (Carol Stream, IL: Hope Publishing, 2003).

9. Fanny Crosby, "Blessed Assurance," *The United Methodist Hymnal,* (Nashville: The United Methodist Publishing House, 1989), 369.

10. Frank, *Soul of a Congregation,* 99.

CHAPTER 3: MOZYING

1. Parker J. Palmer, *The Promise of Paradox: A Celebration of Contradictions in Christian Life* (Notre Dame, IN: Ave Maria Press, 1980), 74.

2. *Choongsuh* is a pseudonym for this church, whose members preferred to remain anonymous and whose names, likewise, appear as pseudonyms.

3. After the Immigration and Nationality Act of 1965, a large number of Koreans began to immigrate to the United States. The number of Korean immigrants continued to increase throughout 1970s and reached its peak in the mid-1980s. From the end of 1980s to the present, this number has gradually declined. U.S. Department of Homeland Security, *Yearbook of Immigration Statistics: 2008* (Washington, DC: U.S. Department of Homeland Security, Office of Immigration Statistics, 2009), 11–15, table 2.

4. I use the term *second generation* interchangeably with the term *offspring of the first generation. Second generation* refers to both American-born and foreign-born children of the first generation and encompasses those who are in fact the third generation.

5. I borrowed this phrase from the core ministerial motto of the Choongsuh congregation.

6. Korean Christians believe that their spiritual traditions can be expressed as enthusiastic faith, passionate prayer, strong commitment to Christian living, and active involvement in congregational life.

7. In the first two stages of second-generation ministry, parents and their offspring create memories together in the same church; parents support the faith education of their offspring more directly and intimately and witness the process of spiritual growth of their offspring. In the third stage, a congregation splits into two and adult children become independent with the blessing of their parents. Members from an English-speaking congregation and its mother congregation

experience a blessed mutual reciprocity. For example, an English-speaking congregation provides English-speaking teachers for the educational ministries of its mother church (usually the mother churches need educational ministries for children because those churches still include children of the first-generation members). The mother church supports the English-speaking congregation financially or with ministerial and administrative wisdom.

8.   Consequently, Korean American churches have had other types of ministers. Some churches tried first-generation Korean American pastors and educators, meaning principally immigrant pastors and first-generation seminary students who had come to the United States as foreign students. But due to language and cultural gaps, that tactic has not been ministerially and educationally successful. On the other hand, some of the Korean American churches that were open to cultural interaction tried Caucasian pastors who were willing to serve ethnic youngsters and who were sensitive to the value of cross-cultural Christian education. But due to complex culture and language gaps, this has also not always been successful.

9.   Furthermore, not all of the second-generation pastors are willing to serve Korean American congregations. Such pastors often want to work with multiethnic or mostly white membership churches for various reasons, including that they tend to receive more financial support and participate in a better pension system.

10.   Stephen Warner points out, "Typical patterns pertain to Korean American congregations across denominational traditions and across regions in the United States. Korean American congregations are overwhelmingly conservative or 'evangelical' in their theology." Stephen Warner and K. C. Kim, eds., *Korean Americans and Their Religions: Pilgrims and Missionaries from a Different Shore* (University Park, PA: The Penn State University Press, 2001), 44.

11.   The interview with Peter was done in Korean, and I translated our conversation from Korean into English. In translating, I tried to use an oral language style for conveying his vivid and everyday language.

12.   There is great diversity in the way these young leaders answered their vocational calls. The twelve young leaders include: an ordained senior pastor of a second-generation Korean American congregation; an ordained English-language ministry pastor of a Korean church; an ordained minister who is studying at a seminary pursuing an advanced degree; an ordained minister who was an associate pastor of a second-generation Korean American church and now is a missionary to Lebanon; a college pastor of a Korean American church; a worship leader of a multiethnic congregation who is being trained to be a missionary to China by a missionary organization; a chaplain/author, who is also on the administrative staff and athletic director at a Christian high school; a youth pastor of a Korean American church; a youth pastor of a Korean American church who served five years at one place and is currently working at a multiethnic congregation; two missionaries to China; and a missionary to the Philippines.

13.   The Choongsuh youth group had two additional practices that were unique. Although they were once vigorously carried out, these practices, unfortu-

nately, no longer continue. One was reconciliation and the other spiritual shalom. Forgiving and seeking forgiveness from one another strengthened the unity and relationships among youth members. Dave recalls:

> We did this about once a month or something like that. We kids always fight and argue and say things like "I don't like you because you did such and such." In that youth group setting, the youth pastor would call us up one by one, with me standing next to him, and he would make everybody close their eyes. And he would say, "If Dave has offended you or if you have offended Dave and there needs to be forgiveness, raise your hands." So then all these kids would start to raise their hands. And the pastor would say, "Go and make things right." He made us go and pray with each person we had wronged and say, "I am sorry I offended you" and all that kind of stuff. That was amazing. Once a month or if the youth pastor felt that there was a conflict . . . not even that but just whenever relationships needed to be restored, we would do this. And so we would go pray with each other. For example, I might say, "Jane, I am sorry last week I said something really mean about you, and so before God and you I apologize." Sometimes it was like that, but other times somebody might raise their hand and I would wonder, "Why are they raising their hands?" But I would go to them, and they would say something like, "You really offended me when you said this," and I would say, "Oh, I am really sorry to have done that." There was that unity. When I think about our youth group, I think about that unity a lot.

The practice of spiritual shalom is also a unique tradition in the Choong-suh youth group. Members ask about one another's spiritual well-being and share prayer requests. The youth members have experienced spiritual connection with one another through this practice of caring about one another's innermost being. They have done this as a way of really taking care of each other's spiritual shalom, not as a cliché. In addition, through this practice they were able to unite the spiritual and mundane spheres of life. Timothy explains, "It was very normal for two of us students to talk about how we were doing spiritually. . . . Usually we talked about how we were doing with God. It's definitely less common in other youth groups. That was a great thing to share prayer requests at any time and any place and not just in church."

14.   In Korea, an older sister is called "Unni" by her younger sisters and "Nuna" by her younger brothers. An older brother is called "Obba" by his younger sisters and "Hyoung" by his younger brothers. Younger siblings are called by their names or addressed as "Donsaeng(s)."

15.   These college students are those who have practiced mozying within youth groups as mentors, leaders, and teachers of the youth.

16.   Besides the three, I heard about many other methods, such as discipling, challenging, teaching, Bible study leading, and advising.

17. Sharon Parks, *Big Questions, Worthy Dreams: Mentoring Young Adults in Their Search for Meaning, Purpose, and Faith* (San Francisco: Jossey-Bass, 2000), 127.

18. Ibid.

19. Ibid.

20. Confucius, *The Analects*, trans. Simon Leys (Filiquarian, 2006), 5. In this book, sibling love is translated as "brotherly duties," "fraternal submission," or "all brothers are friends."

21. Thomas Edward Frank, *The Soul of the Congregation: An Invitation to Congregational Reflection* (Nashville: Abingdon, 2000).

CHAPTER 4: LIVING TOGETHER

1. Douglas John Hall, *Why Christian? For Those on the Edge of Faith* (Minneapolis: Augsburg Fortress, 1998), 34.

2. Judith A. Berling, *Understanding Other Religious Worlds: A Guide for Interreligious Education* (Maryknoll, NY: Orbis, 2004), 3.

3. Dorothy Bass, ed., *On Our Way: Christian Practices for Living a Whole Life* (Nashville: Upper Room Books, 2010), 149.

4. Maya Soifer, "Beyond Convivencia: Critical Reflections on the Historiography of Interfaith Relations in Christian Spain," *Journal of Medieval Iberian Studies* 1, no. 1 (January 2009): 3. Contemporary historiographers differ on their assessment of the convivencia, arguing that it conjures a romantic picture of interreligious harmony that is more accurately depicted by neutral terms such as *diffusion, borrowing*, and *adaptation*. For the purposes of this chapter, we adopt a revised view of the convivencia that does not imply total harmony but acknowledges that the existence of conflict and violence did not preclude the flourishing of an intercultural society that tolerated mutual expressions of respect, solidarity, and collaboration.

5. Walter Brueggemann, *Hope for the World: Mission in a Global Context* (Louisville, KY: Westminster John Knox Press, 2001), 16.

6. See Eboo Patel, *Acts of Faith: The Story of an American Muslim, the Struggle for the Soul of a Generation* (Boston: Beacon Press, 2007) and the Interfaith Youth Core website at www.ifyc.org. This organization provides training and community organizing for young people around issues of interfaith action.

7. Two programs do this with great intentionality. One is the Interfaith Youth Initiative in Boston, a year-round interfaith peacemaker training program for youth and young adults. The other is Youth Theological Initiative at Candler School of Theology, a summer-intensive program for youth that focuses on Christian theology but also explicitly engages faith in a world of pluralism.

8. Pseudonyms are used for people who appear by first name only. All other people have given permission for their names to be used.

9. Stephanie Spellers, *Radical Welcome: Embracing God, the Other, and the Spirit of Transformation* (New York: Church Publishing, 2006).

10. Phyllis Tickle, *The Great Emergence: How Christianity Is Changing and Why* (Grand Rapids: Baker Books, 2008).

11. Notice, Name, Nurture: A Season of Vocation Care. See www.fteleaders. org.

12. For more information on this growing movement, go to the Axis of Friendship website, http://www.axisoffriendship.org/members.php.

13. Derek Tidball, "The Pilgrim and the Tourist: Zygmunt Bauman and Postmodern Identity," in *Explorations in a Christian Theology of Pilgrimage*, ed. Craig G. Bartholomew and Fred Hughes (Aldershot, UK: Ashgate, 2004).

14. Walter Brueggemann, *Interpretation and Obedience: From Faithful Reading to Faithful Living* (Minneapolis: Augsburg Fortress, 1991), 41–44.

15. Miroslav Volf, *Exclusion and Embrace: A Theological Exploration of Identity, Otherness, and Reconciliation* (Nashville: Abingdon Press, 1996), 74–76.

16. Ibid., 66.

17. Spellers, 17.

18. Volf, *Exclusion and Embrace*, 140–45, quoted in Spellers, *Radical Welcome*, 13.

19. Craig Dykstra and Dorothy Bass, "A Theological Understanding of Christian Practices," in *Practicing Theology: Belief and Practices in Christian Life*, ed. Miroslav Wolf and Dorothy C. Bass (Grand Rapids: Eerdmans, 2002), 21.

20. Ibid., 24.

21. A compelling example of this kind of text study is provided in W. Eugene March, *The Wide, Wide Circle of Divine Love: A Biblical Case for Religious Diversity* (Louisville: Westminster John Knox, 2005). See particularly the chapter entitled "God's Way Made Particular" in which author W. Eugene March persuasively argues that Jesus's words as recorded in John 14:6 ("I am the way, and the truth, and the life. No one comes to the Father except through me") when interpreted in context do not support an exclusivist Christian theology.

22. Fatemeh Keshavarz, "The Ecstatic Faith of Rumi," interview by Krista Tippett, *Speaking of Faith*, April 23, 2009. Available at speakingoffaith.publicradio.org/programs/2009/rumi/ (accessed June 4, 2010).

23. Thomas Edward Frank, *The Soul of the Congregation: An Invitation to Congregational Reflection* (Nashville: Abingdon, 2000), 151.

CHAPTER 5: CONVERGING STREAMS

1. N. Gordon Cosby, "Trust the Stream" (sermon, June 11, 1989), available at Inward/Outward: A Project of the Church of the Saviour, www.inwardoutward.org/2010/03/06/trust-stream (accessed June 4, 2010).

2. All names in this chapter are pseudonyms except the name of the bus and the names of current staff members.

3. Thomas Edward Frank, *The Soul of a Congregation: An Invitation to Congregational Reflection* (Nashville: Abingdon, 2000), 65.

CHAPTER 6: EMBODYING *SANKOFA*

1.   Cornel West, "The Vocation of the Black Christian Intellectual" (paper presented at Union Theological Seminary and Presbyterian School of Christian Education, Richmond, VA, April 23, 2008).

2.   First Afrikan Presbyterian Church (USA) came to my awareness through conversations with Matthew Williams, Associate Director of Fellowships for the Fund for Theological Education. Matthew is a member of this congregation. Portions of a sermon he delivered during my research year appear later in this chapter.

3.   Jeremiah Wright is the retired pastor of Trinity United Church of Christ in Chicago, a church with a long-standing tradition of mentoring young people who pursue pastoral ministry and other vocations of service to the church, community, and world.

4.   Nancy T. Ammerman, "Culture and Identity in the Congregation," in *Studying Congregations*, ed. Nancy T. Ammerman, Jackson W. Carroll, Carl S. Dudley, and William McKinney (Nashville: Abingdon Press, 1998), 78–104.

5.   "Sweet Chariot: The Story of the Spirituals," The Spirituals Project, University of Denver, Center for Teaching and Learning, 2004, http://ctl.du.edu/spirituals/Literature/sankofa.cfm (accessed August 27, 2009).

6.   Dorothy C. Bass, "Ways of Life Abundant," in *For Life Abundant: Practical Theology, Theological Education, and Christian Ministry*, ed. Dorothy C. Bass and Craig Dykstra (Grand Rapids: William B. Eerdmans, 2008), 29.

7.   Ndugu T'Ofori-Atta, discussion with author, July 28, 2009. T'Ofori-Atta is Professor Emeritus of Church and Society and Founder of Religious Heritage of the African World at Interdenominational Theological Center, Atlanta, GA.

8.   Mark Lomax, "Passing the Mantle" (sermon, First Afrikan Church, Lithonia, GA, May 27, 2009), emphasis added.

9.   Mark Ogunwale Keita Lomax, *First Afrikan Church Worship Manual, 2005–2006* (unpublished), 46.

10.   Mark Lomax, discussion with author, November 30, 2009.

11.   Matthew Williams, discussion with author, February 24, 2009.

12.   *First Afrikan Church Worship Manual*, 12–13.

13.   Mark Lomax, *Akwabaa (Means Welcome in Yoruba, a West African Language) to First Afrikan Church*, 8.

14.   I confess that I didn't know this song. Thankfully, my young-adult son, who is an insider to the hip-hop culture, translated for me. He describes this as one of the hip-hop classics.

15.   Mark Chaves, *Congregations in America* (Cambridge, MA: Harvard University Press, 2004), 8.

16.   Jackson W. Carroll, *God's Potters: Pastoral Leadership and the Shaping of Congregations* (Grand Rapids: William B. Eerdmans, 2006), 25–26.

17.   Ibid., 26.

18. Itihari Toure, "The Way Forward: Next Steps to Getting Ready to Do a Good Work" (draft of paper for leadership education and New Officers-Elect Training, First Afrikan Church, Lithonia, GA, Saturday April 4, 2009), 2.

19. For more about Destiny, Sound Sculptress, see http://www.harpist-fromthehood.com.

20. Amenti Alare Sujai and Daniel T. Hembree, *You Are the Jewel in the Stone: A Narrative Resource for Vocational Reflections and Theological Exploration* (Orangeburg, SC: The Center for Vocational Reflection at Claflin University, 2006).

21. Cornel West, *Race Matters* (New York: Vintage Books, 1994), 56.

22. Thomas Edward Frank, *The Soul of the Congregation: An Invitation to Congregational Reflection* (Nashville: Abingdon, 2000), 73.

CHAPTER 7: CALLING AMID CONFLICT

1. Thomas Edward Frank, *The Soul of the Congregation, An Invitation to Congregational Reflection* (Nashville: Abingdon, 2000), 174.

2. In this research, the names of individuals and certain other identifying information has been altered in order to preserve the anonymity of people in the congregations. While St. John's Lutheran Church has given permission for me to identify their congregation and minister by name, other names from these two churches are pseudonymous. All Saints is a pseudonym for the actual Episcopal congregation participating in my study. I appreciate the willingness of all three faith communities, including Clarendon Presbyterian Church about which I do not report here, in partnering with me in this research.

3. My research in this larger project was supported by a grant from the Louisville Institute, whose support I gratefully acknowledge. Andrea Green and Mary Thorpe provided excellent help as research assistants in this project.

4. This paragraph only hints at what was a very complex and politically charged situation that space limitations prevent me from detailing here, but which I will address in a book-length discussion of church conflict, which is forthcoming.

5. *Rostered* is the technical term used by the ELCA to specify pastors who are in good standing and in position to be appointed to pastorates. The ELCA's rules for rostered clergy are spelled out in a document called "Definitions and Guidelines for Discipline of Ordained Ministers."

6. Again, this story is much richer and more complex than can be told in the space of the present chapter. St. John's created a video to tell their story: *In a Time of Trial: The Story of Pastor Bradley Schmeling and St. John's Lutheran Church*, DVD, written by D. Mikkelson (Atlanta: C. Reveille & E. Pictures, St. John's Lutheran Church, 2008).

7. *Practicing Our Faith: A Way of Life for a Searching People* (San Francisco: Jossey-Bass, 1997), xi.

8.   Ibid., 5.
9.   *In a Time of Trial.*
10. Frank, *Soul of a Congregation*, 54.

CONCLUSION

1.   See Robin Marantz Henig, "What Is It about 20-somethings: Why Are People in Their 20s Taking So Long to Grow Up," *New York Times Magazine*, August 18, 2010, http://www.nytimes.com/2010/08/22/magazine/22Adulthood-t.html?_r=1 (accessed August 21, 2010); and Jeffrey Arnett, *Emerging Adulthood: The Winding Road from the Late Teens through the Twenties* (New York: Oxford University Press, 2004).

2.   Robert Wuthnow, *After the Baby Boomers: How Twenty- and Thirty-Somethings Are Shaping the Future of American Religion* (Princeton: Princeton University Press, 2007), 14–16.

3.   Jean M. Twenge, *Generation Me: Why Today's Young Americans Are More Confident, Assertive, Entitled—and More Miserable Than Ever Before* (New York: Free Press, 2006).

4.   Consultation on Young Adults, The Collegeville Institute, July 2010.

5.   Frederick Buechner, *Secrets in the Dark: A Life in Sermons* (San Francisco: HarperSanFrancisco, 2006), 35–37.

6.   The work of Parker Palmer and the Center for Courage and Renewal has been instrumental in shaping these commitments.

7.   Nelle Morton, *The Journey Is Home* (Boston: Beacon Press Books, 1985), 205.

8.   Consultation on Young Adults.

9.   For a description of this process through the life stories of twenty-one contemporary young adults in the United States, see Dori Baker, *Kick Off Your Flip Flops: A Barefoot Practice for Finding Your Purpose*, working title (Louisville, KY: Westminster John Knox, forthcoming July 2011).

10. *National Catholic Reporter*, March 28, 2004. From a prayer written by Father Kenneth Uetner for Cardinal John Francis Dearden in November 1979 but almost ubiquitously known as the Romero Prayer.

11. Sharon Parks, *Big Questions, Worthy Dreams: Mentoring Young Adults in Their Search for Meaning, Purpose, and Faith* (San Francisco: Jossey-Bass, 2000), 158ff.

12. From a lecture given by Jürgen Moltmann on May 20, 2010, as part of the Holy Spirit in the World Today Conference, Holy Trinity Brompton, London. Audio recordings from the main presentations at the conference are now available at the St. Mellitus College website, http://www.stmellitus.org/resources.

13. Shane Claiborne and Chris Haw, *Jesus for President: Politics for Ordinary Radicals* (Grand Rapids: Zondervan, 2009), 99–101.

Bibliography

Ammerman, Nancy T. "Culture and Identity in the Congregation." In *Studying Congregations.* Edited by Nancy T. Ammerman, Jackson W. Carroll, Carl S. Dudley, and William McKinney. Nashville: Abingdon Press, 1998.

Baker, Dori, and Joyce A. Mercer. *Lives to Offer: Accompanying Youth on the Quest for Vocation.* Cleveland: Pilgrim Press, 2009.

Bass, Dorothy. *On Our Way: Christian Practices for Living a Whole Life.* Nashville: Upper Room, 2010.

Bass, Dorothy C., ed. *Practicing Our Faith: A Way of Life for a Searching People.* San Francisco: Jossey-Bass, 1997.

Bass, Dorothy C. "Ways of Life Abundant." In *For Life Abundant: Practical Theology, Theological Education, and Christian Ministry.* Edited by Dorothy C. Bass and Craig Dykstra. Grand Rapids: William B. Eerdmans, 2008.

Berling, Judith A. *Understanding Other Religious Worlds: A Guide for Interreligious Education.* Maryknoll, NY: Orbis, 2004.

Brueggemann, Walter. *Hope for the World: Mission in a Global Context.* Louisville: Westminster John Knox Press, 2001.

———. "The City in the Biblical Perspective." *Word & World* 19, no. 3 (Summer 1999): 236–50.

————. *Interpretation and Obedience: From Faithful Reading to Faithful Living.* Minneapolis: Augsburg Fortress, 1991.

Buechner, Frederick. *Secrets in the Dark: A Life in Sermons.* New York: HarperCollins, 2006.

Campbell, Cynthia. *A Multitude of Blessings: A Christian Approach to Religious Diversity.* Louisville: Westminster John Knox, 2007.

Carroll, Jackson W. *God's Potters: Pastoral Leadership and the Shaping of Congregations.* Grand Rapids: William B. Eerdmans, 2006.

Chaves, Mark. *Congregations in America.* Cambridge, MA: Harvard University Press, 2004.

Chaves, Mark, Shawna Anderson, and Jason Byassee. "American Congregations at the Beginning of the 21st Century: A Report from the National Congregations Study." Durham, NC: Duke University, 2009.

Claiborne, Shane, and Chris Haw. *Jesus for President: Politics for Ordinary Radicals.* Grand Rapids: Zondervan, 2009.

Confucius. *The Analects.* Translated by Simon Leys. Minneapolis: Filiquarian Publishing, 2006.

Crain, Margaret Ann, and Jack L. Seymour. "The Ethnographer as Minister." *Religious Education* 91, no. 3 (Summer 1996): 312.

Dean, Kenda Creasy. "After Youth Group." *The Christian Century,* February 9, 2010.

Denzin, Norman K., and Yvonna S. Lincoln. *Strategies of Qualitative Inquiry.* Third edition. Thousand Oaks, CA: Sage Publications, 2008.

Dykstra, Craig, and Dorothy Bass. *Practice of Faith: A Way of Life for a Searching People.* San Francisco: Jossey-Bass, 1997.

————. "A Theological Understanding of Christian Practices." In *Practicing Theology: Belief and Practices in Christian Life.* Edited by Miroslav Volf and Dorothy C. Bass. Grand Rapids: Eerdmans, 2002.

Frank, Thomas Edward. *The Soul of the Congregation: An Invitation to Congregational Reflection.* Nashville: Abingdon, 2000.

Gifford, Carolyn DeSwarte. "Nineteenth- and Twentieth-Century Protestant Reform Movements in the United States." *Encyclopedia of Women and Religion in North America.* Edited by Rosemary Skinner Keller and Rosemary Radford Reuther. Bloomington, IN: Indiana University Press, 2006.

Hall, Douglas John. *Why Christian? For Those on the Edge of Faith.* Minneapolis: Augsburg Fortress, 1998.

Hick, John. *The Rainbow of Faiths: Critical Dialogues in Religious Pluralism.* London: SCM Press, 1995.

Jackson, Robert. *Rethinking Religious Education and Plurality: Issues in Diversity and Pedagogy.* London: RoutledgeFalmer, 2004.

Jones, Tony. *The New Christians: Dispatches from the Emergent Frontier.* San Francisco: Jossey Bass, 2008.

Kang, S. Steve. "Reflections upon Methodology: Research on Themes of Self Construction and Self Integration in the Narrative of Second Generation Korean Young Adults." *Religious Education* 96, no. 3 (Summer 2001): 408–15.

Killen, Patricia O'Connell, and John De Beer. *The Art of Theological Reflection.* New York: Crossroad, 1994.

March, W. Eugene. *The Wide, Wide Circle of Divine Love: A Biblical Case for Religious Diversity.* Louisville: Westminster John Knox, 2005.

Morton, Nelle. *The Journey Is Home.* Boston: Beacon Press Books, 1985.

Moschella, Mary Clark. *Ethnography as a Pastoral Practice: An Introduction.* Cleveland: Pilgrim Press, 2008.

O'Connor, Elizabeth. *Cry Pain, Cry Hope: Thresholds to Purpose.* Waco, TX: Word Books, 1987.

Niebuhr, Gustav. *Beyond Tolerance: Searching for Interfaith Understanding in America.* New York: Penguin/Viking, 2008.

Palmer, Parker. *The Promise of Paradox: A Celebration of Contradictions in a Christian Life.* Notre Dame: Ave Maria Press, 1980.

Parker, Evelyn. *Trouble Don't Last Always: Emancipatory Hope among African American Adolescents.* Cleveland: Pilgrim Press, 2003.

Parks, Sharon. *Big Questions, Worthy Dreams: Mentoring Young Adults in Their Search for Meaning, Purpose, and Faith*. San Francisco: Jossey-Bass, 2000.

Patel, Eboo, and Patrice Brodeur. *Building the Interfaith Youth Movement: Beyond Dialogue to Action*. Oxford, UK: Rowman & Littlefield, 2006.

Smith, Christian, and Melinda Lundquist Denton. *Soul Searching: The Religious and Spiritual Lives of American Teenagers*. New York: Oxford University Press, 2005.

Smith, Christian, and Patricia Snell. *Souls in Transition: The Religious and Spiritual Lives of Emerging Adults*. New York: Oxford University Press, 2009.

Soifer, Maya. "Beyond Convivencia: Critical Reflections on the Historiography of Interfaith Relations in Christian Spain." *Journal of Medieval Iberian Studies* 1 (January 2009): 19–35.

Spellers, Stephanie. *Radical Welcome: Embracing God, the Other, and the Spirit of Transformation*. New York: Church Publishing, 2006.

Sujai, Amenti Alare, and Daniel T. Hembree. *You Are the Jewel in the Stone: A Narrative Resource for Vocational Reflections and Theological Exploration*. Orangeburg, SC: The Center for Vocational Reflection at Claflin University, 2006.

Tickle, Phyllis. *The Great Emergence: How Christianity Is Changing and Why*. Grand Rapids: Baker Books, 2008.

Tidball, Derek. "The Pilgrim and the Tourist: Zygmunt Bauman and Postmodern Identity." In *Explorations in a Christian Theology of Pilgrimage*. Edited by Craig G. Bartholomew and Fred Hughes. Aldershot, UK: Ashgate, 2004.

Twenge, Jean M. *Generation Me: Why Today's Young Americans Are More Confident, Assertive, Entitled—and More Miserable Than Ever Before*. New York: Free Press, 2006.

Volf, Miroslav. *Exclusion and Embrace: A Theological Exploration of Identity, Otherness and Reconciliation*. Nashville: Abingdon Press, 1996.

Wolf, Miroslav, and Dorothy C. Bass, eds. *Practicing Theology: Belief and Practices in Christian Life*. Grand Rapids: Eerdmans, 2002.

Warner, Stephen, and K. C. Kim, eds. *Korean Americans and Their Religions: Pilgrims and Missionaries from a Different Shore*. University Park, PA: The Pennsylvania University Press, 2001.

West, Cornel. *Race Matters*. New York: Vintage Books, 1994.

———. "The Vocation of the Black Christian Intellectual." Paper presented at Union Theological Seminary and Presbyterian School of Christian Education, Richmond, VA, April, 23, 2008.

Wuthnow, Robert. *After the Baby Boomers: How Twenty- and Thirty-Somethings Are Shaping the Future of American Religion*. Princeton: Princeton University Press, 2007.

This book grows out of the work of Calling Congregations, an ecumenical initiative of The Fund for Theological Education (FTE). Calling Congregations seeks to establish a national network of congregations and church-related partners committed to the cause of cultivating future pastoral leaders. We know that congregations are seedbeds where young people's gifts might be noticed, named, and nurtured for the sake of the church and the world. To support them, Calling Congregations developed VocationCARE, a set of principles and practices that invite congregational leaders to create the conditions where diverse and gifted young people are more likely to hear, respond to, and serve God's call in their lives. VocationCARE is an acronym that points to four communal practices:

C—Create hospitable space to explore Christian vocation;

A—Ask self-awakening questions;

R—Reflect theologically on self and community; and

E—Explore, enact, and establish ministry opportunities.

Resources that support VocationCARE include Web-based tools, consultation, conferences, retreats, and other learning events. An additional book—with a working title of *Kick Off Your Flip-Flops: A Barefoot Practice for Finding Our Purpose* (Louisville, KY: Westminster John Knox Press, 2011) by FTE Scholar-in-Residence Dori Baker—assists congregations in leading theological reflection with youth and young adults. To learn more about FTE, a nonprofit advocate for excellence and diversity in pastoral ministry and theological scholarship, visit www.fteleaders.org.